8

The Ancient World: Source Books

General Editor: Peter Walcot
Professor of Classics, University of Cardiff

Leadership and the Cult of the Personality

Edited with an Introduction by

JANE F. GARDNER
Lecturer in Classics, University of Reading

Dent, London
Hakkert, Toronto

© Introduction, translations and commentary,
J. M. Dent & Sons Ltd, 1974

Made in Great Britain
at the
Aldine Press · Letchworth · Herts
for
J. M. DENT & SONS LTD
Aldine House · Albemarle Street · London
First published in 1974

Published in Canada, the United States of
America and its dependencies by A. M. HAKKERT
LTD, 554 Spadina Crescent, Toronto M5s
2J9, Canada

This book is set in
9 on 10 and 10 on 11 point Fournier 185

Dent edition
Hardback ISBN 0 460 10788 7
Paperback ISBN 0 460 11788 2

Hakkert edition
Hardback ISBN 0 88866 549 0
Paperback ISBN 0 88866 550 4

Library of Congress Catalog
Card No. 74 80346

Foreword

Although few today study Greek and Latin at school or college, there has never been a more widespread interest in classical civilization and culture. How academically respectable is such an interest unless it is reinforced by an ability to read the Greek and Latin languages? Certainly it is crucially important that a student should have a direct contact with the primary evidence, that is, the evidence offered by what our ancient authorities say themselves. Yet this need may be met be thy provision of sound translations, for these can go a long way towards supplying an acceptable alternative to an actual knowledge of Greek and Latin. It is no longer possible to argue, as it was possible in antiquity, that a man can attain mastery of all branches of learning; the sheer complexity of the modern world forces us to be selective in education as in so much else. It is not reasonable to expect the student to be conversant with a variety of languages, but it would be absurd if we restricted our studies to the exclusive consideration of those speaking and writing our native tongue. In fact, if an effort to guide a student's interest is to be really constructive, we are obliged to do more than just supply adequate translations; we must also be willing to collect together as representative a selection of the relevant evidence in translation as is possible. What then is left to the student? A great deal. Questions are posed and evidence is presented, but the student finds the answers himself. The student must think for himself, and his thoughts will not be casual or ill-founded if he and his colleagues can and do make frequent reference to the primary evidence which it is the purpose of this series of source-books to collect and to translate.

PETER WALCOT

Contents

Preface

The main theme of this book is the tendency of human societies to single out certain individuals and place them in positions of authority, and to find justifications for doing so. The individual's pre-eminence may rest on a formal constitutional basis or on the susceptibility of the people in general to certain appearances and types of behaviour which betoken, or are believed to betoken, the possession by a man of certain qualities which make him superior to his fellows and therefore deserving of their deference or even obedience. The qualities need not actually be there for this charisma to be created; it is sufficient that the accepted symbols of them are present. The possession of office is one of the means of the creation of charisma, but by no means the only one.

In early monarchies, as described in Homer, the kings are already subject to some political restraint, but at the same time there is some suggestion of divine authorization for their position. The powers of the Spartan kings are restricted, but their privileges are carefully maintained and with them the political stability of the state. There are signs in fifth-century Greece of attempts to produce a justification of monarchic rule in terms of the common good. At the same time, reaction to democratic pressures by ambitious politicians produces exploitation of emotional and irrational responses in the citizens—the fostering of a 'personality cult'.

Fourth-century Greek theory, in disenchantment with actual constitutions, takes refuge in the notion of the ideal individual as ruler, leaving vague his relationship to the law. With the establishment of Hellenistic monarchies, theory turns to justification of monarchic rule in quasi-mystical terms, with the king regarded as, inter alia, the embodiment of the law. Examples of Hellenistic practice illustrate the extreme development of opinion-moulding and exploitation of response in forms whose blatancy in part reflects the political situation.

Development of monarchical control in Rome provides an object-lesson in manipulating the forms while altering the realities of government. The cult of the personality is used as a technique of gaining acceptance, while the content given the cult is carefully controlled. By the end of the first century A.D. elaborate justifications of the principate as an institution appear alongside laudation of an individual *princeps*.

Christian examples show rejection of the idea of the divinity of emperors and a certain sensitivity about the relations between Church and State; particularly notable, however, is the way in which the eloquence of Christian leaders is applied to providing divine warrant for the temporal position of the emperor, extending even to the notion of a 'special relationship' between him and God.

There are at least two grounds of justification for drawing upon the literature of ancient Greece and Rome to illustrate the theme. One is that these societies are at the basis of the tradition in which Western European political institutions developed. The other contrary one is that these societies are now so remote from us that their very unfamiliarity may enable us to perceive unexpected parallels with modern societies and events, and so give us insights into the meaning of modern developments.

In translating the passages cited, I have sought to avoid the two main pitfalls awaiting a translator. Concern with the quality of one's English prose may result in the use of vocabulary and idioms having external associations with concepts developed only in recent times, or belonging to a developed system of ideas which appears in the ancient writer only in a much less sophisticated form. Conversely, the translator may attempt to preserve the 'flavour' of the passage—the structure of the thought and the degree of sophistication—by adhering closely to the syntactic structure and level of diction of the original; and the result in English may well be stilted, unidiomatic and grotesque. Whether I have fallen into the ditch on either side (or both), I leave the reader to judge.

JANE F. GARDNER

Select Bibliography

Barker, E. *The Political Thought of Plato and Aristotle* (Dover, 1959).

Baynes, N. H. *Constantine the Great and the Christian Church* (Proceedings of the British Academy, 1929; Haskell, 1972).

Brown, P. *The World of Late Antiquity* (Thames & Hudson, 1971; Harcourt, 1971).

Brunt, P. A. *Social Conflicts in the Roman Republic* (Chatto & Windus, 1971; Norton, 1971).

Carter, J. M. *The Battle of Actium: the rise and triumph of Augustus Caesar* (Hamish Hamilton, 1970).

Chadwick, J. *The Decipherment of Linear B* (Pelican, 1958; Cambridge University Press, 1970).

Connor, W. R. *The New Politicians of Fifth-Century Athens* (Princeton, 1971).

Dvornik, F. *Early Christian and Byzantine Political Philosophy*, 2 vols. (Dunbarton Oaks, 1966).

Finley, M. I. *The World of Odysseus* (Pelican, 1972; Viking Press, 1965).

Forrest, W. G. *The Emergence of Greek Democracy* (Weidenfeld & Nicolson, 1966; McGraw, 1967).

Gelzer, M. *Caesar: Politician and Statesman* (Blackwell, 1968; Harvard University Press, 1968).

Hammond, M. *The Antonine Monarchy* (American Academy at Rome, 1959).

Hammond, N. G. L. *History of Greece to 322 B.C.* (Oxford, 1967).

Hignett, C. A. *A History of the Athenian Constitution to the end of the fifth century B.C.* (Oxford, 1952).

Holmes, T. R. *The Architect of the Roman Empire*, 2 vols. (Oxford, 1928, 1931).

Jones, A. H. M. *The Later Roman Empire*, 3 vols. (Blackwell, 1964).

Jones, A. H. M. *Sparta* (Blackwell, 1967; Harvard University Press, 1967).

Jones, A. H. M. *Augustus* (Chatto & Windus, 1970; Norton, 1971).

Jones, A. H. M. *Constantine and the Conversion of Europe* (Pelican, 1972).

Mahaffy, J. P. *A History of Egypt under the Ptolemaic Dynasty* (Methuen, 1899).

Parker, H. M. D. *A History of the Roman World from A.D. 138 to 337* (Methuen, 2nd edn, 1958; Barnes and Noble, 1958).

Salmon, E. T. *The Roman World from 30 B.C. to 138 A.D.* (Methuen, 6th edn, 1968; Barnes and Noble, 1968).

Scullard, H. H. *From the Gracchi to Nero* (Methuen, 3rd edn, 1970; Barnes and Noble, 1970).

Scullard, H. H. *History of the Roman World 753 to 146 B.C.* (Methuen, 3rd edn, 1961; Barnes and Noble, 1969).

Scullard, H. H. *Scipio Africanus, Soldier and Politician* (Thames & Hudson, 1970; Cornell University Press, 1970).

Setton, K. M. *Christian Attitude towards the Emperor in the Fourth Century* (Columbia University Press, 1941).

Sutherland, C. H. V. *Coinage in Roman Imperial Policy 31 B.C. to A.D. 68* (Methuen, 1951; Barnes and Noble, 1971).

Syme, R. *The Roman Revolution* (Oxford, 2nd edn, 1952).

Tarn, W., and Griffith, G. T. *Hellenistic Civilisation* (Methuen, 3rd edn, 1966; St Martin, 1952).

Taylor, L. R. *The Divinity of the Roman Emperor* (American Philological Association, 1931).

Taylor, L. R. *Party Politics in the Age of Caesar* (University of California, 1961).

Wace, A. J. B., and Stubbings, F. H. *A Companion to Homer* (Macmillan, 1962).

Wirszubski, Ch. *Libertas as a Political Idea at Rome during the Late Republic and Early Principate* (Cambridge, 1950).

Introduction

'The Cult of the Personality' is what Humpty Dumpty would doubtless have called a portmanteau-title. Purists may complain that entire sections of this book contain no reference at all to 'cult' in the religious sense, or to the personality of any individual, or even to 'personality-cult' in the sense in which the phrase became current in the Stalinist era and is still used today in reference to the publicity treatment given certain politicians both in the West and in the East. All these elements do find a place in this book, but they do not constitute its totality. An attempt has been made to present these as parts of a complex phenomenon: the persistent tendency, in different periods and in societies with widely differing constitutions, to create and maintain—and, moreover, to justify—a situation in which, whatever the nominal constitutional position, an individual can be made to stand out as both the possessor of authority and thereby the appropriate object for the respect and deference of his fellow citizens. It seems as though authority in the abstract is not enough; the human mind seems to demand a personification of that authority as the focus for his respect and reverence, and prefers to honour the ruler, rather than the rule of law. The connection with the religious impulse is obvious and, as will be seen, this tendency produced at times an assertion of the divinity, or at least divine sponsorship, of the ruler. Its secular manifestations, however, are no less striking or important, and considerable portions of this book are devoted to texts in which theoretical justifications of monarchic rule are set forth, and others illustrating ways in which the possession of power by a particular individual has been facilitated or justified by means of techniques of enhancing his impressiveness in the public view, of adding glamour to the man and his position.

For such techniques to work, there must be a predisposition to belief in the reality of the kind of superiority of which they try to create the impression. Even in societies avowedly democratic and egalitarian, there is found this readiness, and even eagerness, to acknowledge the natural superiority, and therefore deserved pre-eminence, of an individual—up to a point, at least. The histories of Julius Caesar and of Augustus and his successors as head of the Roman Empire, show the care needed to tread the political tight-rope in what was, nominally, a republic; and in ancient Athens the point is illustrated by the contrast between acceptance of a Cimon or a Pericles and the ambivalence of attitude towards an Alcibiades. 'Alcibiades was a celebrity among the Athenians,' says Thucydides (6.15), 'and he indulged his enthusiasm for horse-rearing and other expensive pursuits beyond his means. This, in fact, later on played no small part in the downfall of Athens. For people in general became alarmed at his extremism, both in the physical excesses of his way of life and in the frame of mind in which he acted on all occasions. They thought that he was aiming at a tyranny, and rejected him. Although in public life his management of the war was excellent, everyone found his conduct in private life objectionable; so they entrusted affairs to others, and soon ruined the city.'

The passages translated are taken from writers in Greek and Roman society at various periods from the dark ages of post-Mycenaean Greece to the early centuries of the Christian Roman Empire, since it is from this tradition that modern ideas on political philosophy, in Western European countries and others whose political development has been influenced by them, have their origin. The theories of kingship in certain ancient oriental societies had a limited and indirect, and relatively late, influence in the Greco-Roman world.

The kind of society which appears in the earliest extant literature of the Greco-Roman world presents a very different view of kings from that of Persia or Egypt. Geography may have had much to do with it. The physical characteristics of Greece more or less compelled the development of small political units, with people living in close proximity. Visibility and accessibility are inimical to glamour—a lesson not lost on Pericles, for example. As the units grew larger, the ruler less and less known to his subjects by personal sight and experience, the more it was expected that the holder of such great power should be a superior being, and the more elaborate the dress, the behaviour and the ceremonial by which he was set apart from and raised above his subjects. Athenaeus' account of a royal procession indicates that the Ptolemies realized the value of shows in impressing the populace. The culmination was the rigid, gorgeous formality of the Byzantine court.

Also, the more complete the power of the monarch, the more definitely do theoretical writers assert a connection between the individual ruler and the ruling power in the universe, making the monarch's position part of the natural order. This can be seen in texts from the Hellenistic period and from the Christian empire. It is questionable how far such statements were of religious importance, but politically they were very important indeed. Was this a good or a bad thing? Did the value of the political stability afforded outweigh the possible undesirability of the authoritarianism that the invocation of such sanctions was bound to encourage? The concept of treason can be dangerously widened—or narrowed.

It is a pity that we have no records of the early stages of political life in ancient Greece. The society depicted in Homer (and even that glimpsed hazily in the Linear B tablets, perhaps) is one in which the concept of a 'kingly class' is already as important as that of a king. There are commoners and there are nobles—that is, potential kings; and the relations between each of these groups and the king are different. Thersites' own companions side with Odysseus against him, in support of the established order; and Thersites and his like could never aspire to *be* a king, unlike the noble suitors of Penelope. Divine ancestry characterizes the 'heroes'; in addition, the king has received his sceptre from Zeus. The hereditary principle holds, but is under attack.

During the Dark Ages before about 800 B.C., with the development of city life, monarchies were superseded in all but the remote parts of Greece by aristocratic régimes. Sparta retained her kings, but with restricted powers and as part of a rather elaborate constitution, described further below. The care taken to maintain the dignity (as distinct from the power) of the kingship at Sparta is notable; at the same time, actual power, when conferred on any other individual Spartans, was given only grudgingly and for strictly limited periods (as, for instance, to admirals in war or commanders of special expeditions, such as Brasidas in 424–2 B.C.). The Spartan constitution was the most stable in antiquity, but at a considerable price in terms of loss of international power and waste of talent and initiative among her people.

The development of Athens was very different. Like other major

Greek cities, she had a prolonged period of conflict among leading aristocratic families (including some of the newer aristocracy of wealth), and ultimately a *coup d'état* resulting in the establishment of one of these nobles, Peisistratus, as tyrant. 'Tyrant', originally a Lydian loan-word, was first used by the Greeks merely to denote a sole ruler established by extra-constitutional means; it subsequently acquired the connotations of cruelty and depotism. In the tyrannies, there was concern to secure acceptance of the ruler and his heirs by providing some further justification of his position. For instance, a birth legend was created for Cypselus of Corinth (Herodotus 5.92 ff.), just as, later, for Alexander, Caesar, Augustus. Peisistratus at Athens resorted to play-acting—a tall girl, handsomely dressed, rode into Athens with him on a chariot, and it was announced that the goddess Athena was escorting him into the city. The technique here may be childish and crude, but the principle is essentially the same as that used by the political rebels against Rome who supported Jesus, the Parliamentarian leaders who opposed Charles II, or the emperor Constantine who claimed a vision of the Holy Cross.

Within a generation or two after Peisistratus, however, the constitution at Athens changed radically. After the downfall of Peisistratus' son, Cleisthenes established at Athens a constitution designed to put an end to aristocratic faction by preventing any one section of the aristocracy from acquiring too much political influence, and also reducing the power of the aristocracy as a whole relatively to the rest of the people. The chief executive magistracies were still confined to the propertied classes, but the deliberative and judicial bodies in the state were totally reorganized. The clan-based Ionic tribes were abolished and their place was taken by ten new tribes based on artificial geographical divisions. Each tribe chose fifty representatives who formed the Council, which served as the chief administrative body in the state and was probouleutic to the Ecclesia, the assembly of all citizens which was the sovereign legislative body. The principal developments in the constitution thereafter were: the institution of ostracism, whereby individuals whose policies were thought dangerous could be sent into exile, without loss of property or civic rights, for ten years; the replacement of election by sortition in the appointment of the principal magistrates and officials, with some exceptions, of which the most important were the *strategoi*, the generals commanding the tribal regiments in the army, who were elected annually; the transfer from the Areopagus (the council of ex-archons, in office for life) to the Council and the Ecclesia of most of its judicial powers; and the introduction of pay for state service. In the radical democracy at Athens, the theory was that the whole people was sovereign, governing directly through the assembly, and that all citizens were equally capable of participating in ruling and had an equal opportunity of doing so.

Such, at any rate, was the theory. Practical necessity, as we have seen, obliged the Athenians to waive the rule of sortition for offices requiring special ability, and so to retain election for military commanders. The result was that this replaced the archonship as the office to which the more able and ambitious sought appointment, and this, combining with the increasing importance of the *strategia* as a result of the development of Athens' naval empire, the Delian League, made it a position of power and influence. Tenure was annual, but, unlike other magistracies, it was open to re-election. Pericles held the office for some fifteen years, and during that period was virtual head of state.

It is a fact worth noting that, in the generation after Cleisthenes' reforms, the archonship, and subsequently in the fifth century, the *strategia*, tended, where we have records, to be held by very much the same sort of people as had ruled in Athens before. The tendency is most marked in the earlier half of the century, but by no means disappears later. Pericles himself was from the same family as Cleisthenes; so was Alcibiades. Thucydides the historian (general in 424 B.C.) and his relative Thucydides, son of Melesias (Pericles' leading opponent in the 440s), were distantly connected with Cimon. The extracts quoted from Plutarch's *Lives* of Cimon and Pericles show the importance of the 'grand manner' in influencing the Athenian populace. The anecdotes of outré behaviour he tells in his *Life of Alcibiades* give an idea of the fascination exercised by this flamboyant young aristocrat. More than once, he lists the qualities that most impressed the populace. The fullest list is in chapter 16. It comprises Alcibiades' voluntary donations, his contributions to public shows, his ancestry, his oratorical skill, his physical strength, his good looks and his military prowess. These qualities in him, says Plutarch, made the Athenians ready to forgive him his lapses, and find excuses for them. Conversely, it was cast up as a slur against men like Cleon and Hyperbolus that they were 'in trade'.

What won Cleon his eminence was primarily his skill in oratory.

This, we have just seen, was one of the qualities that counted in
Alcibiades' favour, and Pericles also was an exceptionally powerful
orator. This was at the root of their influence. Athenian democracy
was direct government—the people, met in assembly, listened to those
who cared to speak on matters at issue, and decided on the spot. A
criticism frequent in Greek authors from Thucydides onwards is that
the Athenian assembly was wont to be influenced by a showy per-
formance, rather than by careful weighing of arguments. Continuity
of policy was hard to achieve, and, worse still, there gradually developed a divorce between power and responsibility. A skilful orator
might exercise real power in that his persuasions brought the people
to adopt the policies he advocated; responsibility for their success or
failure, however, was laid at the doors of the generals who were
assigned to their execution. This was the difficulty in which Nicias
found himself, in Sicily; in the council of war after the disastrous
defeat at Epipolae in 413, when the other generals were for retreating,
Nicias refused, partly because he believed there were some grounds
to hope the Syracusans might surrender, partly, Thucydides says
(7.48), because he was afraid of reactions at Athens. The Athenians'
judgments were readily influenced by clever speeches. The soldiers
who now, in Sicily, were urging a return home would like as not
accuse them at Athens of having been bribed to withdraw; he said
he knew the character of the Athenians, and he would take his chance
there in Sicily and, if necessary, be killed, rather than risk condemnation at Athens by an unjust verdict. Less than ten years later, that
was the fate of a group of generals, who had been in command at
Arginusae; and Alcibiades' final disgrace was engineered in the same
way.

The last third of the fifth century, the so-called 'age of the Sophists',
was the beginning of a period of intellectual inquiry and challenge.
One of the subjects in which these travelling specialists purveyed
instruction was the art of oratory. Its importance for a city like Athens
is obvious. The citizen could learn to express his views effectively in
public; put another way, money could help to buy skills which could
go some way to compensate for the lack of other advantages—noble
birth, for example—denied by nature. Equally, the Sophists fed and
catered for the growing interest in discussion and inquiry into matters
of moral and political philosophy. Already in the fifth century, as we
see in chapter 3, there were doubts as to whether radical democracy

could correspond in practice to the theory. These doubts were further reinforced by experience of shortcomings of the kind described in Thucydides. Furthermore, in the course of the fifth and increasingly in the fourth century, men's concern at the instability of existing constitutions, and their wish for some solution to the problem, grew. Even Athens had two oligarchic revolts in the course of the Peloponnesian war. Many other states were even less stable, and swung to and fro in the storms of faction-fighting between oligarchs and democrats. Their situation was made even worse by the recurrent inter-state warfare of the fourth century, and a persistent economic crisis which impoverished the cities. Civic spirit seemed to be declining, and personal self-interest making stronger claims.

Theoretical discussions searching for a constitution that would be both just and stable tended to end by envisaging an ideal monarchy, or, in the case of Plato's *Republic*, a caste of ideal rulers (conflict among whom presumably was obviated by their complete imbibement of knowledge of the Good). In the actual world, admiring eyes began to be cast on actual monarchs who had notably provided strong and successful leadership. Xenophon wrote admiring monographs on King Agesilaus of Sparta, and on Cyrus, founder of the Persian might. The orator Isocrates wrote a eulogy of Evagoras, the ruler of Salamis in Cyprus, who successfully held the Persians at bay; his companion works, 'To Nicocles' and 'Nicocles', addressed to Evagoras' son, are a kind of handbook on the duties of a model ruler, and the advantages of a monarchy for its subjects. Another strong ruler was Dionysius I, who made himself tyrant in Syracuse. The Greek world might condemn him for being a tyrant, but they could not but admire and approve his success in saving the Greeks in Sicily from Carthaginian domination.

Events overtook the theorists. The conquests of Philip of Macedon, then of his son Alexander, and the subsequent wars among Alexander's former generals, resulted in the subjection of the greater part of the Greek world to a number of strong monarchs, each controlling large and powerful kingdoms. Political theorists of the Hellenistic period go further than either Plato or Aristotle had gone. A king, *qua* king, is a kind of representative of, or intermediary on his subjects' behalf with the ruling principle of the universe. Plato had hoped that philosophers might become kings; to the authors preserved in Stobaeus, kings are philosophers, or more.

Ruler-worship, originating in the eager flattery of the conquered, was welcomed by the successors of Alexander for its political advantage, and ruler-cult became established, particularly in the Seleucid and Ptolemaic kingdoms. The Antigonids of Macedon were never worshipped in their own country (where their rule rested ultimately on election, not conquest), but received divine honours in various conquered Greek cities. The worship of the gods of the Olympian pantheon was still maintained in the Greek world, but without that sense of spiritual awe that had once produced legends illustrating the dangers of human presumption, and these gods no longer appeared among men; the kings were present and visible, with the power of benefaction. The dividing line between human and divine was, in any case, rather blurred. All over the Greek world, not only the heroes of Homeric legend, but early kings and founders of cities, were given heroic honours—that is, offerings were made at their actual or supposed tombs, and their help and protection sought. The town of Amphipolis, in the late fifth century B.C., paid similar honours to the dead Brasidas as 'founder' and so did some of the Greeks of Asia Minor to Lysander, apparently in his lifetime (Plutarch, *Lysander* 18), a generation later. The body of Alexander, taken by Ptolemy to Alexandria, was given similar honours. In some ways, the cult of heroes resembled that of Christian saints, in that they were not themselves, strictly, gods, but nonetheless received offerings and were believed to have superhuman powers to aid and help the living.

The heroes of old had been of semi-divine origin, and even some of those long formally recognized as gods had had a mortal parent—Heracles, for instance, Dionysus and even Apollo and Artemis. Alexander too had become a god. The bestowing of divine honours upon the living ruler might not therefore constitute a very great offence to religious feeling. It both reinforced and provided a justification for the authority of the ruler, and was politically useful to him for that reason. In title, the prominence given to the idea of the king as Saviour and Benefactor is notable—perhaps initially the voicing of an anxious hope, acknowledging the real facts of power, as much as an expression of gratitude; in the established cults, it serves to make the point that the king is the fount of all patronage. Ruler-worship also becomes a standard method of demonstration by the conquered of willingness to submit. 'The Goddess Rome' was already being worshipped at Smyrna in 195 B.C., in gratitude for protection against

Antiochus; by the first century B.C. the offer of divine honours by Greek cities to Roman governors of the Eastern provinces had become a commonplace. In those regions, the ground was already laid for Roman emperor-worship.

The attitude of the educated classes in the Hellenistic kingdoms to the deification of their monarchs is not easy to determine. They were unlikely to take seriously the paying of divine honours to a man, as to one of the Olympian gods, although, paradoxically, that very disbelief which had emptied the Olympian religion of what little spiritual influence it might ever have had and turned speculation towards philosophy apparently made them willing to accept king-worship as a political measure. Philosophical writers, such as Diotogenes and Ecphantus, found ways of reconciling it with the answers philosophy was providing to questions on the nature and purpose of the world and the supremacy of Reason.

Of Hellenistic literature, maddeningly little has been preserved. The two major surviving poets, Theocritus and Callimachus, both belong to the early period, the first half of the third century. Theocritus' poem on Philadelphus is translated in chapter 7 below. The point at which he stops short, as said there, is significant for the time and the place; perhaps equally significant, however, is the lengths to which he *is* prepared to go. Callimachus, also, refrains from actually calling the king a god. However, in his *Hymn to Apollo*, he says, 'Who wars with my king, wars with Apollo'; and he did write a graceful piece, known to us in extensive fragments, and in the Latin version of Catullus, supporting the court astronomer Conon's flattering identification of a group of stars in the area circled by Ursa Major, Boötes, Virgo and Leo. Queen Berenice, the daughter of the king of Cyrene, was the wife of Ptolemy Euergetes. His sister, also named Berenice, and her husband the King of Syria were murdered by the latter's divorced wife Laodice, who set her son upon the throne. Soon after his marriage, Ptolemy set off upon a war of vengeance; the lock of hair which Berenice vowed to the gods she duly offered up, on his return, in the temple of Arsinoe Aphrodite. It mysteriously disappeared; and Conon flatteringly alleged its metamorphosis into the group of stars aforementioned. Callimachus' poem adopts this identification and makes the lock express its bitter regret at being severed from the queen's head, even as the price of stardom.

In a more serious vein, Callimachus writes in his *Hymn to Zeus*

that Zeus chose for his special patronage the best among men—not
sailors or warriors or minstrels, who were assigned to lesser gods, but
kings. Callimachus' own king—of course—is better than other kings,
but there is no suggestion that he, any more than the others, is divine.
His rule is, however, taken for granted and given the very powerful
backing of sponsorship by Zeus. How later poets treated ruler-cult
we do not know.

The writings of Euhemerus (who was in the service of Cassander
from 311 to 298 B.C.) both illustrate the extent of the development of
rationalism among the intellectual classes, and perhaps indicate how
it was possible for ruler-cult to find acceptance among them. Euhemerus said that the gods—including even the oldest gods of Olympian
mythology, Uranos, Kronos and Zeus—were men who had done
great service to mankind, and so had come to be venerated. If gods
were really men after all, why should not men be called gods?

Early Rome was ruled by kings; traditionally, there were seven of
them from the foundation by Romulus to the expulsion of the last of
them, Tarquinius Superbus—coincidentally, at the same time as the
expulsion of the tyrant at Athens. Most of the traditional record is
legendary, but some of the religious and political institutions probably do date back to the regnal period, and the history of the later
kings preserves some traces of the actual domination of the Etruscan
federation over Rome. Our principal surviving sources for the history
of the kings and of the early Republic are the early part of Livy's
history, and of that of his uncritical contemporary Dionysius of Hali-
carnassus, and Cicero's *De Re Publica* (mainly on constitutional matters). These narratives themselves are filtered through a succession of
previous writers. Cicero cites the *Origines* of the elder Cato; Livy
used both the early first-century B.C. authors Valerius Antias and
Licinius Macer, the latter a virulent opponent of Sulla, whose political
prejudice coloured much of his presentation of early history in a way
still detectable at second hand in Livy (for instance, in the section on
the apotheosis of Romulus). However, these surviving accounts, even
if their standing as historical fact is dubious, are valuable to us as
evidence of what Romans themselves believed about their country
and its past. Romulus, as the founder of the state and therefore its
greatest benefactor, traditionally became a god, even though later
scepticism demurred.

After the expulsion of the kings, there was a prolonged struggle—lasting, all in all, more than a century and a half—between the two categories of people in the Roman state, the patricians, the original ruling class, and the plebeians. In the early stages, the commons were rebelling against the economic exploitation to which they were subjected and the operation of the cruel debt laws (a contest described in Livy in terms strongly coloured by the troubles of the first century B.C.), and then engaged in securing certain political rights. This has two basic aspects. The common people were given magistrates of their own, the *tribuni*, and, ultimately, the agreement that resolutions passed by their own popular assemblies should be regarded as having the force of law. Not all plebeians were poor, however. In Rome, as in Greece, there developed a second aristocracy, outside the old aristocracy of birth, and these claimed a share in governing the state. Ultimately the magistracies, and so the Senate, were open to men of plebeian family as well as to patricians.

Polybius, writing in the mid second century B.C., claims Rome as an actualization of the ideal mixed constitution, with the two consuls as the monarchic element, the Senate as the aristocratic and the people as the democratic. This is a very misleading picture. By the mid second century the Senate, although technically only the advisory body to the magistrates, was the real controlling body in the state. It provided continuity, while magistrates changed annually. At first *de facto*, and later, certainly by the last century of the Republic, with fixed property qualifications, only the wealthy citizens could undertake the (unpaid) magistracies. The people elected them, but, aided by the Roman voting system, the upper-class Romans soon developed ways of influencing the vote, ranging from direct bribery (frequently legislated against) and intimidation, through patronage to the use of lavish methods of self-advertisement, e.g. in the giving of public games while in office as aedile. Electioneering was taken very seriously by an upper-class Roman; it was vital to his political career. The *Commentariolum Petitionis*, or 'Electioneering Handbook', attributed to Cicero's brother and written sometime during the first century B.C., lays great emphasis on the building up of a body of influential friends and persons under an obligation to one, who can influence the votes of their clients and dependents. The giving of spectacular shows, e.g. in one's capacity as aedile, or in celebration of a military triumph, was also of great importance for future elections. The voters had to be wooed.

Theoretically the people was sovereign. In practice, bills were put to the citizen assembly for approval only if they first had the approval of the Senate. The tribunes (strictly officers of the people, and not part of the hierarchy of State magistracies) came from the same wealthy class that made up the Senate and filled the magistracies. Their veto over a magistrate's actions came to be used rather as a weapon in faction-fighting inside the Senate than in defence of the individual citizen against arbitrary mistreatment.

So long as the members of the Senate continued to respect the interests of their order as a whole, this complicated system, based on the unchallenged authority of the Senate, could continue to work. The real threat to it lay in direct appeal to the people, away from the Senatorial authority, by individuals. Scipio Africanus' success in the Hannibalic War made him a national hero; none the less, his career was ominous for the Republic. Popular enthusiasm for a flamboyant young warrior gave him his first major command, unconstitutionally. A still more direct attack on Senatorial control was made by the Gracchi, who both in turn used their office as tribune to realize the sovereignty of the people and by-pass the Senate altogether. These are the two factors that dominate Roman politics in the last century of the Republic, from Marius to Caesar—the use of tribunes to thwart Senatorial authority, and the holding of prolonged military commands, useful both in themselves as sources of power, and as the means of building up a reputation with the voting populace at home. The political catchwords of the period were *optimates* and *populares*, respectively the champions of the Senatorial monopoly of government, and the defenders of the interests of the people (or, as their opponents preferred to put it, those who bribed the people with promises of corn and land in return for votes). There were real and severe social and economic distresses in Italy at the time, and one must believe that some at least of the so-called *populares*—in particular Caesar (though I have my doubts about Pompey)—were sincere in their wish to relieve them. Nevertheless, the political struggles were principally concerned with personal ambitions, particularly those of a certain few individuals. Sulla as dictator did his best to shore up the old order by removing much of the tribunes' power; but this was speedily restored after his retirement—the tribunate was too useful a political weapon.

Politics in the twenty years leading to the outbreak of the Civil War was a bitter power struggle, in which the main weapons were the tribunes' power of veto and legislative initiative through the popular assembly, influencing of the popular vote by agrarian legislation and more or less direct bribery, and, to an increasing extent, the use of direct physical intimidation within the city of Rome itself. Two men, Gnaeus Pompeius Magnus and Gaius Julius Caesar (and, until his death in 53, a third, Marcus Licinius Crassus), secured a predominating position in the state, each holding long-term military commands. The core of aristocrats at the centre of conservative resistance ultimately succeeded in driving a wedge between the two, and formed an alliance of expediency with Pompey. In the Civil War, however, Pompey was killed, the 'Republican' cause (Caesar having been declared a public enemy) lost, and Caesar was left in control. The Republican constitutional machinery continued to function, but real power was in the hands of Caesar, who was officially designated *dictator*, an extraordinary magistracy, which he held at first on an annual basis, and then, in the year of his death, was designated dictator in perpetuity. Officially, Rome was still a Republic; in practice, everything depended upon the will of Caesar, whose impatience with opposition and failures of tact lent substance to the beliefs of hostile critics that he intended to establish himself as actual king at Rome. However, he was a popular hero, both for his military successes abroad and for the reforms he instituted at Rome. There was no way to oust him by constitutional means, and so resort was had to assassination. To remove Caesar, however, was to remove merely a symptom, not the cause, of the political ills of the Republic, and civil war continued until another strong man won power by force—and held it by force, by tact towards the nominally governing class, and by manipulation of public opinion.

The last is by no means the least important. The lavish and showy honours voted Caesar are strongly reminiscent of the glaring ostentation by which the Hellenistic kings were set apart from and above their subjects, and Dio's account captures something of the highly emotional atmosphere at Rome in the aftermath of the Civil War. Some proposals, he thinks, were the fruits of adulation and/or panic, and others, in due course, of a calculated assault on traditional republican sentiment.

What is clear, however, is that the real opposition to Caesar was not among the populace at large, but was confined to a section of the governing class—although it is less clear whether their prime motive was love of the Republican constitution or concern for maintenance of the status and powers of their class. Augustus' early rise was in no small measure made possible by popular enthusiasm and veneration for the name of Caesar—the popular hero, then martyr and so, with deification, 'hero' also in the Greek sense (demigod). Later he acquired his own heroic aura. The provision of peace and a degree of material prosperity went a long way, as Tacitus indicates (*Annals* 1.2), to secure acceptance of his rule, and this was buttressed by a system of grants of special powers and titles, with careful avoidance of obvious violation of the republican constitution. At the same time as the reality of power was secured, public opinion was manipulated by enhancement of his image.

Coinage provided one of the readiest and most widely disseminated vehicles for propaganda (Sutherland, *Coinage in Roman Imperial Policy*); other public manifestations are detailed in the texts in chapters 9 and 10. Not least important was the part played by poets of the period. While usually stopping short of directly calling Augustus a god, in his lifetime, they skirt very close to it; and there is much comparison with particular gods and heroes, or assertion that the emperor is under their special patronage. More than a hint is borrowed from Hellenistic writers.

A few examples will have to suffice here. Ovid and Virgil, as is well known, used the tradition—employed by Julius Caesar himself at an early stage in his political career (Suetonius, *Divus Julius* 6)— of the descent of the Julian family from Aeneas' son, Iulus, and so ultimately from Venus. Ovid compares Augustus not only with Rome's founder Romulus but also with Heracles and Bacchus (i.e. Dionysus), and draws a parallel between Jupiter, father of the gods and ruler of the universe, and Augustus, father of men and ruler of the world. Horace says Jupiter rules in heaven; and when Augustus adds Britain and Persia to the empire, he will be considered a present god (*praesens divus*—almost a direct translation of *epiphanes*, 'Manifest'); and in the *Epistles* he compares Augustus with former benefactors of mankind—Romulus, Liber (i.e. Dionysus again), Castor, Pollux and Hercules—who attained divinity after death, while Augustus' *numen* (power, might—normally of gods), he says, is worshipped while he is still alive. And while the whole of Virgil's *Aeneid* is a kind of allegory of Augustus as Rome's man of destiny, the statement is most clearly made in the prophetic vision of Rome's destined future which closes the sixth book, with the advent of Augustus inaugurating a golden age.

In theory, Augustus was not the master of the Roman state, but its agent, given special administrative powers. He had 'restored the Republic' and government by the Senate and People of Rome, and he himself was merely the 'leading citizen' (Princeps). Modern historians tend to speak of the early empire, up to about Hadrian, as 'the Principate'; the next stage as 'the Monarchy'; and ultimately 'the Dominate'. This reflects the developments consequent upon the centralization of authority. Power itself becomes increasingly centralized. Already by the reign of Tiberius, the popular assemblies had effectively ceased to function; in the course of the second century A.D., senatorial debate and voting were gradually replaced by simple unanimous acclaim for proposals put by the emperor. Ultimately, even that function was unnecessary, as imperial edicts and rescripts with the force of law became more and more the regular method of governing. The Senate continued to exist for centuries, no longer as an effective governing body, but as an exclusive and prestigious 'order', constituting the highest social class (next to the imperial family itself) in the empire, from which the chief civil and military officials were drawn. Legal writers as early as the second century found a formula for reconciling the situation with the fiction of a continuing Republic. The emperor was the source of law because the people by the *lex regia* conferring the *imperium* had delegated all its authority to him. Symbolic of this act of delegation at a later period, and necessary for the formal establishment of each emperor, was the acclamation of the Senate at his accession.

As the emperor's rule became increasingly autocratic, so the ceremonial forms which surrounded him and set him apart became increasingly formal and elaborate. The 'cult of the personality' becomes more and more marked, but with increasing emphasis on 'cult' and less on 'personality'—or, in other words, it is not so much a particular emperor who is idolized, for his own characteristics, but 'the emperor', the details of whose personal history are cited in eulogies as illustrations of the virtues inherent as it were by definition in an emperor. Eusebius' eulogy of Constantine, quoted in chapter 12, provides a good example of this kind of formalism. In the fifth chapter of the oration, Eusebius is ostensibly talking about the character of Constantine, and, besides piety and devoutness, the qualities he ascribes to him are goodness, justice, bravery and temperance—the classic cardinal virtues. The 'cult' aspect in ceremonial became more and more marked. Diocletian (A.D. 284–305) is sometimes credited with the introduction of the ceremonial of *proskynesis*, or prostration on entering the emperor's presence, but it may have been in use as early as the reign of Aurelian (A.D. 270–275); it was soon combined with 'adoration of the purple', kissing of the hem of the garment of imperial purple, which only the emperor was entitled to wear. The word *dominus* ('master') first appeared on coins in the fourth century. The vocabulary of religion came to be used, not only in flattering addresses to the emperor, but in the everyday terminology of the imperial administration. The imperial Minister of Justice is the 'Quaestor of the Sacred Palace', the imperial Minister of Finance is the 'Count of the Sacred Largesses', the Chamberlain is the 'Steward of the Sacred Bedchamber', and so on.

Christianity changed little. The actual divinity of the emperor was, of course, denied; but the emperor's authority even over Church affairs was for a very long period accepted in at least part of the empire; and as far as his temporal authority was concerned, Christian writers went out of their way to assert that monarchy was the form of government that fulfilled God's intention for mankind, and that the monarch was the representative and agent of the will of God. Conspiracies and rebellions against the throne could and still did happen; and once the successor had the formal acknowledgment of the Senate, all the titles and reverence accorded to his predecessor were his, in his turn.

I. Early Monarchy

HOMERIC

Homer is our earliest literary evidence for social organization in the Greek world. Before that, we have only the scrappy and tantalizing information of the Linear B documents from Knossos and Pylos. Between Homer and the documents there are resemblances in terminology, but a difference in the social order they depict.

Both at Knossos and Pylos there was one person referred to as *wanax*, apparently the monarch. *Basileus* (the normal Greek word for 'king') appears as the title of a relatively minor local ruler. In Homer, we find the verb *anassein* ('to rule') and *anax*—usually in the phrase *anax andrōn* ('ruler of men')—used of persons also referred to as *basileis*.[1] The striking feature of Homeric terminology is the multiplicity of *basileis*, apparently heading independent, autonomous states. John Chadwick suggested (*The Decipherment of Linear B*, Cambridge, 1958) that during the Dark Age the great monarchies had disappeared and only petty chieftains survived.

Certainly, many passages both in the *Iliad* and the *Odyssey* raise doubts as to whether *basileus* really corresponds to our 'king' or 'monarch', and as to the precise status of the kingship. Alcinous, the host of Odysseus in Phaeacia, says there are twelve other *basileis* in the island. The position of Agamemnon in the *Iliad* is ambiguous. He is both ruler of a Greek city, Mycenae (as Odysseus is of Ithaca, Menelaus of Sparta, and so on), and in some sense leader of the combined Greek forces, although his authority does not seem to be unchallengeable in either capacity. Again, in the passage from the *Odyssey* below, it is clear that hereditary succession is by no means accepted in Ithaca as conferring an indisputable right to the throne; yet, on the other hand, one must wonder why, during Odysseus' long absence, no one else has yet seized the throne. What is the importance of Penelope?

However, we do not have an impression of total inconsistency. The society depicted in Homer recognizes distinctions of rank, status and

[1] After Homer, *anax* is a title of gods.

I

authority, and also limitations on authority, and the two passages translated here provide some of the best material for attempting to analyse
these.

Agamemnon before Troy

Agamemnon, to make trial of the morale of the Greeks, gave out that
he had had a divine instruction in a dream to prepare to leave Troy. To
his chagrin, the men responded by rushing to start their preparations for
departure. Odysseus acts to bring the situation under control. He calls an
assembly, which apparently has its rules of procedure. The part played by
Thersites is striking—most so, perhaps, in the reaction evoked in his
comrades when he is thumped by Odysseus. Homer's stress on his physical
grotesqueness might in part prepare us for this; still, he is one of them—
why is class solidarity lacking here?

Homer, *Iliad* 2. 166–277.

So spoke Hera, and grey-eyed Athene obeyed her and went down
quickly from the heights of Olympus. She soon came to the swift
ships of the Achaeans, and then she found Odysseus, equal of Zeus
in counsel, standing there. He did not lay hand on his black, well-
benched ship, because grief had come upon his heart and spirit. Grey-
eyed Athene stood beside him and said: 'Son of Laertes, of the line
of Zeus, much-devising Odysseus, are you going to flee like this on
your benched ships home to your own dear land, and leave to Priam
and the Trojans Argive Helen of the lovely arms, for whose sake
many Achaeans died in Troy, far from their own country? Go now
through the host of the Achaeans, delay no more, and with your
gentle words try to hold each man, and not let them drag their curved
ships to the sea.'

So she spoke, and he recognized the voice of the goddess and broke
into a run, throwing off his cloak (which his herald picked up, Eury-
bates of Ithaca, who attended him), and went straight to Agamemnon,
son of Atreus, and took from him the ancestral staff, never-perishing,
and went with it among the ships of the bronze-clad Achaeans.

Whenever he met someone who was a king (*basileus*) and a prominent man, he would stand beside him and try with mild words to
restrain him, saying: 'My dear fellow, it is not seemly for you to be
afraid, like a coward. Sit down yourself, and make the rest of your
people sit; for you do not yet clearly know the intentions of the son of

Atreus. Now he is merely testing you, but presently he will strike the sons of the Achaeans. Did we not all hear what he said in the council? Beware in case he grows angry and does some harm to the sons of the Achaeans. The kings nurtured by Zeus are proud in spirit, and their honour is from Zeus and Zeus, god of counsel, loves them.'

But whenever he saw a man of the people and found him shouting, he would strike him with his staff and reprove him, saying: 'Fellow, sit still, and listen to what others have to say, who are better than you. You are unwarlike and weak, and of no account either in war or in the council. By no means can all we Achaeans be kings here. It is not a good thing to have many chiefs; let one be chief, one king, to whom the son of crooked-counselling Cronos has given the staff and judgments, so that he may take thought for his people.'

So he went through the army as a chief; and they hurried again from the benched ships to the meeting place with a din, as when the billow of the roaring sea thunders on a long beach and the deep roars.

The rest sat down and stayed in their places, but one alone kept chattering, Thersites the out-spoken, whose mind was stocked with many unruly utterances, upbraiding the kings, idly and not in any orderly fashion but whatever he thought would make the Achaeans laugh. He was the ugliest of all those that came to Troy; he was bandy and lame in one foot, his shoulders were hunched, drawn together over his chest, and his head was misshapen, with only a scanty growth of hair. He was most hateful to Achilles and to Odysseus, because he would rail at those two; but now he cried out again shrilly, abusing lordly Agamemnon. The Achaeans were exceedingly angry with him, and seethed inwardly. But he bawled out and began to upbraid Agamemnon: 'Son of Atreus, what are you vexed about, or what do you lack? Your huts are full of bronze, and there are many women in your huts, chosen spoils, that we Achaeans give to you first of all, whenever we take a citadel. Or are you wanting gold as well, which some man of the horse-taming Trojans shall bring you out of Ilium as ransom for his son, whom I or one of the Achaeans has bound and led away? Or do you want a young woman to make love with, one whom you will keep apart? It is not fitting for one who has command to bring the sons of the Achaeans to harm. 'You poor fools, shameful wretches, Achaean girls, no longer men, let us go home with the ships, and leave him to digest his prizes here in Troy, so that he may know whether we are of any help to him or not, to him who now has dishonoured Achilles, a far better man than he—for he took away, and keeps, Achilles' prize, having wrested it from him. But indeed there is not wrath in Achilles' heart; he does not care—otherwise, son of Atreus, you would now do outrage for the last time.'

So spoke Thersites, railing at Agamemnon, shepherd of the host. But lordly Odysseus came to him quickly and glaring under his brows at him spoke harshly, saying: 'Ranting Thersites, you are a shrill talker; but be quiet, and do not try to combat by yourself against the kings. I say there is no mortal man worse than you, of all that came with the son of Atreus to Troy. Therefore, you should not lay your tongue to the kings as you talk, putting reproaches on them, and keeping an eye on your return home. We do not yet know how these things will turn out, and whether we sons of the Achaeans shall return well or badly. You keep upbraiding Agamemnon, son of Atreus, because the Danaan warriors give him many gifts, while you jeer. I tell you, and it shall be fulfilled—if I find you again raving as you were now, then may Odysseus' head no longer sit on his shoulders, nor may I be called any longer the father of Telemachus, if I do not take you and strip you of your cloak and tunic that cover your indecency and send you howling to the swift ships, drubbed shamefully out of the meeting place.'

So he spoke, and struck his back and shoulders with the staff. Thersites cringed, and a big tear fell from him. A bloody weal rose up on his back from the blow of the gold studded staff. He sat down, frightened and in pain, looking helplessly as he wiped away a tear. The Achaeans, though they were annoyed with him, laughed merrily, and one said to another: 'I tell you, Odysseus has before now done countless glorious deeds as leader in good counsel, and directing in war; but now he has done the best deed of all among the Argives in stopping this scurrilous babbler from talking. Never again will his proud spirit set him on to rail at the kings and abuse them.'

Telemachus' Speech

At the start of the *Odyssey*, Telemachus, Odysseus' son, is just coming to maturity. At the prompting of the goddess Athena, he determines to act to stop the depredations of the suitors in his house. The proposed meeting of the assembly does take place the next day, but all that happens is that Telemachus repeats his complaints. The people are not moved to take sides, although more is at stake than the misuse of the goods of one nobleman's household by other nobles.

Odyssey 1. 365–404

The courtiers clamoured in the shadowy hall, every one eager to be Penelope's bedfellow. Telemachus addressed them sensibly:

'Suitors of my mother, men overbearing and arrogant—for the moment let us enjoy our meal and let there be no disturbance, since it is a good thing to listen to a minstrel like this one, with a god-like voice. In the morning, let us all go and sit in the assembly, so that I may speak out directly and bid you leave these halls. Find meals elsewhere; eat your own substance, going from house to house in turn. However, if you think it better and more desirable that one man's substance should be destroyed without atonement, devour on; I shall appeal to the everlasting gods, in hopes that Zeus may grant requital; and then it will be you who will be destroyed in the house, without atonement.'

So he spoke, and they all sat biting their lips and marvelled at the boldness of Telemachus' speech. Then Antinous, son of Eupeithes, answered him: 'Telemachus, indeed the gods themselves are teaching you to talk big and bluster. May the son of Cronus never make you king in sea-girt Ithaca, which is your inheritance by birth.'

Sage Telemachus answered, 'Antinous, you may marvel at my words—this too I would wish to achieve, if Zeus granted it. Or do you say that this is the worst thing that could happen in man's life? To be a king is no bad thing: quickly his house becomes rich and he himself receives more honour. But there are many other kings of the Achaeans in sea-girt Ithaca, young and old, and one of them might possess this rule, since Odysseus is dead. However, I shall be master in my own house and halls, which lordly Odysseus got for me.'

Then Eurymachus, son of Polybus, replied: 'Telemachus, it rests on the lap of the gods who is to be king in sea-girt Ithaca. Possess your own property and rule in your own house, and may no man come and shamefully wrest your goods from you by force, so long as Ithaca is inhabited.'

SPARTA

Kingship in historical Sparta was hereditary in two houses, the Agiads and the Eurypontids. The Spartans themselves had a story that the dual kingship originated from the twin sons of Aristodemus, the Heraklid. The city was physically constituted by a group of villages, and it has been suggested that the true origin of the dual kingship was in the two earliest founded communities.

The following passage from Herodotus gives nearly all the information we have about the positive powers of the kings. In the latter part of the fifth century at least, we know from Thucydides, the king's wish in the matter of going to war could be overruled by the assembly. Three Spartan kings and one regent were deposed in the course of that century. Two of the five *ephors* elected annually by the citizens accompanied the kings on military expeditions, and on more than one occasion a king was obliged to accept the company of an advisory commission.

Of the authority of the Gerousia, or Council of Elders, we know little —there is no clear evidence in our sources of positive action by them. In the mid seventh century, according to the obscure text of the Rhetra, or enactment, quoted by Plutarch in his *Life of Lycurgus*, the assembly was given some rights of discussion, and a rider—the text of which is equally obscure—apparently limited these rights by giving kings and elders (or kings-with-elders) a power of veto.

The Spartan constitution was the wonder of the Greek world for its stability. The idea gaining ground in the fifth century that stability in a constitution would be ensured if a proper balance were found among the three alleged basic types of constitution, i.e. monarchy, oligarchy and democracy (rule by one, by a few and by the people at large), seemed to find exemplification and proof in Sparta, and Sparta became the stock example of the 'mixed constitution' in fourth-century and later theory, until Polybius in the second century B.C. tried to make Rome fit the model.

Such theories, however, do not explain why the kingship was maintained, and maintained in so exclusive a form, at Sparta. The reader may feel himself still, to a certain extent, in the atmosphere of the Homeric world in the description of the Spartan kingship written by Herodotus in the mid fifth century B.C. Various possibilities may be considered. The necessity to keep control of a hostile subject population (the helots) constituted a more or less permanent national emergency. The attractions normally inherent in monarchy elsewhere were perhaps lacking in Sparta, so that the crown was not an object of ambition or a stimulus to revolution. The full citizen population was, by the terms of the constitution, more than usually homogeneous in social and economic status, a factor which may have reduced pressure for radical change in the forms of government. But still —why keep the kings at all?

Herodotus 6

56. These are the privileges the Spartans gave their kings: two priest-hoods, those of Zeus Lacedaemon and Zeus Uranius; the right of making war on whatever country they wish—none of the Spartans is to prevent this on pain of being held accursed. In campaign the kings are the first to advance, the last to retreat. One hundred picked men guard them, and they are allowed to use as many cattle as they please on their expeditions. They receive the skins and chines of all the cattle that are sacrificed.

57. These are their privileges in war; in peace, they are allowed the following. If there is a public sacrifice, the kings are the first to sit down to the banquet and they are served first, receiving twice as much of everything as the other diners. They make the first libation and they receive the hides of the sacrificed animals. On the first and seventh days of every month each is given, at the public expense, an unblemished sacrificial victim to sacrifice at Apollo's temple, and a bushel of barley meal and a Spartan quart of wine. At all the games they have front seats reserved for them. It is their privilege to appoint whomever they wish of the citizens as responsible for handling the interests of foreigners, and to choose two 'Pythians' each. The Pythians are envoys to the Delphic oracle, and they dine with the kings at public expense. If the kings do not attend the state dinner there is sent to them at home two quarts of barley meal each and a half-pint of wine. When they are present they are given double quantities of everything. They are honoured in the same way when they are invited to dinner in private houses. They also keep all oracles, of which the Pythians also are cognizant. The kings also have sole power to judge certain legal matters, namely the following only: if an heiress has not been betrothed by her father, the king decides who is to have the right to marry her; and they have charge of the public roads. If anyone wishes to adopt a child, he must do so in the presence of the kings. They sit in deliberation with the twenty-eight elders; if they are absent, their next of kin among the elders take over the privilege of the kings, casting two votes and their own as a third.

58. These are the privileges accorded publicly by the Spartiates to the kings in their lifetime. When they die, there are the following honours: horsemen proclaim the event throughout Laconia, and in the capital women go round beating cauldrons. When something of this sort

occurs, two free persons from each household must put on mourning, one man and one woman, on pain of heavy penalties if they do not comply. One custom that is observed by the Lacedaemonians at the deaths of their kings is the same as among the barbarians in Asia—in fact, most of the barbarians observe the same custom on the deaths of their kings. When a king of the Lacedaemonians dies, then not only Spartans but a specified number of local inhabitants from all over Lacedaemon are obliged to come to join in the mourning. When they and the helots and the Spartiates are assembled for this purpose, to the number of many thousands, men and women together strike their foreheads earnestly, wailing as though they could never be sated with mourning, and declaring always that the deceased king was the best ever. When a king dies in battle, they make an effigy of him and carry it out on a richly draped bier. When they bury him, there are no public meetings or elections for ten days, during the whole of which period they mourn.

59. Another custom in which they resemble the Persians is that when a king succeeds on the death of his predecessor, the new king cancels all debts owed by any Spartan to the king or to the public treasury. Likewise in Persia the newly installed king remits arrears of tribute to all the cities.

EARLY ROME

The passage taken from the first book of Livy's history concerns the first occasion of succession to the throne at Rome—always a tricky moment in any monarchy. The account belongs to legend rather than fact, but not to any one simple legend. Livy is writing at a late stage in the tradition, when the legends had been modified and multiplied both by centuries of political development and by the prejudices of previous historians. One *might* also fancy that one could detect in Livy's presentation of this stage in the history of Rome a covert justification of the succession of Octavian to the position of Caesar, and allusions to the deification of the latter and the position of spiritual leadership and policy of national moral regeneration cultivated by the former. However, it would perhaps be going too far to attribute to Livy himself any deliberate intention of propaganda for the new régime; although he valued the peace Augustus' success had brought to Rome and Italy, Livy seems to have refrained from close association with the 'court circle'.

Romulus disappears, rather than dies—just the sort of ending one might expect for a hero, especially an eponymous founding hero. The story of the apotheosis is found as early as Ennius (239–169 B.C.). The epiphany is a feature characteristic of Greek, rather than Roman, religion and perhaps a Hellenistic addition. Julius Proculus was probably given a place in the story by Julian family tradition during their long time of obscurity before the first century B.C.

Livy's account of the end of Romulus is a blend of these favourable traditions, doubtless strengthened by the success of the Julii in the first century B.C., and of others less favourable, relating to the political history of the Senate. There is a hint of a tradition going back at least to the second-century writer Fabius Pictor that the announcement of the apotheosis was contrived by the Senators; and the version that had Romulus actually murdered by the Senators clearly belongs to the political quarrels of *populares* and *optimates*, as a slur on the Fathers. The account of the institution of the interregnum and the selection of a new king seem to be a reading back into pre-Republican history of the claims asserted by the Senate since at least the second century B.C. to over-all control in the state and of the—basically conflicting—assertion of ultimate popular sovereignty. At the same time, divine approval is sought for the person designated as king. Are we to interpret this as meaning that Livy's contemporaries or predecessors entertained belief in the 'divine right' of kings? The most ancient kings were both priests and warriors, leaders of their tribes in dealings both with men and gods, and this function did not quickly disappear. The consuls were conceived of as the successors to the powers and duties of the kings, and although in historical Rome they are not the only magistrates with the right of taking auspices, theirs are the senior auspices. Is the story of the selection and inauguration of Numa, then, in a sense part of the aetiology of the consulship?

Still, there is some ambiguity here. We shall observe later how tradition and aetiological legend could be used to 'sanctify' the position of Augustus.

Livy 1

16. These exploits merited immortality. Later, he was holding a meeting in the Campus Martius near the Marsh of Capra, to review the army, when suddenly a storm blew, with great claps of thunder. The king was covered in a cloud so thick that he was invisible to those assembled; and Romulus was seen no more on earth. The terror of the Roman warriors abated at length when the stormy weather gave way again to clear skies, calm and light. When they saw the royal throne empty, they believed the story of the Senators standing nearest, that

he had been swept off on high by a whirlwind; but as though stricken with grief at bereavement they maintained for some time a mournful silence. Then, with a few taking the lead, they all demanded that Romulus should be hailed as god, born of a god, king and father of the city of Rome. They prayed to him for peace, asking him always to look favourably upon and deliver his own offspring. I believe that at that time too there were some who secretly alleged that the king had been torn to pieces by the Senators—for this rumour also got about, though in covert hints only. However, the former story secured acceptance because of admiration for the man, and the immediate awe. Also it is said that further credence was given to the tale as the result of one man's contriving. During the city's distress at the disappearance of the king, and its hostility to the Senators, Julius Proculus, aware of the prevailing temper, conceived the shrewd idea of coming forward and addressing the assembly. 'Citizens,' he said, 'Romulus, the father of this city, at dawn today suddenly came down from heaven and presented himself before me. I was awe-struck. I prepared to do reverence to him, entreating to be allowed to look at him, and he said: "Go, report to the Romans that it is the wish of the inhabitants of Heaven that my Rome shall be head of the world; that the Romans therefore look after their military resources, and let them be assured, and pass on to their posterity the assurance, that no human strength can resist Roman arms." And when he had said that he went away aloft.' It was remarkable how readily his recital was believed, and how much the belief in Romulus' immortality did to alleviate mourning for him among the populace and the army.

17. Meanwhile, the thoughts of the Fathers were occupied by ambition and the struggle for the kingdom, though it had not yet come to a contest of individuals, since no-one in the new population was greatly pre-eminent. The contest was between factions. Those of Sabine descent thought that one of their number should be made king, because after the death of Tatius there had not been a king from their side, and they were afraid that, despite their having equal partnership in the state, they might lose the right to hold the command. The old Romans rejected the idea of a foreign king. Opinions were divided, but all were agreed in wanting to have a king, as they had not yet any experience of the sweetness of freedom. Then the Fathers were assailed by fear that if the state were left without a ruler, the army without a leader, while many of the surrounding states were hostile, some external power

might attack. So, it was agreed that there ought to be some government, yet no one could entertain the idea of yielding to another. So the hundred Fathers combined together. They made up ten decuries and appointed one man from each to hold supreme power. Ten men ruled. One had the emblems of power and the lictors; his period of office was limited to five days, and this went round them all in rotation. The monarchy was interrupted for a year; this period received in consequence the name still applied, *interregnum.* Then the plebs began to complain that they had a manifold servitude, as a hundred masters had been created instead of one; and it seemed that they would not put up with anyone else save a king appointed by themselves.

When the Fathers realized what was stirring, they thought it best to offer what otherwise they would lose, and they sought to ingratiate themselves by giving supreme power to the people, without, however, conferring more power than they retained. For they decreed that when the people appointed a king, this would be ratified if the Fathers gave their authorization. Today also when laws are proposed, or the conferment of offices, the same right is exercised, though only as a matter of form. Before the people go to vote, the Fathers give their authorization, while the outcome of the voting is still uncertain.

Then the interrex summoned a meeting and said: 'May it be good, blessed and fortunate. Citizens, appoint a king. This is the Fathers' decision. Then, if you appoint someone who is worthy to be reckoned second after Romulus, the Fathers will give their consent.' The people were so pleased by this that, not to seem outdone in generosity, they decreed and commanded merely that the Senate should determine who should rule at Rome.

18. At that time, the justice and devoutness of Numa Pompilius were renowned. He lived at Cures in Sabine territory and was, by the standards of that time, a man most learned in divine and human law. For want of another explanation, credit has been falsely given for creation of this branch of learning to the Samian Pythagoras, who one hundred years later, in the reign of Servius Tullius, is acknowledged to have had schools of young men, interested in his studies, around Metapontum, Heraclea and Croton. But even if they had been contemporaries, how could any word have reached the Sabines from those places? Or in what language could there have been communication, to rouse anyone to desire of learning? Or under what protection could one man reach there, through so many tribes differing in lan-

guage and manner of life? So, I think that it was through his own disposition that his mind was cast in a virtuous mould, and that he was
taught, not so much by the arts of foreigners as by the severe and stern
discipline of the ancient Sabines, than whom there was no more incorruptible race. When the Romans heard the name of Numa, although it
appeared that to take a king from the Sabines would result in access
of power to them, none the less no one ventured to nominate either
himself or anyone else of his own group, nor indeed any of the Fathers
or the citizens, in preference to him. Everyone voted that the kingdom
should be bestowed on Numa Pompilius. He was summoned; he gave
orders that, just as Romulus received kingship at the founding of
Rome as a result of augury, so the gods should be consulted about
him too. Then an augur, who was subsequently honoured by being
given this priesthood as a public office for life, led him to the citadel
and sat him on a rock facing south. The augur sat to his left with head
veiled, holding in his right hand a smooth staff, hooked at the end,
which they called a *lituus*. Then after taking sights over the city and
the countryside, he prayed to the gods and measured off areas from
east to west, and said that those on the right were southward, those
on the left northward, and took a notional boundary as far away as the
eye could reach. He passed the lituus into his left hand, laid his right
on Numa's head, and prayed: 'Father Jupiter, if it is lawful for this
Numa Pompilius whose head I hold to be king at Rome, give us a
definite sign within those limits I have set.' Then he described verb-
ally the signs he wished to be given. When they were given, Numa
was declared king, and left the place of augury

II. Fifth-Century Greece:
Constitutional Theory

Towards the middle of the fifth century evidence begins to appear of the development in the Greek world of political theorizing. According to Aristotle a certain Hippodamus of Miletus who, like Herodotus, went to join the new settlement at Thurii, wrote on constitutional theory.

The historian Herodotus (3.80–82) gives an account of a debate which he alleges took place between Darius (later King of Persia) and six others, after their successful revolt against the usurper Gaumata. Three speakers are quoted, Otanes advocating a democratic government for the Persians, Megabyzus an oligarchy, Darius monarchy. Herodotus is insistent that the debate as he renders it occurred, although the content he gives it has nothing to do with the theory or practice of government in the Persian empire. We cannot positively deny that any debate at all occurred; but the questions it would most appropriately have handled would be e.g. whether to continue the present system of a conglomeration of states with satraps and subject-rulers under one central authority, the Great King, or to disband the empire into its constituent states. The alternatives discussed here are those that would be appropriate to a single Greek city-state. The debate is very brief and condensed. Many crucial assumptions are made and the society assumed is Greek rather than Persian.

Two main themes emerge—first, the division of types of constitution into a basic three and, secondly, the status of law. The latter is a twofold theme. Otanes' speech and the passage from Euripides both make explicit the theme of the contrast between arbitrary rule and the rule of law (which we shall find further discussed by Aristotle in a later chapter). The other theme, whether law can or should be challenged or altered by citizens, occurs frequently later. There are examples later in this book; and perhaps the most famous example of all comes in the discussions which Plato represents Socrates as holding in prison during his last days.

The two passages that follow may be considered as reactions to radical democracy as practised at Athens from the mid fifth century B.C., as much as theories of monarchy or sovereignty.

EURIPIDES

The story of the play is set in the immediate aftermath of the attack of the Seven Champions against Thebes. The Thebans refused to release the Argive dead for burial, and King Adrastus of Argos came with the mothers of the slain chiefs to ask Theseus, King of Athens, for help. King Creon of Thebes sent a herald to warn Theseus against giving help.

Euripides' play was probably produced first in 424 B.C. Whether direct allusion was intended to the current international situation in Greece, with the approaching end of the Thirty Years' Peace between Argos and Sparta and serious developments in the Peloponnesian War, need not concern us here. The passage in question disregards verisimilitude—Theseus, a legendary king of antiquity, is given words that support, and assume the existence of, a fully developed democracy at Athens—Euripides, of course, is writing for an Athenian audience.

The herald is given strong arguments against direct democratic government, to which no direct answer is made in Theseus' speech. Comparison might profitably be made with the passage from Aristotle's *Politics* (written in the latter part of the fourth century B.C.) immediately following, to consider whether Athenian democratic practice did provide any real safeguards against the defects mentioned. The end of the herald's speech hints at an important factor—is a belief in actual numerical equality really predominant in men's minds in a democracy, or are men always vulnerable to, or even actively looking out for, examples of Weberian *charisma*: 'a certain quality of an individual personality by virtue of which he is set apart from ordinary men and treated as endowed with supernatural, superhuman or at least specifically exceptional qualities'? Chapter 3 will afford some examples of conscious image-building by politically ambitious individuals.

Euripides, *The Suppliants*, 399–449

Herald: Who is tyrant of the land? To whom am I to proclaim the words of Creon, who rules over the land of Cadmus since the death of Eteocles by the sevenfold gates at the hand of his brother Polynices?

Theseus: First, stranger, you began your speech falsely in seeking a tyrant here. The city is not ruled by one man, but is free. The people is lord, succeeding annually in turns, not giving the greatest weight to wealth, but the poor man too having equal power.

Herald: In yielding this one point you allow us the advantage, as in dice. For the city from which I come is ruled by one man, not by the mob. No one feeds the city's conceit with words and twists it this way and that for his own gain, saying what is pleasant and very agreeable at the moment, but harmful later, and then by fresh denunciations disguising his own earlier mistakes and evading retribution.

In any case, how could the populace, who never direct their reasoning aright, guide the city on the proper path? Time, not haste, enables better understanding.

Moreover, a poor man, even if he is not actually a dolt, would be too busy with his own concerns to attend to public business. Indeed, it is noxious to the better class, when a low fellow wins repute by charming the people with his tongue, when he was nothing before.

Theseus: This herald is a clever fellow, a quibbler with words. But, since you have entered into this contest, listen. You were the one who started the debate.

Nothing can be more inimical to a city than a tyranny, where—to take the most important point—there are no public laws, and one man rules, who has established the law by himself alone. This is not equitable. Where the laws are written down, the weak man and the wealthy have equal justice, the weaker has the same right to speak as the well-off, when he is abused, and the lesser man, when he has justice on his side, prevails over the greater. This is what freedom says: 'Does anyone wish publicly to present some useful counsel to the city?' He who wishes to to so, wins fame, he who does not is silent. What could be more equitable in a state?

Moreover, where the people is sovereign over the land, it takes pleasure in its youthful citizens growing up. But a king thinks these his enemy. Of the best men, those he thinks to have some sense he kills, fearing for his tyranny. How could a city still be strong when it lops off and destroys its valiant youth, like the bloom of a meadow in spring?

ARISTOTLE AND RADICAL DEMOCRACY

Power concentrated in the hands of an individual or of a small number may be regarded by the rest of the people as dangerous. On the other hand, individuals are unequal in various respects; Aristotle examines the consequences of assuming that this is not so. It is not easy to determine whether rules of the kind he describes are intended to nullify certain inequalities by making the possession of certain qualities irrelevant for the conduct of public business, or whether they are simply a consequence of the determination to prevent concentrations of power. The answer may be a mixture of the two. Have the Herald's objections been met, or are there perhaps still loopholes left?

Aristotle, *Politics*

1317b. The basis of the democratic constitution is liberty. (This is what is usually said, as though it is only under this constitution that men partake of liberty; for this they say is the objective of democracy.) One characteristic of liberty is to rule and be ruled in turn. For democratic justice is equality—but numerical equality, not equality according to merit; and on this conception of justice, the majority must be sovereign, and whatever is the wish of the greater number, this prevails and is justice—for they say that each of the citizens must be treated equally. So in democracies it turns out that the poor are more powerful than the rich, because they are more numerous and the rule of the majority is sovereign. This, then, is one mark of liberty, which all democrats specify as a criterion for the constitution. Another is to live as one wishes. This they say is an effect of freedom, since not to live as one wishes is the life of a slave. Therefore this is a second defining characteristic of democracy. Next comes not being ruled—preferably by anyone at all, but failing that to rule and be ruled in turn, and this contributes to liberty, on a basis of equality.

Given these principles and rules of this kind, the following are democratic: all officials are chosen from all; everyone rules everyone else in turn; the lot is used to assign offices, either all or those which do not need expertise and skill; there is no property qualification for office, or a very small one, and the same man is not to hold office twice, or very rarely and only in the case of a few offices, except military ones; all offices, or as many as possible, are to be of short tenure; justice is to be administered by the whole people or persons drawn from the whole people, and is to deal with everything, or with the most important and vital matters, such as auditing of magistrates' accounts, constitutional matters and private contracts; and the assembly is to be sovereign over everything or over the most important matters, but no official is to have authority save over the most trivial matters (and of offices, the most democratic is membership of the council, except in states where public pay is not available for all, for, if it is, they deprive this office also of its power, for the people, if it receives state pay, takes all decisions upon itself, as was said previously in our earlier exposition); then another criterion is that there should be state pay, preferably for all—the assembly, courts and magistrates —or, failing that, for the magistrates and the courts and council and the scheduled assemblies, or such officials as must take meals together. Moreover, since the defining features of oligarchy are noble birth and wealth and education, those of democracy seem to be the opposite, low birth, poverty and lack of education. Again, no offices are to be perpetual, and if any such survive from the old order, its powers are to be curtailed and it is to cease to be elective and be decided by lot.

1318a. So these are the common features of democracies, and from what was agreed to be democratic justice (that is, that all should be equal, on an arithmetical basis) there results what seems most like democracy, and the demos or sovereign people. For it is equality that the poor should not have more power than the rich and the poor should not be sovereign alone, but everyone equally and arithmetically, for in this way one would impose equality and freedom would exist in the constitution.

III. Self-Promotion in a Republic

For an ambitious man, the theoretical equality of citizens of a constitution-ally governed country, whether, in a radical democracy, among all, or, in Republican Rome, among those eligible for office and membership of the Senate, could be frustrating. Fortunately, theory was not borne out by practice nor were votes won solely by the rational presentation of policies but by other appeals of a less rational kind. One approach was appeal to the self-interest of the electors; there were various others, many of which could loosely be summed up as the creation of a personal charisma—with or without the supernatural element. This is particularly evident in the stories told of Pericles and Scipio, although the grand style of Cimon surely appealed to more than simply the cupidity of the Athenians.

Cimon, Pericles and Scipio have certain things in common which enabled them to succeed where a Thersites never could, and that although Pericles shares with Thersites one advantage in particular which he could turn to account to off-set the particular advantages of a man like Cimon. What worked the magic for them, and not for Thersites?

What these men did is stated, and some of the reasons, real or alleged, for their behaviour. Why this produced certain effects on the minds of the general public deserves consideration. Is a theoretical belief in equality perhaps less deep-seated and influential than certain other tendencies?

Cimon belonged to the aristocratic Athenian family of the Philaidae; his father had been a general at Marathon. Cimon's successes as general in command of Athenian and Delian League forces between 478 and 462 doubtless did much to enhance his political prestige. His politics, however, were not in sympathy with radical democracy, and in 462 B.C., when con-stitutional reforms at Athens coincided with a rebuff by Sparta, Cimon, who had advocated aid to Sparta and led the Athenian force sent to Ithome, was ostracized.

In his youth, said Plutarch, Cimon led a drunk and disorderly life and showed no interest in a literary education. Pericles, on the contrary, was keenly interested in philosophical studies; he also possessed outstanding gifts as an orator. He also was an aristocrat; his mother was the niece of

Cleisthenes the Alcmaeonid, promoter of the first major democratic reforms at Athens.

Scipio belonged to the patrician Roman family of the Cornelii. His uncle was consul in 222 B.C., his father in 218. Through his mother, he was connected with the patrician Aemilii. In 218, he saved his father's life in battle; in 216 as military tribune he rallied the survivors of the Roman defeat at Cannae. His election as curule aedile was in 213 B.C. Three years later the Roman people chose him by popular acclaim to command the Roman army in Spain with proconsular *imperium*, although he had held no qualifying office; this is the occasion of the speech reported in the Livy passage.

CIMON

Plutarch, *Cimon*

10. Cimon was already a wealthy man, and his expense-allowance as general, which appeared to be a profit he had honourably earned from campaigning, he spent still more honourably upon the citizens. He took down the fences from his estates, so that strangers and needy citizens could help themselves freely to the fruits, and provided at his home every day a dinner that was plain, but sufficient for a large number of people, so that any poor man who wished could come in and receive maintenance that cost him no effort and left him free to attend exclusively to public affairs. Aristotle says that he did not provide this dinner for all the Athenians, but only for the members of his own deme, Lacia. He customarily was attended by a number of young men, handsomely dressed, and if Cimon met any of the older citizens poorly dressed one of the young men would change clothes with him; this sort of occurrence impressed people. The young men were also supplied with plenty of small change, and they would go up beside decently turned-out poor people in the market place and silently slip some coins into their hands. This is probably what Cratinus the comic poet refers to in *The Archilochians* when he says: 'And I Metrobios, the clerk, prayed that I might spend a sleek old age, feasting all the time, with the god-like man, most philanthropic to strangers, best of all the Greeks that ever were till now, Cimon. But he has passed on first and left me.'

Moreover, Gorgias of Leontini says that Cimon acquired money in order to spend it, and spent it so as to win honour. Critias, who was one of the Thirty, prays in one of his elegiac poems for 'the wealth of the Scopadae, the magnanimity of Cimon and the victories of Arcesilaus the Lacedaemonian'.

Indeed, we know that Lichas the Spartan won renown among the Greeks solely because he used to entertain foreigners to dinner at the Gymnopaedia; but the lavishness of Cimon surpassed even the ancient hospitality and generosity of the Athenians. The Athenians of old, as the city justly prides itself, taught the rest of the Greeks to sow seed for food, to find springs of water and to kindle fire, when men were in want of all this; but Cimon made his house as it were the public hall for all the citizens, and in the country he allowed strangers to take first pick of the ripe fruit and every other good thing in season, and, in a way, he restored to their lives the legendary age of Cronos when everything was shared. Some people said this was mere flattery of the mob and demagogy, but they were refuted by his general political stand, which was aristocratic and favoured Sparta. When Themistocles began to push democracy too far, Cimon joined Aristides in resisting him; later he opposed Ephialtes, when the latter, to win popular favour, tried to destroy the Council of the Areopagus; and though he saw that all the other politicians, except Aristides and Ephialtes, were filling their coffers from public funds, he remained impervious to bribery and corruption, and right to the very end always spoke and acted honestly and without thought of gain.

PERICLES

Plutarch, *Pericles*

5. Pericles had an extreme admiration for this man (Anaxagoras), and becoming steeped in the so-called higher philosophy and exalted speculation it seems that he cultivated a dignified mien and a lofty style of speech, kept pure from all low and vulgar buffoonery. Not only that, but the composure of his face was unbroken by laughter, his walk was smooth, his mantle was carefully arranged and not disturbed by any occurrence while he spoke, and the modulation of his voice was controlled. By all these and other similar means he made a great impression on the populace.

Indeed, on one occasion he endured the reviling and insults of some low, licentious fellow in the agora for a whole day without replying, continuing meanwhile to conduct pressing business. When evening came, he went off homewards calmly, followed by the man, who was heaping all kinds of abuse on him. When he was about to go in, it being already dark, he told one of his servants to take a light, escort the man and see him to his home. The poet Ion says that Pericles' behaviour was disdainful and conceited and that his haughtiness was mingled with a great deal of arrogance and contempt for others, while he praises Cimon for being agreeable, compliant and urbane in his dealings in society.

But we may dismiss Ion, who expects virtue, like a tragic tetralogy, to have always a touch of the satyr-play in it. On the other hand, Zeno reproved those who decried Pericles' dignified bearing as mere popularity-hunting and conceit, and said that they should do something of the sort themselves, since the imitation of noble qualities might imperceptibly turn them into a habit and make them admired.

7. Pericles when young was inclined to give the people a wide berth. For he was thought to resemble the tyrant Peisistratus in appearance, and the sweetness of his voice and fluency of his speech made the very old men astonished at the likeness. As he was wealthy and of good family and had powerful friends, he was afraid of being ostracized, and so kept clear of politics, but on military service he was courageous and ready to take risks. Then, when Aristeides was dead and Themistocles in exile, and Cimon was kept away by frequent campaigning outside Greece, then Pericles began to devote himself to the people, taking the part not of the wealthy and few but of the poor and many (although his own nature was by no means to be an adherent of the *demos*). But, it seems, he was afraid of incurring suspicion of tyrannical leanings, and seeing that Cimon was aristocratic and was an outstanding favourite with the upper-class Athenians, he wooed the masses, to win security for himself and also strength to oppose Cimon. And immediately he changed the fashion of his way of life. He was seen going along only one street in the city, that leading to the agora and the council chamber. He refused all dinner invitations and all such friendly social engagements. In fact, during all his long political career he never went to dine with a friend, except that he did attend the wedding-feast given by his great-uncle Euryptolemus, but stayed only until the libations were poured, then left. For social occasions

are apt to overcome dignity, and it is hard to preserve an impressive solemnity in familiar company; but true virtue is the more beautiful the more it is seen, and the daily life of good men does not so rouse the admiration of outsiders as it does that of close friends.

He avoided regular contact with the people and satisfied their curiosity only at intervals, not speaking on every matter, nor attending the assembly constantly, but, as Critolaus says, reserved himself like the state galley Salaminia for great occasions, and employed friends and other speakers on other matters. One of these people they say was Ephialtes, who broke the power of the Council of the Areopagus, 'pouring out,' said Plato, 'for the citizens a large and unmixed draught of the wine of freedom', the result of which, the comic poets say, was that the people grew unruly like a horse and would no longer obey, but bit at Euboea and leapt upon the islands.

SCIPIO

Polybius 10

2. As I am about to relate Scipio's actions in Spain, and in short everything he accomplished in his life, I think I ought first to inform my readers of the character and natural endowments of the man. For the fact that he became almost the most famous man who had ever lived up to his own day makes many people desire to know what he was like, and what was the nature or the training that served as the basis for so many remarkable achievements; and they are compelled to remain in ignorance or under false impressions because those who have given accounts of him have gone far wide of the truth. The soundness of what I now say will be evident to those who are able by means of my account to appreciate the most glorious and most hazardous of his exploits. All other writers represent him as a man favoured by fortune, who generally succeeded in his enterprises contrary to expectation and by mere chance. They assume that such men are somehow more divine and more deserving of admiration than those who always act with deliberation. They are unaware that one of the aforesaid conditions deserves praise, the other congratulation, the latter being common to all and sundry, while praise properly belongs to those who reason well and

have intelligence, and that these are the men whom we should consider most divine and most dear to the gods.

In my opinion, the nature and outlook of Publius strongly resemble those of the Spartan lawgiver Lycurgus. For we must not suppose either that Lycurgus in formulating the Spartan constitution acted from superstition and referred everything to the Pythia, or that Scipio won such ascendancy in his country by following dreams and omens. However, both of them saw that the majority of men are reluctant to accept anything strange and do not venture on formidable undertakings without the hope of help from the gods. So Lycurgus made his own plans more acceptable and persuasive by adducing the utterance of the Pythia in their support. Likewise Publius made the men under his command more confident and zealous in facing dangerous exploits through encouraging the belief that he was acting under some divine inspiration. That he did everything with calculation and premeditation, and so the outcome of all his undertakings was as planned, will be clear from what I am about to say.

3. It is agreed that Scipio was beneficent and magnanimous; but that he was also shrewd and circumspect and kept his mind fixed on his aim, no one would agree save those who lived with him and saw his nature absolutely clearly. One of these was Gaius Laelius, who from his youth participated in every word and deed of Scipio's, to the end. It is Laelius who has created in me this impression of Scipio, as what he says appears plausible and consonant with Scipio's deeds. For he says that the first signal action of Publius was at the time when his father had a cavalry engagement with Hannibal near the river Po. At the time, it appears, Scipio was in his seventeenth year and this was his first emergence into public life. His father attached to him, for safety, a picked band of cavalry, and when Scipio caught sight of him in the battle, surrounded by the enemy, seriously wounded, and accompanied by only two or three horsemen, he at first set about urging his companions to go to his father's rescue, but they hung back for some time because of the press of the enemy around them, and so he himself, it seems, charged recklessly and boldly against the encircling opponents. Thereupon the rest were obliged to attack, and the enemy were terrified and dispersed, while Publius, thus unexpectedly rescued, was the first to address his son in the hearing of all as his preserver. This service gained Scipio an acknowledged reputation for courage, but thereafter he was careful of exposing himself to per-

sonal risk in times of danger, when his country's hopes of her entire welfare depended upon him; and this is the characteristic not of a commander who relies on fortune, but of one who is sensible.

4. After this, his elder brother Lucius was a candidate for the aedile-ship, which is about the most distinguished office open to young men among the Romans, the custom being to elect two patricians. On this occasion, as there were several candidates, for a long time Scipio did not venture to offer himself as candidate for the same office along with his brother. As the election approached, Scipio reckoned from the inclination of the populace that his brother would not easily gain the office, while he saw the people had a great deal of good-will towards himself; and supposing that the only way that his brother would achieve his aim would be if both of them came to an agreement and made the attempt together, he arrived at the following plan. Observing that his mother was going around the temples and sacrificing to the gods on behalf of his brother (he had only her with whom to concern himself, as his father at that time happened to depart for Spain where he had been appointed commander in the aforesaid campaign), he assured her that he had twice had the same dream. For he, it seemed, had been elected to the aedileship along with his brother and they were going up from the Forum to their house when she met them at the door and welcomed them with embraces. She was affected by this as a woman would be, and exclaimed something like, 'Would I might see that day.' Said he, 'Would you like us to try, mother?' And she agreed, never thinking that he would dare but supposing that he was merely making a joke in the circumstances, for he was very young. So he asked her to get a whitened toga ready for him at once, as this is customary for candidates. What she had said was not in her mind at all, and Scipio first got his white toga and then, while his mother was still asleep, he presented himself in the Forum. The populace, owing to the unexpectedness and to his previous popularity, received him with pleasure and enthusiasm, and afterwards when he went to the appointed place and stood beside his brother not only did the multitude confer the office on Publius, but on his brother also for his sake, and they arrived home both having become aediles. When the news of the event suddenly came to his mother she was overjoyed and came and met the young men at the door and welcomed them ecstatic-ally, so that as a result everyone who had heard of the dreams believed that Publius had converse with the gods not only in his sleep but even

more in reality by day. It was nothing to do with a dream at all, but, as he was kind and generous and affable in greetings, he calculated on his popularity with the people. So by accommodating himself appropriately to the disposition of the people and of his mother he not only achieved his aim but also had the reputation of acting under some kind of divine inspiration. For those who are unable to discern accurately circumstances, causes and dispositions, either because of poor natural endowments or from inexperience and laziness, ascribe to the gods and to chance what is accomplished through shrewdness by calculation and foresight.

Livy 26

19. When Scipio observed that the Romans were anxious and worried after their precipitate action, he called a public meeting. There he spoke about his youth and the command bestowed on him and the war in prospect, with such spirit and enthusiasm as to rekindle and renew their diminished ardour and fill them with a more assured hope than is wont to be engendered by reliance on a man's promise or reasoning based on expectation of his success. For Scipio was remarkable not only for his genuine virtues but for the skill he had since youth developed in displaying them. He usually behaved in public as though his actions were prompted by visions in the night or inspired by divine admonition—either because he himself was in some way the slave of superstition, or in order to have his commands and recommendations acted on without delay, as though they were the deliveries of an oracle. Also, he had worked on men's minds from the very beginning; once he had formally come of age, he undertook no public or private action on any day until he had first gone to the Capitol, entered the temple and sat down, and spent some time there, usually alone, in private. He observed this practice throughout his life and so—whether deliberately or not—gave credence among some people to the wide-spread notion that he was of divine stock. Men recalled the story earlier spread about Alexander the Great, which was equally baseless and fantastic, that he had been conceived as the result of intercourse with a snake, and that the apparition of this prodigy had often been seen in his mother's bedroom and when men came in it suddenly glided away and vanished. He himself never tried to scotch

belief in such marvels, but rather enhanced it by skilfully refraining both from denial and from overt affirmation. Many other tales of the same sort, some true, others invented, raised men's admiration for this young man to an extraordinary degree; and in reliance on these the state now entrusted so weighty a task and so great a command to one by no means of an age to bear it.

IV. Fourth-Century Theory: The Monarch and the Law

During the fourth century, the increasing difficulties of the city-states and the inadequacy of democracies to deal with them had effects both on practice and on thought. As to the former, new régimes came and went—oligarchies, federations with representative government, and tyrannies. Theorists, concerning themselves more and more with the search for the ideal constitution, were agreed in dismissing democracy. This, however, inevitably raised once again the question of the relation between the ruler, or rulers, and the law. In a full democracy, there was no basic conflict between the two, the rulers being also the ruled, and making the law for themselves. Where one man, or a limited number, had the *power*, where should the *sovereignty* be—with the ruler or the law? And what, in any case, was the sanction of the ruler's position?

THE ADVANTAGES OF MONARCHY

One school of thought is represented by Isocrates, who in the course of his long life became convinced that the city-states had had their day, and that strong central control, as represented by a Philip of Macedon or an Evagoras of Cyprus, was the only way to secure peace and prosperity. Philip he hails as the saviour of Greece, and terminator of her destructive quarrels.

However, he does not stop there. In the pair of companion speeches written soon after 372 B.C. for the benefit of Nicocles, son and successor of Evagoras of Cyprus, he produces a defence of monarchy as a constitution desirable in itself.

In the first speech, Isocrates speaks of how absolute power should be used, describing the ideal king in terms rather reminiscent of Plato's philosopher-kings. The king should be a model of virtue, acting according to the best philosophical theory, just and temperate, abiding by the laws and himself modifying them in the interests of justice and good government. The late Evagoras, it is implied, was such an ideal ruler, and his son

27

is exhorted to take advice from philosophers in his kingdom, so as to be
as much as possible like him. (One may recall Plato's attempts to guide
the tyrant of Syracuse.) The fact of power as the sanction of rule is passed
over.

The second speech is put into the mouth of Nicocles himself, addressing
his subjects on how they ought to behave. This incorporates a series of
arguments justifying monarchy as the best form of constitution. It is
interesting and instructive to compare the arguments here with those
Isocrates uses at *Areop.* 20–28 and *Panath.* 130–133, 143–148, to demonstrate the superiority of the Solonian 'democracy' (more accurately,
timocracy) at Athens. At the end of chapter 15, a disclaimer is inserted;
in the rest of the argument, it is ignored, and the character of the monarch
is taken for granted. But if a particular king is not an ideal of virtue, what
becomes of the arguments then?

Isocrates, *Nicocles*

11. You have heard Isocrates put one side, how a tyrant ought to
behave; now I shall try to expound the corollary, how subjects should
act—not that I aspire to outdo Isocrates, but I am the most appropriate person to speak to you of these matters. For if you mistook
my intention because I had not made it clear what I wanted you to do,
I would not be justified in being angry with you; but if I had stated in
advance what I wanted and none of it was done, then I would quite
rightly take to task those who did not obey.

12. In order to encourage and persuade you to be heedful of my word
and obedient, I think the best way would be not simply to give advice
by reeling off the various items, and then having done—rather, I
should demonstrate to you first that you ought to welcome the existing constitution not only because you must, nor because we have
always lived like this, but because it is the best of constitutions, (13)
and then that I hold rule here not illegally nor as a usurper but right-
fully and justly in virtue of my earliest forefathers and of my father
and in my own right. Once I have demonstrated all this, then surely
anyone would consider that he deserved the severest penalty if he did
not obey my advice and injunctions.

14. Concerning constitutions, then, since I am taking this as my starting point, I think all agree that it is most dreadful to have worthy
people and bad valued equally, but most just to make distinctions and
not to give unlike people the same treatment but to deal with each

and honour him according to his worth. (15) Now oligarchies and democracies aim at equality among those who have the franchise, and in these constitutions it is regarded as a laudable state of affairs that no one can have the advantage over anyone else—which, of course, benefits the bad. Monarchies, on the other hand, accord most to the best, secondly to those next, third and fourth and so on correspondingly. This perhaps is not actually established in practice everywhere, but such at any rate is the intention of the constitution.

16. Now everyone would admit that tyrannies more than other governments make distinctions between men of different natures and performances. What sensible man would refuse to participate in a constitution where his worth would not pass unnoticed, and he would not be lumped in with the masses without being recognized for what he is? What is more, we would be right in judging such a constitution to be milder, in as much as it is easier to attend to the views of one man rather than to try to please many varying dispositions.

17. So, one could demonstrate in many ways that it is pleasanter and milder and more just, though it is obvious from what I have already mentioned. Concerning its other virtues, the superiority of monarchy over other constitutions in adopting and implementing the best policies could readily be seen if one took their most important practices and examined them in comparison with each other. Where magistrates enter upon office for a year, they become private individuals again before they acquire knowledge of public affairs or experience in handling them; (18) whereas those who remain constantly in charge of the same duties, even if they have less natural ability, at least far excel everyone else in experience. Again, the former neglect many matters, because each leaves them to someone else, while the latter think nothing beneath their notice, because they know that they are responsible for everything's being done. Furthermore, in oligarchies and democracies those in office harm the interests of the people as a whole through their rivalry among themselves; but those in monarchies, having no one to envy, in all circumstances do the best they can.

19. Again, in other constitutions they are always late in acting, because they spend most of their time on their own concerns, and when they come to a meeting, one will find them more often falling out than taking counsel together; but in tyrannies, where there are neither assemblies nor times appointed for them, the rulers are at work day and night and miss no opportunity, but do everything at the right time.

20. Again, those others are malicious, and wish their predecessors and successors to manage the state as badly as possible, so that their own reputation may be enhanced; while monarchs, being in authority all through their lives, are always benevolent.

21. But this is the chief difference: the former treat the state's interests as though they were the concern of others, monarchs as their own concern; in choosing advisers, the former take the most foolhardy of the citizens, the latter choose out the most sensible; the former esteem those who have the gift of mob oratory, the latter those who know how to handle affairs.

22. Not only are monarchies superior in routine, everyday circumstances, but they embrace every advantage in wars as well. For tyrannies are better able than other constitutions to raise armies and use them effectively for surprise, and to win people over by persuasion, force, bribery and other means of conciliation. One can be assured of this from their actions as well as their words.

23. First, we all know that the power of the Persians grew so great not because of the intelligence of the people, but because they honour kingship more than any other race. Secondly, the tyrant Dionysius took over Sicily when the rest of it was in a state of upheaval and his own city under siege, and not only did he release it from its present dangers, but he made it the greatest of the Greek states.

24. Again, the Carthaginians and Lacedaemonians, who are the best governed people in the world, are oligarchies in domestic affairs, but ruled by kings in war. One could point also to the fact that the city which most hated tyrannies, when it sent out many generals failed, but when it took risks under a single leader succeeded.

25. Yet how could one show more clearly than through such examples the supreme excellence of monarchy? For those states which have always had monarchs are seen to have the greatest powers; that the best of the oligarchies in their most serious undertakings appoint in some cases a sole general, in others a king, who has command of the armed forces; but states that hate tyrants, when they send out many commanders, succeed in nothing.

26. To take an old example—it is said that the gods too have a king, namely Zeus. If this story is true, then clearly the gods also prefer this type of constitution, and even if no one knows the truth of it for certain, and this is merely what we conjecture and suppose to be the case, still it is an indication that we all give pre-eminent honour to

monarchy; for we would never say that that was the practice among the gods, if we did not think it was better than all others.

PLATO AND THE SCIENCE OF RULING

Plato, in the *Politicus* ('Statesman'; written about the middle of the fourth century), operates on a much more theoretical plane. He is less concerned with justification of monarchy as an existing institution than with establishing that the ideal rule must be a monarchy or at most a very narrow oligarchy. As usual, however, we are dealing with the Ideal Ruler and Ideal Law. Does Plato favour absolute monarchy in practice? Is the relationship of which he approves between actual ruler and actual law parallel to that between their respective Ideals? And why is it that the former, the Ideal ruler, might conceivably, he seems to think, exist in practice, but not the latter?

Plato, *Politicus*

291 *Stranger:* We agree that monarchy is one of the forms of government?

Young Socrates: Yes.

Str.: And after monarchy I suppose one would mention rule by the few.

Y.S.: Certainly.

Str.: And is not the third form of government the rule of the multitude, named democracy?

Y.S.: Certainly.

Str.: These are three; but do they not somehow become five, as they produce from themselves two additional names?

Y.S.: What?

Str.: When people pay attention to the presence in them of compulsion and voluntariness, and poverty and wealth, and law and lawlessness, they divide them in two, and they apply two names to monarchy, as having two forms—tyrannical and kingly.

Y.S.: Well?

Str.: And where a state is controlled by the few it is called an aristocracy or an oligarchy.

Y.S.: Quite so.

Str.: Whereas with democracy, whether the majority rule with

292 or without the consent of those who possess property, and whether they observe the laws scrupulously or not, still no one is ever in the habit of changing the name.

Y.S.: True.

Str.: Well then. Do we not suppose that one of these constitutions—defined according to the distinctions between one, few, many, wealth and poverty, compulsion or consent, written constitution or absence of law—is the right one?

Y.S.: Why not?

Str.: Then let us examine more closely, taking this line.

Y.S.: What line?

Str.: Do we abide by what we said at first or dissent from it?

Y.S.: What do you mean?

Str.: We said, I believe that kingly rule was one of the sciences.

Y.S.: Yes.

Str.: And not of all the sciences, but we chose out one involving judgment and command.

Y.S.: Yes.

Str.: And in the science of command we distinguished one part concerned with inanimate products and one with living creatures. And so by subdividing in this way we always progressed up to this point, always bearing in mind that it is a science, but not yet able to define it sufficiently accurately.

Y.S.: Quite right.

Str.: Then we think that the distinction should not be that of few or many, willing or unwilling, poverty or wealth, but of what kind of knowledge—that is, if we are going to follow our previous argument.

Y.S.: But we surely must.

Str.: So now we must consider this, in which of these forms of government there is produced the science of ruling men, which is pretty well the hardest science to acquire and the greatest. For we must find it, in order to see what persons must be distinguished from the wise king, persons who claim to be good statesmen and persuade many, but are nothing of the sort.

Y.S.: Yes we must, as the previous argument requires.

Str.: Now, do you think the multitude in a state is capable of acquiring this knowledge?

Y.S.: How could it?

Str.: But in a state of a thousand men would one hundred or even fifty be capable of acquiring it?

Y.S.: No, because then it would be the easiest of the skills; for we know that a city of a thousand men could not produce that number of champion draughts players who could match all other Greeks, still less that number of kings. For the man who has the science of kingship, whether he rules or not, must, according to our previous argument, be called kingly.

293 *Str.:* That was an apt reminder. And following on this I suppose we must look for the right rule in one or two or a very few men, whenever such rule occurs.

Y.S.: Certainly.

Str.: And these men, whether they rule with the consent of their subjects or not, whether they have written laws or not, and whether they are rich or poor, must, as we think now, be considered to be exercising their rule according to some science. To a very large extent this is how we think of physicians. Whether they treat us against our will or with our consent, whether they cut or cauterize or cause us pain in any other way, whether they have written precepts or not, whether they are poor or rich, nonetheless we call them physicians, so long as they direct us in virtue of some art or science, purging us or reducing us in some other way or even building us up, so long as those who treat their patients do so for the benefit of their physical health, making them better than they were, and so preserve them. In this way, I believe, and in no other we shall determine this to be the only true definition of the rule of the physician or any other kind of rule.

Y.S.: Quite so.

Str.: So, it seems, among forms of government, that one is pre-eminently correct, and is the only right one, in which one finds that the rulers are really in possession of science and do not merely seem to be so; and whether they rule according to laws or without laws, over willing or unwilling subjects, whether they are poor or rich, none of this is to be taken into consideration at all on any right method.

Y.S.: Excellent.

Str.: And if they purge the state for its good by killing or banishing some of the citizens or make it smaller by sending out colonies, like a swarm of bees, or if they make it larger by bringing in other citizens from elsewhere, so long as they make use of science and justice in preserving it and make it better than it was, so far as they can, then that must, at that time and according to those characteristics, be considered the only right form of government; and all the other forms must be described as not being legitimate or really existent, but merely imitating that one. Those we call well-governed imitate it better, the others imitate it worse.

Y.S.: Everything else you have said, stranger, seems reasonable. But it is hard to accept the statement that government should be carried on without laws.

Str.: You took the words out of my mouth, Socrates. I was just
294 about to ask you whether you agreed with all of this or whether you objected to anything that was said. Now clearly we will want to discuss the question of the rightness of government without laws.

Y.S.: Certainly.

Str.: Yet in a way it is clear that law-making is part of the science of kingship; but the best thing is not that the laws should be powerful, but that the man should be, who is wise and kingly. You understand the reason?

Y.S.: What reason do you mean?

Str.: Because the law could never, by laying down exactly what is noblest and most just for all at once, prescribe what is best; for the dissimilarities between men and between circumstances, and the fact that virtually nothing in human affairs is ever static, does not allow any science of any sort to put forward one simple rule to cover everything and all occasions. You agree?

Y.S.: Oh, yes.

Str.: Yet we see that this is almost exactly what the law aims at. It is like a stubborn and ignorant man who allows no one to do anything contrary to his own command nor to question it, not even if something new occurs to someone that is better than the rule he himself laid down.

Y.S.: True; the law, as it is, treats each of us exactly as you have said.

Str.: So a simple rule of universal application could not be appropriate when applied to things that are never simple?

Y.S.: That seems likely.

Str.: Then why is it necessary to make laws at all, if the law is not absolutely right? We must ask the reason for this.

Y.S.: Yes.

Str.: Now, we have here, as they have in other cities, classes for practising athletics, running and such-like, to prepare for contests.

Y.S.: Yes, lots of them.

Str.: Now, let us recall to mind the instructions given by skilled trainers in command of such classes.

Y.S.: What sort of thing?

Str.: They think there is no room for going into detail with each individual and prescribing what is appropriate for each person's physique. They think they must use more rough-and-ready methods and give a general instruction which will benefit the physique of the majority.

Y.S.: Very good.

Str.: So they allot equal exercises to entire classes and start them off and stop them at the same time, in running or wrestling or any other sort of physical exercise.

Y.S.: That is so.

Str.: Now, we are to believe that the law-maker, who is to have
295 charge over the masses and look after justice and contracts, will never be able, by issuing general rules to cover all of them, to assign precisely what is appropriate to each individual.

Y.S.: Probably not.

Str.: But I think he will lay down a law for the majority and in general, and so applying only roughly to individuals, whether he issues written laws, or follows unwritten ones, i.e. traditional customs.

Y.S.: Right.

Str.: Yes. Quite right. For how could anyone sit beside each individual all his life and command exactly what is proper for him to do? Any one of those truly possessing the kingly science, if he could do this, would hardly, I believe, put obstacles in his way by producing those written laws we spoke of.

Y.S.: Not according to what has been said, at least.

Str.: Or rather, not according to what is going to be said.

Y.S.: What is that?

Str.: Something like this. Let us suppose that a doctor or a trainer is going away and will, as he thinks, be away a long time from those under his care. If he thinks his pupils or patients will not remember his instructions, will he not want to write down memoranda for them?

Y.S.: Yes.

Str.: And what if he is away less time than he expected and comes back? Would he not dare to replace those written instructions with others, if others happened to be better for his patients because the winds or something else by act of God had unexpectedly changed from what usually happens? Would he be stubborn and think that no one must transgress the old rules, neither he himself by issuing others, nor his patient by venturing to do anything other than what was written, in the belief that these rules were medically sound and healthful and anything else was unhealthy and unscientific? If anything like that happened in science and true art on any matter, would not such regulations incur the greatest ridicule?

Y.S.: Assuredly.

Str.: Then if someone has issued written laws about just and unjust and noble and base and good and bad, or laid down unwritten laws for the herds of men that are tended each in their cities according to the laws of the law-givers, and if a scientific law-giver or someone like him arrives, is he not to be allowed to 296 enjoin anything different? Or would this prohibition not seem truly as ridiculous as that other?

Y.S.: Yes.

Str.: You know, then, the argument put forward in such cases by most people.

Y.S.: I can't think of it just at the moment.

Str.: It seems a reasonable one. For they say that if someone knows of laws better than those of their forbears, he should make laws for his own city if he can persuade it, but not otherwise.

Y.S.: Well, is that not right?

Str.: Perhaps. But if he does not persuade and uses force to impose the better laws, then, tell me, what name are we to give this force? But we cannot answer this yet, without first looking at our previous example.

Y.S.: What do you mean?

Str.: If someone who himself truly knows his craft does not persuade his patient, and contrary to the written instructions compels the patient, whether a child or a man or even a woman, to do what is better, what name will be given to this compulsion? Will we not call it anything sooner than allege it is an error, contrary to science and dangerous to health, as the phrase is? And the person subjected to compulsion in such a matter could correctly say anything, save that he was treated, by the physicians who compelled him, in an unhealthy and unscientific way.

Y.S.: Most true.

Str.: Now, what do we call an error in political science—baseness and wickedness and injustice, right?

Y.S.: Certainly.

Str.: So, suppose people force others, contrary to written law and traditional custom, to do what is more just and better and nobler than the previous system. If someone wants to reproach such people for such compulsion, then, tell me, if he is not to be an utter laughing-stock, must he not say anything always, rather than that those who underwent compulsion at their hands were treated basely and unjustly and wickedly?

Y.S.: Most true.

Str.: Do we say the compulsion was just if it was exercised by a rich man and unjust if by a poor one? Or, irrespective of whether he persuades or not, whether he is rich or poor, whether he contravenes written laws or not, if he does what is beneficial, then on such matters ought not this to be the truest standard of proper management of a city, according to which a wise and good man will manage the affairs of the ruled? Just as a pilot always keeps a watch on the welfare of the ship and the sailors, not setting

297 down any written regulations, but applying the science as law, and saves his fellow sailors, likewise, in the hands of those capable of ruling thus, there would be good government when they make science stronger than the laws? And whatever wise rulers do is not a mistake, so long as they observe one great principle, and by using wisdom and science always in dispensing the greatest justice to those in the city they are able to preserve them and make them, as far as possible, better than they were.

Y.S.: One cannot object to what has now been said.

Str.: And there is something else that cannot be objected to.

Y.S.: What?

Str.: That no multitude whatsoever could ever acquire such science and become capable of managing a state wisely, but our one right form of government must be sought in a small number, a few, or one person, and the other forms must be classed as imitations, as was said a little while ago, some imitating better, some worse.

Y.S.: How do you mean? I didn't properly understand before, either, what you said about imitations.

Str.: Yet it is no light matter if, after setting this argument going we drop it and do not proceed and show the error that arises in relation to it nowadays.

Y.S.: What is that?

Str.: What must be examined is something like this; it is not simple or easy to see, but let us try to grasp it. Consider: there is this one right constitution which we have spoken of; so you see that the others must preserve themselves by following the written laws of this one, doing what nowadays is praised, though it is not the most correct way.

Y.S.: Namely?

Str.: That no one should venture to do anything contrary to the laws in the city, and that anyone who does should suffer death and all the most extreme penalties. This is the good way and the most correct way, as a second-best, once one departs from the first form already spoken of.

Let us recount how what we called the second-best way comes into being.

(The Stranger returns to the analogies of the pilot and the physician. Suppose that a society conceived a mistrust of its pilots and physicians. Suppose it then decided to limit their authority and prepared a system of laws to be binding upon them; and began to select them by lot and call them to account year by year, and insist on their practising the sciences only according to the laws laid down, and indict anyone who studied these sciences otherwise than by the laws on a capital charge, as a corrupter of the youth. This, it is agreed, would lead to the destruction of the sciences. Suppose, further, that their practitioners broke the rules for reasons merely of cupidity or the like; this situation would be still worse. Therefore—returning to politics—the safest course for a state, as a second-best, is to allow no violation whatsoever of its laws.)

300 *Str.:* Now we said, if we remember, that the man who had knowledge, the true statesman, would by his science do much, in his activities, without regard to written regulations, whenever something seemed better to him, though it was in contravention of the regulations he had written down and sent to men elsewhere.

Y.S.: Yes, we did say that.

Str.: Now if a man or a number of men, who have laws established, were to try to do something contrary to the laws, as being better, would they not be doing, so far as they could, the same thing as our true statesman?

Y.S.: Certainly.

Str.: But if they did this without knowledge then they would be trying to imitate the truth, but they would imitate it very badly; and if they did possess the science, then this is not an imitation but the real thing?

Y.S.: Entirely.

Str.: Now, earlier we agreed that it was not possible for any multitude whatsoever to acquire the science.

Y.S.: Yes.

Str.: So, if there is a science of kingship, the numbers of the wealthy and the people as a whole could never acquire this science of government.

Y.S.: No, how could they?

301 *Str.:* So, such constitutions, it seems, if they are going to the best of their ability to imitate well the true government under the one man who rules with science, must never, once their laws are established, do anything contrary to the written law and ancestral custom.

Y.S.: Excellently said.

Str.: Now, when the rich imitate this government, we call it an aristocracy; and when they disregard the laws, oligarchy.

Y.S.: Probably.

Str.: Again, when one man rules according to the laws, imitating the man who knows, we call him a king, not making a distinction in name between the man who rules with science and the one who rules by opinion, if they both follow the laws.

Y.S.: Yes, we probably do.

Str.: So, if one man, who truly has science, rules, he will be called by the same name, king, and nothing else. As a result, the five names of the forms of government mentioned just now have become one only.

Y.S.: So it seems.

Str.: When one man rules, and does not act in accordance with laws or customs, but claims, like the man with science, that he should act contrary to written law to do what is allegedly best, and it is some desire or ignorance that directs this imitation, then is not each such man to be called a tyrant?

Y.S.: Yes.

Str.: So, we say, a tyrant has come into being, and a king and oligarchy and aristocracy and democracy, because people are discontented under the one monarch, and do not believe that anyone could ever be worthy of such an office, so as to have the will and the capacity to rule with virtue and science and dispense real justice and equity to all, but rather that he will harm and kill and injure whomever he wishes at any time. For if such a one as we describe came into being he would be welcomed and dwell here governing us to our happiness in the one truly right form of state.

THE ARGUMENTS FOR KINGSHIP

The two Aristotle passages that follow deal respectively with the themes of Law and Power. The first (*Politics* 1284a ff.) forms an instructive comparison both with the *Nicocles* and with the *Politicus*. Aristotle distinguishes four types of known monarchy, differing in the degree of their limitation by law and in the attitude of the ruled. He precedes this discussion with a paragraph on the Ideal individual. It should be noticed that the sanction for rule by the Ideal monarch is different in kind from that for the others, as is his relation to law—'such people are themselves a law'—and Aristotle does not preclude the possibility of such a person's existence. It will not be long before we find theorists writing of the king as being the source of law, 'living law', *qua* king.

He then presents at some length the arguments for and against monarchic rule, particularly those against. In the end, his appeal is to 'natural fitness' —a concept that might seem not so widely different from Plato's.

Aristotle, *Politics*

1284a. If, however, there is one person so pre-eminent in respect of his exceptional excellence (*arete*)—or more than one, but still not enough to make up a whole city—so that there is no comparison between his—or their—*arete* and political power and that of all the rest, then such people are not counted part of the city. It would be unjust to reckon them on an equal footing with the rest, when they are so unequal in the respects mentioned; for such a person is like a god among men. So it is clear that laws must be applied only to those equal in birth and influence, and that over such people there is no law, for they themselves are a law. Anyone who tried to legislate over them would be ridiculous. They might reply as Antisthenes said the lions did when the rabbits began making demagogic speeches, calling for equality for all. This is why democratically governed cities have instituted ostracism; for these cities appear to aim above all at equality, and so they ostracized those who seemed outstandingly powerful because of wealth or connections or some other political advantage, and they removed them from the state for limited periods of time. There is also a legend that the Argonauts had some such reason for leaving Heracles; for the Argo refused to carry him with the others, as far surpassing the other rowers. So one must not simply assume the rightness of the censure passed by those who criticize tyranny and Periander's advice to Thrasybulus (the story is that Periander uttered no word in reply to the messenger who had been sent to him for advice, but cut off the exceptionally tall stalks of corn and made the field level; and the messenger did not know the reason for this action, but reported it to Thrasybulus, who understood that he ought to remove the pre-eminent men). This is beneficial not solely to tyrants, nor are tyrants the only people who do it; it is the same with oligarchies and democracies. Ostracism has something of the same effect, in cutting down the eminent and sending them into exile. The same thing is done to cities and to peoples by those who have power over them—as for instance the Athenians did to the people of Samos and Chios and Lesbos, whom they humbled, as soon as they were firmly in control, despite the agreements. The Persian king likewise often cut down the Medes and the Babylonians and others who were proud because they had once possessed an empire.

1284b. This problem is general in all constitutions, even the right ones; for the divergent forms do it because they aim at private advantage, but it does also happen in constitutions aimed at the common good. The same principle is seen in the arts and sciences in general.

A painter will not allow the foot of an animal to be disproportionately big, even if it is extremely beautiful, nor will a shipwright allow a prow or any other part of the vessel to do so, nor will a chorusmaster allow someone who sings better and more beautifully than the rest of the chorus to join in with the others. Therefore, nothing in this practice prevents monarchs from being in harmony with their cities while using it, so long as their personal rule is beneficial to the city. Therefore the argument for ostracism does have some political justice, in the case of admitted pre-eminence. It would be better if a legislator could so frame the constitution in the first place that there was no need of such surgery; but next best, if it so turns out, to try to set things right by some such correction. This did not happen in the cities in question; they did not have regard to the particular interests of the city, but used ostracism as a weapon in factional fighting. Now in the divergent constitutions it is clear that it is beneficial and just in specific instances, but it is also clear, perhaps, that it is not just absolutely. Even under the best constitution, there is much uncertainty as to what should be done, not in the event of pre-eminence in other qualities, such as strength or wealth or powerful connections, but if someone should excel in *arete*. For no one would say that such a person should be driven out and expelled, but neither would they agree to his holding office, for it would be as if they were to claim to rule over Zeus, and demarcate his sphere of power. The remaining, and natural, alternative is that all should obey such a person willingly, so that such people would be perpetually kings in their cities.

Perhaps after what has been said it would be well to pass over to an examination of kingship, which we say is one of the correct constitutions. We must consider whether it is in the interests of good government for a city or country to have a king, or whether some other constitution is preferable, or whether it is beneficial for some places and not for others. First one must determine whether all kingship is of one kind or whether there are several different varieties.

1285a. It is easy to ascertain that the term covers several different types, and that the nature of the rule is not the same in all. That in Laconia appears to be a kingship of the kind controlled by law, but the kings are not in control of everything. They are commanders in war when they go out of the country, and also certain religious matters are allocated to the kings. This kind of kingship is a sort of plenipotentiary generalship, held in perpetuity. They have not the authority to take life, except for cowardice, as for instance in ancient times on military expeditions, by the exercise of summary justice. Homer shows this. Agamemnon put up with abuse in the assemblies, but when they had gone out on expeditions, he had the power to inflict death; for he says, 'Whomever I catch away from the battle . . . he will have no hope of escaping dogs and vultures, for I have the power of death.'

So this is one kind of kingship, generalship with life tenure. Some instances of this run in families, some are elective. There is also another kind of monarchy, of which there are some instances among the barbarians. These all have power very like that of tyrants, but they are bound by law, and hereditary. As barbarians are by nature more slavish than Greeks, and Asiatics than Europeans, they put up uncomplainingly with despotic rule. This, then, is why they are tyrannical. The reasons for their stability are that the monarch is hereditary, and rules by law. Likewise their guard is a royal one, not that of a tyrant; for kings are guarded by their own citizens, bearing arms, tyrants by foreigners. Kings rule by law and over willing subjects, whereas tyrants rule over the unwilling—so the former have guards drawn from the citizens, the latter guards against the citizens.

So there are these two kinds of monarchy, and another is that which existed in ancient times among the Hellenes, called *aisumnetes*. This is, roughly speaking, an elective tyranny, which differs from the barbarian model not in that it is not guided by law, but only in that it is not hereditary. Some held this office for life, some for limited periods or with limited functions. For instance, the Mytilenaeans once chose Pittacus to counter the exiles led by Antimenides and the poet Alcaeus. Alcaeus says in one of his drinking-songs that they chose Pittacus as tyrant—he upbraids the people, saying 'They set up the ill-begotten Pittacus as tyrant over the weak and ill-fated city, thronging to praise him.'

1285b. Constitutions of this type, then, are or were tyrannical, in that they were despotic, but regal, in that they were elective and with the consent of the ruled. There is a fourth type of regal monarchy, that found in heroic times, when kings were legal and hereditary and ruled by consent. Men gained positions of eminence as benefactors of the people, either through skills or prowess in war, or because they gathered people together or provided land for them, and so they became kings by popular consent and handed on the position as hereditary to their successors. They had control of the command in war and of sacrifices, save those reserved to the priests, and in addition they gave judgment. Some swore an oath, others did not; and oaths were confirmed by holding out the sceptre. So in ancient times they ruled over everything in the state, both domestic and foreign matters. Later the kings gave up some of these functions, and the common people took some over. In some cities, only the sacrifices were left to the kings, and where there was still a kingship worth the name, they retained only command in foreign wars.

These are the types of kingship, four in number. One existed in heroic times. This was rule by consent, but in the hands of specified people; and the king was general and judge and had control of religious affairs. Second is the barbarian type. This is a despotic rule, based on law, dependent on birth. Third, the one called *aisumnetes*—an elective tyranny. Fourth, the Spartan type. This is more or less a hereditary perpetual generalship. These differ from each other as indicated.

There is a fifth kind, where one person has responsibility for everything, in the way that each tribe or each city is sovereign over its common concerns. This is a kingship established for management, for just as domestic management is a kind of kingship over a house, so kingship over one city or tribe or more is a kind of domestic management. There are virtually two types of kingship that need to be considered, this one and the Spartan. The rest, which are numerous, lie somewhere in between, having less complete control than total kingship, and more than the Spartan; so these are the two we must consider. Of one, we must ask whether it is a good thing for a city to have a perpetual military commander, chosen by birth or class, or not; and of the other, whether it is a good thing or not to have one man in control of everything.

1286a. Inquiry into this type of military office would appear to be a legal rather than a constitutional matter (for it can occur in all types of constitution), so we shall leave it aside initially. However, the remaining kind of kingship is a type of constitution, and so we must examine it and run through the difficulties inherent in it. The starting point of the inquiry is whether it is better to be ruled by the best man or the best laws.

Those who think kingship is beneficial say that the laws merely give general injunctions but do not give directions according to circumstances as they arise, just as in any sort of art it would be silly to direct proceedings by written rules, and in Egypt doctors can change their treatment after four days, although if they do so sooner it is at their own risk. Clearly, therefore, the best constitution is not the one that follows written rules, that is, laws, for the same reason. All the same, the rulers must have a general principle. Something in which the emotional element is lacking is better than something in which it is innate. Now, the law does not contain emotion, whereas every human spirit necessarily does. Perhaps someone might say that, in compensation, the individual will decide better about particular cases. Clearly, he must be a lawgiver, and laws must be established, but these laws should not be binding where they go astray (though otherwise they should). On matters where law is unable to judge at all, or to judge well, ought the best man to rule, or all the citizens? As it is, they come together and try cases and deliberate and give judgments, all of which are on particular cases. Now, if one compares them individually, then probably any one of them is inferior to the best man; but a city is made up of many people, and so, just as a feast to which many have contributed dishes is better than one plain meal, so a multitude often judges better than one single person.

Moreover, the crowd is less corruptible. As with a larger body of water, so a larger number is less corruptible than a few. Also an individual may be mastered by anger or some other emotion, and his judgment would necessarily be impaired, whereas in the other case it would be hard for everyone to be angry and to make a mistake. The multitude, however, must consist of the free men, not acting beyond the law, except where the law is of necessity deficient. If this is not easy in the case of many men, but nevertheless there are a greater number of good men and good citizens, then would one man be less corruptible as ruler, or those who are more in number but all good? Obviously, the latter.

1286b. A possible objection is that they would be prone to faction, whereas a single ruler would not. Against this, however, one should perhaps set the fact that they are honest in spirit, just as he is. If, then, the rule of the majority, when they are all good men, is to be considered an aristocracy, and that of one man kingship, then aristocracy would be preferable to kingship for cities, whether the power has armed might attached to it or not, if it is possible to find a number of men of like nature. This perhaps was the reason for there being kings in the old days, that it was rare to find men who greatly excelled in virtue, especially as the states they lived in were small. So they used to make men kings because of their benefactions to the community, which are the actions of good men. When it came about that there were many men equally excellent, they tolerated this state of affairs no longer, but looked for some common arrangement, and established a constitution. Then men grew worse and began to enrich themselves at the community's expense, and this one may assume was the origin of oligarchies, because they brought wealth into esteem. Then they changed, first to tyrannies and then to democracy; for by confining the government always to fewer persons, out of greed for gain, they made the people stronger; and the latter attacked them, and set up democracies. Now that cities have become larger, perhaps it is no longer easy for any form of constitution save a democracy to come into being.

Well then: if one were to posit that kingship was best for the cities, what about the children? Ought the family to be kings, hereditarily? If the children turned out as some do, it would be disastrous. You might say that the king, having power to decide, will not hand over to his children; but one cannot readily trust in this, for it would be a difficult thing to do, one requiring superhuman virtue.

Another difficult point is that of armed force. Should someone who intends to be king have some force about him to enable him to compel those who will not obey his rule? How is he to exercise command otherwise? Even if he is supreme according to law, and does nothing voluntarily to transgress the law, none the less he needs force to safeguard the laws. Perhaps, though, this is no difficult matter to determine, in relation to such a king. He must have a force, sufficient to overpower an individual or a group of people, but still less than the majority in the state. Therefore the ancients, when setting up what they called an *aisumnetes* in a city, or a tyrant, gave him a bodyguard. When Dionysius asked for guards, someone advised him to give the Syracusans the same number of guards.

1287a. Now our discussion has arrived at the king who rules in all matters according to his own will, and him we must examine. The king who rules according to law does not represent a separate type of constitution, as we said (for perpetual generalships can occur in all sorts of constitutions, in democracy and aristocracy for instance, and many put one man in charge of administration—there is an office of this sort at Epidamnus and to a lesser extent at Opus). However, concerning absolute monarchy, that is, where the king rules entirely according to his own will, some think it contrary to nature to have one man sovereign over all the citizens, when the state is made up of like people; for people like in nature must, according to nature, have the same justice and the same esteem. Therefore just as it is physically harmful for unequal persons to have equal nurture or clothing, so it is with honours, and conversely with equal persons. It would not be just for any of them to rule, any more than to be ruled, but they should take it in turns. This is law; for law is regulation. Therefore it is preferable that the law should rule rather than any one of the citizens, and on the same principle if any people are better at ruling they should be made guardians and servants of the laws. For one must have some offices, but they say it is not just for one man to rule when all are alike.

Again, as has been said before, if the virtuous man is worthy to rule because he is better, two good men are better than one—see the proverb, 'When two go together' (*Iliad* 10. 224), and the prayer of Agamemnon, 'Would I had ten of like mind' (*Iliad* 2. 372). And some magistrates, like the dikast, even have power to judge some matters which the law is unable to determine. (I presume no one will dispute that, where the law is competent, it is the best authority to judge.) Some things, then, can be compassed by the laws and others cannot. It is these latter that disconcert us, and make us ask whether it is preferable that the best law should rule or the best man, for matters which admit of deliberation are those on which legislation is impossible. Opponents of monarchy, however, do not deny the need for a man to judge these matters; but they say that there should be not merely one man but many.

The individual judges well when he has been instructed by the law; and it might appear absurd that in judging he should perceive better with two eyes and two organs of hearing, and in action do better with two feet and two hands, than many men do with many. In fact, the monarchs make many eyes and ears and hands and feet their own, for they share their rule with those who are well-disposed to their rule and to themselves. If these people are not well-disposed they will not act in conformity with the monarch's policy. If they are friendly to himself and his rule, and if a friend is one's equal and like oneself, then, if the monarch thinks these people ought to rule, what he thinks is that those equal to and like himself ought to rule. These are more or less the arguments of those who argue against kingship.

However, this may be true in some respects and not in others.

There is such a thing as natural fitness for control by a master, and likewise fitness to be controlled by a king, and fitness to be a citizen, and this is just and beneficial. But no one is by nature fitted to be the subject of a tyrant, or of any other deviant type of constitution, for they are contrary to nature.

1288a. From what has been said it is clear that where men are equal and like it is neither beneficial nor just that one should be in supreme control, neither when there are no laws but he himself acts as law, nor when there are laws, whether he and his subjects are both good or both bad, nor even when he himself is superior in virtue—except in a certain way. What this way is, must be said, although in a way it has been said already.

First we must define what is meant by fitness for government by a king, fitness for aristocratic government and fitness for republican government. Now, the populace fitted for government by a king is one whose nature is such that it can produce a family outstandingly suited by its excellence (*arete*) for political leadership. One fitted for aristocracy is one which can produce a family capable of exercising rule over free men, the government being in the hands of those who are leaders in political office by virtue of their *arete*. And the people fitted for republican rule is one in which there naturally arises a citizen class capable of ruling and being ruled in accordance with a law which assigns office, according to status in wealth, to the well-to-do.

So, whenever a whole family or some one individual is so preeminent in *arete* as to surpass all the others, then it is right that that family should be the ruling one and have control of everything, and that individual the king. For as has been said before this is so not only in accordance with the principle of justice usually adduced by those setting up constitutions, aristocratic, oligarchic and, what is more, democracies, all alike (for they all base their claims on superiority, though not the same superiority), but also in accord with what was said already. It would not be seemly to kill such a person, or exile or ostracize him, nor to expect him to be ruled in his turn; for it is not natural for a part to excel over the whole, and someone who is so preeminent does out-top the rest. All that is left, then, is to obey such a man, and to give him authority, not when his turn comes, but absolutely.

Let this, then, be our decision concerning the types of kingship, the differences between them, whether they are beneficial to cities or not, and to what cities and in what conditions.

DANGERS TO MONARCHY AND SAFEGUARDS

The argument of the second passage is complex and will repay analysis. Aristotle is concerned here not with justification of monarchic rule but with the relationships and feelings between ruler and ruled in different types of monarchy. The real theme is the search for stability. Monarchy as such will not ensure stability, but some kinds apparently are more stable than others. Do the reasons lie entirely in the character of the individual ruler?

Monarchs themselves—as Aristotle points out—are often made, not born, and therefore at some time in their lives were among the ruled. Is the king's power really less vulnerable than that of the tyrant? The tyrant, it seems, can become less vulnerable by turning himself into a 'king'. Is this really so? The answer perhaps depends on whether we think Aristotle has taken us back to the realms of the ideal, or whether he is saying that stability is to be found in the rule of law.

Aristotle, *Politics*

1310b. It remains to speak also of monarchy, the causes of its destruction and the means by which it is preserved. What happens in the cases of monarchies and tyrannies is very much like what has already been said about constitutional governments. Kingship corresponds to aristocracy, and tyranny to a blend of the last form of oligarchy and democracy. This is why tyranny is most harmful to its subjects, because it comes out of two evils and has the deviations and errors of both sorts of constitution. Both types of monarchy take their origin in their opposites. Kingship arises to help the nobles against the common people, and the king is chosen from among the nobles on account of pre-eminence in *arete* or in actions arising from *arete* or pre-eminence of that kind, and the tyrant arises out of the common mass of the people, in opposition to the notables, to prevent the people suffering injustice at their hands.

This is clear from what has actually happened. Practically all tyrants have started as demagogues, winning the people's trust by their attacks on the notables. Some tyrannies were set up in this way when the cities had already grown great, others in earlier times when kings over-stepped their traditional powers and tried to claim more despotic authority. Others arose from men chosen for the highest offices (for in ancient times the peoples used to appoint magistrates and sacred envoys for long terms), and some from oligarchies which chose one man to hold the highest offices. It was possible for men to achieve the change to tyranny in all these ways easily, if they but wished, because they already had power, some through the office of king, others through other high office. For instance, some such as Pheidon of Argos became tyrant when they already held the kingship; Phalaris and the Ionian tyrants were in high office; Panaetius at Leontini, Cypselus at Corinth, Peisistratus at Athens, Dionysius at Syracuse and others likewise were already demagogues.

As we have said, then, kingship corresponds to aristocracy, for it depends on worth, either from personal *arete*, or birth, or benefactions, or these together with power. All those who achieved this honour did so after they had conferred or were able to confer benefits on their cities or peoples. Some, like Codrus, had prevented their being en-slaved in war; some, like Cyrus, had freed them, or had settled or acquired territory, like the kings of the Lacedaemonians, the Mace-donians and the Molossians.

1311a. A king wants to be a guardian, to prevent the possessors of property from suffering any injustice, or the people from being ill-used in any way; whereas tyranny, as has been said often, pays no regard to the common good except in so far as it serves its own inter-ests. Tyranny aims at what is pleasant, kingship at what is noble. Hence tyrants exact money, whereas kings rather seek honour, and a king is guarded by his own people, a tyrant by foreigners.

That tyranny combines the bad points both of oligarchy and demo-cracy is obvious. From oligarchy it has the setting up of wealth as an aim (since this is the only way to maintain the bodyguard and the luxurious living), and complete distrust of the people (which is why they confiscate weapons). Other features common to oligarchy and tyranny are ill-treatment of the masses, expulsion and segregation. From democracy, tyranny takes the habit of fighting against the not-ables and destroying them, both in secret and openly, and exiling them on the grounds that they plot against the people and obstruct its rule; for it is from the noble class that conspiracies arise, some wishing to rule themselves, others not to be slaves. Hence the advice of Periander to Thrasybulus, lopping off the loftier stalks, meaning that the more outstanding citizens should always be made away with.

Therefore, as has been stated, more or less, the origins of revolution in popular governments and in monarchies must be deemed to be the same. Many subjects attack monarchies because of injustice and fear and contempt (and, in the case of injustice, particularly because of insult), and sometimes also because of seizure of private property. Also the aims of the rebels are the same, in tyrannies or kingships and in constitutional governments. Monarchs have great wealth and honour, which all men strive for.

Some attacks are made against the person of the ruler, others against his authority. Those provoked by insult are made against his person; insult takes many forms, all of which occasion anger, and angry men usually attack for the sake of revenge rather than to gain superiority. For instance, the attack on the Peisistratids was because they insulted Harmodius' sister and treated Harmodius himself contemptuously; and Harmodius attacked for his sister's sake and Aristogeiton for the sake of Harmodius.

1311b. Men plotted against Periander, the tyrant in Ambracia, because when he was drinking with his favourite he asked in he had conceived yet by him; Pausanias attacked Philip because the latter allowed him to be insulted by Attalus and his associates; the attack on Amyntas the Little by Derdas was because Amyntas mocked at his youth; and the attack of the eunuch on Evagoras of Cyprus arose from a sense of insult, for he murdered Evagoras because Evagoras' son took away his wife. Many attacks have occurred because of personal indignities inflicted by monarchs. For instance, Crataeus, who attacked Archelaus, had always chafed at their association so that even a slight excuse sufficed; or the reason may have been that Archelaus went back on his agreement and did not give Crataeus one of his daughters, but gave the elder, when he was hard-pressed in a war against Sirrhas and Arrhabaeus, to the King of Elimeia, and the younger to his son Amyntas, thinking that thus Amyntas would be least likely to quarrel with his son by Cleopatra; but the origin of the estrangement was in Crataeus' resentment because of their physical affair. Hellenocrates of Larisa joined in the attack for the same reason. Archelaus took advantage of his youth, but did not keep his promise to restore him to his home, and so Hellenocrates thought that Archelaus' affair with him had been intended merely to violate him, and was not the outcome of erotic passion. Pytho and Heraclides of Aeneus killed Cotys to avenge their father, and Adamas rebelled against Cotys because of the outrage he suffered, in that as a boy he had been castrated by Cotys.

Many have been enraged by the indignity of physical beatings and have destroyed or attempted to destroy those in power, whether magistrates or kings. In Mytilene, the Penthelidae went around striking people with their staves, and Megacles and his friends attacked them and made away with them. Later, Smerdis killed Penthilus, after he had been beaten and dragged away before the eyes of his wife. Decamnichus was a ringleader in the attack on Archelaus, and foremost in egging on the attackers. The ground of his anger was that Archelaus had given him to Euripides the poet to be flogged, because Euripides was angry at his saying that his breath smelled. Many others have overthrown or plotted against their rulers for similar reasons.

Fear is another motive. This, we said, was one of the causes both in the case of constitutional governments and of monarchies. For instance, Artabanes killed Xerxes from fear of the charge about Darius. He had killed him without Xerxes' orders, thinking Xerxes would forgive him because he was dining and would forget.

1312a. Sometimes the cause was contempt. Someone attacked Sardanapalus after seeing him combing among the women (if the tales people tell are true; and even if it is not true of him, it might well be true of someone else). Dion attacked Dionysius the younger out of contempt, seeing how the citizens despised him and how he was always drunk. Even some of the friends of rulers attack from contempt, despising them for their trustfulness, and thinking they will not be detected. Also those who think themselves capable of seizing rule attack, in a sense, out of contempt; for, as they believe they can do it, this leads them to despise the danger, and encourages them to attack. Thus, military commanders attack monarchs. For instance, Cyrus attacked Astyages out of contempt both for his way of life and his power, for his power had weakened, and he was living luxuriously. Likewise, Seuthes the Thracian, when a general, attacked Amadocus. Some attack for more than one motive, for instance, contempt and gain, as in the case of Mithridates' attack on Ariobarzanes. This—i.e. contempt—is particularly the motive for attempts by those who are naturally daring and have military command under a monarch, for courage accompanied by power is daring; so they attack thinking that through the combination of power and boldness they will prevail.

In the case of persons actuated by ambition, the motive works differently from the cases previously described. Some attack tyrants seeing the great rewards and honours there are to be gained; but those impelled by ambition do not decide to take the risk for such reasons. They attack monarchs to obtain, not the monarchy, but glory, just as they would engage in any other exceptional deed through which they would gain notoriety and renown among men. However, men who act on this motive are very few in number, for there must be an underlying disregard for self-preservation, if concern for safety is not to prevent action. These men must share the belief of Dion, although it is not easy for many to hold it. Dion marched against Dionysius saying that, however far he would get, it would suffice him to have had that much part in the deed, and if, for example, it should befall him to die when he had barely set foot in the country, he would regard that as a good death.

1312b. One way in which tyranny, like each of the other forms of constitution, is destroyed is from outside, if some state with an opposed constitution is stronger; for obviously the will to destroy will be there, because of the opposition of principle, and what men wish to do they all do if they are able to. The opposing constitutions are: democracy, which is opposed to tyranny as, in Hesiod's phrase, 'potter is against potter' (for the final form of democracy is tyranny), and kingship and aristocracy because of the opposed nature of the constitution. Thus the Lacedaemonians overthrew many tyrants, and so did the Syracusans, at the time when they were well-governed. One way, though, is from itself, when the participants in it disagree, as, for instance, the tyranny established by Gelon and recently that set up by Dionysius. Gelon's was destroyed when Thrasybulus, brother of Hieron, encouraged Gelon's son and egged him on to pursue pleasure, in order to rule himself, and the son's relatives banded together to prevent the entire destruction of the tyranny, while securing only that of Thrasybulus; however, some of the band took the opportunity and expelled them all. Dion used military force to expel Dionysius, his relative, and won the support of the people, and then he was killed.

So there are two chief reasons for which tyrannies are attacked, namely hatred and contempt. One is always present, namely hatred of tyrants, but many coups result from contempt. An indication of this is that most of those who have acquired tyrannies have maintained their rule to the end, but their successors almost all finish at once, because in living for enjoyment they breed contempt of themselves and give many opportunities to assailants. Also anger must be included as part of the hatred against them, for in a way it produces the same kind of deeds. Often it leads more directly than hatred to action, because men attack more vigorously since this emotion does not pause to reason (and in particular men yield to their tempers because of insult; this was the reason for the downfall of the Peisistratids and many others), whereas hatred does reason more. For anger is accompanied by painful emotion, which makes it hard to be rational, whereas hatred is free from such emotion.

To put it briefly, the reasons that we have spoken of as causing the downfall of unmixed and extreme oligarchy and of the final form of democracy must all be assigned also for the destruction of tyrannies, since these constitutions are really 'delegated' tyrannies. But kingship is least prone to destruction from outside, and so it is longlasting. Most monarchies that fall are destroyed from within themselves. They perish in two ways, either from a dispute between those who participate in rule, or when the king attempts a more tyrannical way of rule, claiming wider powers and transgressing the law. Kingships do not come into being nowadays; what does is rather monarchy or tyranny. For kingship is rule by consent, with authority over the more important matters; but there are many men of equal ability and no one so outstanding as to fit the stature and dignity of the office, and for this reason men are not willing to submit. If they are deceived or forced into doing so, then this is seen at once to be a tyranny.

1313a. In hereditary kingships one must add to the causes of destruction already stated the fact that many contemptible kings arise, and though they do not have the power of a tyrant but the status of a king they act overweeningly. Their overthrow is easy, for if men refuse to accept his rule, a king is no longer a king but a tyrant over unwilling subjects. So monarchies perish from these and similar causes.

Their preservation is clearly due to the opposite causes, roughly speaking. Let us take these separately. Kingships are preserved by making them more moderate; the less the extent of the king's powers, the longer the office as a whole must last, for the kings themselves become less despotic and more equal in temper to their subjects, and the less they are resented by their subjects. This is why kingship lasted a long time among the Molossi, and the Spartan kingship has endured because in the beginning the office was divided in two, and later

Theopompus introduced various measures to moderate its power, and in particular set up the ephorate as a check on it (for by reducing the power of the kingship he lengthened its life, so that in a way he did not diminish it but increased it). It is said that when Theopompus' wife asked him if he was not ashamed to hand on the kingship to his sons lesser than he received it from his father, he replied, 'Not so; for I hand it on more durable.'

Tyrannies are preserved in two entirely opposite ways. One is the traditional method, according to which most tyrants manage their rule. They say that in most respects it was created by Periander of Corinth, and it also derived many elements from the Persian rule. This method includes the measures of preservation spoken of some time ago—cutting off the outstanding and destroying the proud. 1313b. Also there is a ban on any banqueting clubs or associations or education or anything of the sort; a guard is kept on anything that generates strong feelings, pride and confidence; schools or other places of assembly for discussion are not allowed to develop; everything is done to keep all men, as far as possible, strangers to one another (for familiarity breeds greater mutual confidence); and people in the city are always to be in public and hanging around the palace doors, for in this way their activities will least admit of concealment and by growing accustomed to this servility they will develop habits of humility in thought—and all other such practices of Persian and barbarian tyrannies (for they all have the same effect). Also, they try not to let anything any of the subjects may say or do pass undetected, but they have spies, like the so-called *provocatrices* at Syracuse, and the 'Listeners' sent out by Hiero to wherever there was a gathering or discussion (for men are less outspoken through fear of such spies, or if they do speak out, they are less concealed); and quarrels and strife between friends are encouraged, and between the nobles and the populace, and among the wealthy. Likewise, it is a practice of tyranny to impoverish the subjects, both in order to maintain the tyrant's guard and also not to allow the people leisure from day to day for plotting. An example of this is the pyramids in Egypt, as also the votive offerings of the Cypselids and the temple-building at Olympia by the Peisistratids and the works of Polycrates at Samos, all of which have the same effect, to keep the subjects busy and poor; likewise the exaction of taxes, as at Syracuse, for in the time of Dionysius men paid in their entire property in the space of five years. Also the tyrant en-

courages war, so that the people will not be idle and will constantly
need a leader. Moreover, kingship is preserved by friends, but it is
typical of tyranny to mistrust friends, believing that while all have
the wish they above all have the power [sc. to destroy it].

Moreover, all the features that occur in the final form of democracy
favour tyranny, e.g. female dominance in the homes (so that they may
inform outside against the men), and undisciplined behaviour of slaves
(for the same reason). The women and slaves do not plot against the
tyrants, and if they are flourishing they must be well-disposed both
to tyrannies and to democracies (for the people also wishes to be
monarch).

1314a. Therefore both look with favour on the flatterer. In democracies, this is the demagogue (for he is the flatterer of the people) and
with tyrants it is the men who fawn upon them, this being the office
of flattery. This is why tyranny likes base people, for tyrants like being
flattered, and no man of a free spirit would do it; honourable men
love a ruler or do not flatter him. Besides, the base are useful for base
deeds—as the proverb says, 'Nail drives out nail.' It is typical of a
tyrant not to like anyone with pride or a free spirit, for the tyrant
thinks he himself alone has the right to be like that. He thinks that
anyone else who shows these qualities is detracting from his pre-
eminence and the tyrant's position of mastery; therefore tyrants hate
such men, as being subversive of their rule.

These, then, are the characteristics of tyranny and the way its rule
is preserved, and no wickedness is lacking there. All of it is comprised
in three categories—since the tyrant has three aims, one being to keep
his subjects humble (for a mean-spirited man will not plot), the second
to keep them mistrustful of one another (for a tyranny will not be
overthrown until men have confidence in each other, and so tyrants
fight against men of good character, regarding them as dangerous to
their régime, not only because such men disapprove of despotic rule
but because they are loyal to themselves and to their fellow citizens
and do not inform against each other or the other citizens); and,
thirdly, to keep them from having any power to act (for no one
attempts without the power, and so if they lack the power they will
not attempt to overthrow the tyranny). So these are the three aims
towards which the policies of tyrants are directed, and one could refer
all a tyrant's actions to these principles—mutual mistrust, incapacity
for action and mean-spiritedness.

So this is one way in which tyranny is safeguarded. The other follows a method more or less the opposite of the aforesaid. One can grasp its nature by considering the downfall of kings; for just as one way of causing a king's downfall is to make his rule more tyrannical so one way of preserving a tyranny is to make it more like kingly rule, being careful, however, to maintain one thing, i.e. the power, so that the tyrant may rule whether his subjects will or no—for if he lets slip the power, then he loses his tyranny too. This must remain as a basic principle, but in other respects he should take action, or appear to, in careful imitation of kingly behaviour.

1314b. First, he must appear to be careful about the public funds, not to be squandering them on the sort of lavish presents that the populace resent, when rulers take from the hard-earned fruits of their labour and give lavishly to mistresses and foreigners and craftsmen. They must produce accounts of income and expenditure, as indeed some tyrants have done already. By managing in this way a ruler will appear to be a steward and not a tyrant, and he need not fear ever being short of money when he has control of the state. Indeed, for tyrants who go abroad on campaign, this is safer than leaving their wealth amassed together, for there is less likelihood of its guardians trying to seize power. These guardians are a cause of more fear to the tyrants, when they are out of the country, than the citizens—for the citizens go with them, but the guardians of the treasury stay behind. When the tyrant levies taxes and exacts liturgies, he must appear to do so for the administration of the nation and, whenever necessary, for military emergencies, and in general he must present himself as guardian and treasurer of a public fund and not a private one.

He must appear not harsh but dignified, that is he must inspire respect rather than fear in those he encounters. This is not easy to manage if he is a contemptible person, so even if he studies no other virtue he must attend to military prowess and win himself a reputation for that. Also, not only must he not be seen to do any outrage to any of his subjects, boy or girl, but the same applies to his courtiers, and their wives also must behave properly towards other women, for many tyrannies have been destroyed by the insulting behaviour of women. As far as bodily pleasures are concerned he must behave in a way opposite to the behaviour of some contemporary tyrants, who not only start their enjoyments at dawn, but carry on for days on end and actually want to show off their behaviour to others, to be marvelled at for their felicity and happiness. He should preferably be moderate in such things, or else he should avoid parading them—for it is not the sober man but the drunkard, not the vigilant man but the slumbering, who is vulnerable to attack. He must do the opposite of almost all the things already mentioned. He must fit out and adorn the city as though he were a trustee and not a tyrant. Also, he must always appear particularly zealous in observance of the worship of the gods, though not to the point of foolishness.

1315a. People are less afraid of illegal treatment at the hands of such men, if they think their ruler is god-fearing and pays regard to religion, and they are less ready to conspire against him, since they think he has the gods on his side. He must honour those who show goodness in any respect, so that they will not think that they could possibly have received greater honour among citizens who were self-governing. Such honours he himself should dispense but punishments he should inflict through the media of officials and law-courts.

A general safeguard for all monarchies is to make no one man great but, if any, several (for they will watch one another), and if he must make someone great, certainly not anyone of bold spirit, for persons of such a disposition are most forward in all enterprises. If he decides to remove someone from power, he should do it gradually, and not take away all his standing at once. Again, he must carefully avoid all forms of outrage, and two in particular, viz. corporal punishments and offences against the young. He must be particularly careful of this in relation to men of ambition; for whereas lovers of money are upset by any slighting of them regarding wealth, the ambitious and honourable take very ill any slur upon their prestige. So, he should either refrain from employing such men, or should appear to inflict chastisement in a paternal way, and not contemptuously. In his associations with the young, he should seem to act with passion and not because he has the power, and in general he should buy off what are considered dishonours with greater honours. Among those who make attempts upon his person the most formidable and most to be guarded against are those who are not concerned about saving their own lives, if they can destroy him. So he must exercise particular caution towards those who think that they themselves or those under their care are being outraged; for such men attack in anger, and do not spare themselves—as Heraclitus said, it is hard to fight against anger, for it will pay the price of life.

And since cities consist of two parts, the poor and the well-off, what is most essential is that both should believe that they owe their preservation to his rule, and neither be wronged by the other, and, whichever is the stronger, its personal support is to be won for his rule—for if this is secured the tyrant will have no need to set slaves free or confiscate weapons, because one of the two parts of the state, added to his power, will suffice to make it stronger than its assailants. It is unnecessary to discuss these matters individually; the general aim is clear.

1315b. He must appear to his subjects to be not a tyrannical ruler but an administrator and king, not an expropriator but a trustee, and in his way of life to seek not excess but moderation. He should associate in a friendly way with the men of note, and make himself popular with the commonalty. As a result, not only will his rule inevitably be nobler and more enviable, because he will rule better subjects and not men humiliated, and will not be continually hated and feared, but also his rule will last longer and he himself in his character will be excellently disposed towards virtue, or at least half virtuous, and will not be wicked or semi-wicked.

V. Alexander and the Development of Absolutism

Histories of Alexander's Eastern campaigns, and particularly the *Anabasis* of Arrian (written in the second century A.D. but using some sources contemporary with Alexander), give a vivid picture both of the somewhat unstable and violent temperament of Alexander and of the effect upon him of nearer acquaintance with the atmosphere of Persian royal circles, which contrasted strongly with the rather free-and-easy, egalitarian atmosphere of Macedonian military court circles.

The passages quoted illustrate both Alexander's own wish to create a new image of himself on the model of the Great King, and the reactions of his court. What is not clear is the intentions of Alexander and, to some extent, of his court. Is it the office of king that is being exalted, or are ways being sought of enhancing the splendour of a particular king, Alexander? Both may be true.

The ceremonial and display used by the absolute monarch of the Persian empire to impress his subjects had certain elements foreign to Greek ways of thinking. Can one determine from Arrian's account whether Alexander himself or those at his court actually intended certain ceremonials to be interpreted as cult acts to a divinity ('"cult" of the personality' in a rather special sense), that divinity being Alexander, and not solely to imitate procedure at the Great King's court?

There has been much debate among modern scholars on the question whether Alexander himself seriously wished to be regarded as a god. Students might profitably consult, as arguments on either side, the essay by W. W. Tarn, *Alexander the Great*, vol. II, appendix 22 (C.U.P., 1948) and the reply by J. P. V. D. Balsdon, 'The "divinity" of Alexander' (*Historia* I, 1950, 363–388), both reprinted in *Alexander the Great: the main problems*, ed. G. T. Griffith (Heffer, 1966). Decisive, if true, would be the statement of Plutarch and Aelian that Alexander in 324 B.C. sent to the League of Corinth a request for divine honours. Tarn affirms that he did; Balsdon denies. The Egyptians regarded the Pharaohs as sons of a god. Was the priest at the shrine of Ammon addressing the man Alexander, or the successor to Pharaoh? The Greeks regarded obeisance as an honour paid to Gods—did the Persians? And did Alexander?

At a drinking party, certain flatterers and toadies compared Alexander to his face with Castor and Pollux, sons of Zeus, and with Heracles. Cleitus, who had for some time been concerned at Alexander's increasingly barbaric style of life, objected, praised Philip and reminded Alexander how he himself had once saved his life. Alexander, himself by now far gone in drink, grabbed a spear, threw it at Cleitus and killed him. This is the bereavement for which consolation was required. The tale of Anaxarchus the Sophist, in Arrian's interpretation, has significance both in relation to earlier discussions of the relation between the monarch and the law, cited above, and to theories such as those of the Hellenistic writers in the following chapter.

Arrian, *The Anabasis of Alexander*, IV

9.7. Some say that Anaxarchus the Sophist was summoned to give Alexander consolation; and when he came and found him lying moaning, he laughed at him, and said Alexander did not know that the wise men of old made Justice sit by the throne of Zeus for this very reason, that whatever act is done by Zeus is done with Justice—and likewise the acts emanating from a great king should be considered just, firstly by the king himself and then by all the rest of mankind.

By saying this he consoled Alexander for the time being, but I say that he did him great harm, even greater than the trouble that weighed upon him at the time, if indeed he gave this opinion as that of a philosopher, that the king need not seriously attempt to pick out just deeds and do them, but that whatever a king does and however he does it, we must think it just.

For the story goes that Alexander even wanted people to do obeisance (*proskynesis*) before him, as he entertained the idea that Ammon was his father, rather than Philip, and he was already emulating the customs of the Persians and Medes both in the change in his clothes and the general alteration in his style of life. Moreover, he had no lack of people who gave in to him on this, to flatter him, and in particular Anaxarchus, one of the Sophists at his court, and Agis of Argos, an epic poet.

10. However, Callisthenes of Olynthus, a pupil of Aristotle and a man of rather boorish disposition, did not approve of these things. To that extent I myself agree with Callisthenes; but I do not think Callisthenes' remark (if the record of it is true) at all seemly, that Alexander and Alexander's deeds were dependent upon himself and his writing. He said that he had not come to Alexander to win glory himself, but to

make Alexander renowned among men. Moreover, he said, Alexander's share in the divine did not depend on Olympias' false story about his conception, but on whatever he himself would record of Alexander and publish to mankind. Some also relate that Philotas once asked him whom he thought the Athenians most honoured, and he answered Harmodius and Aristogeiton, because they killed one of the two tyrants and put an end to the tyranny. Philotas asked him again if it was open to a tyrannicide to go and find refuge among any of the Greeks he wished, and Callisthenes replied that even if he could find a safe refuge nowhere else, yet he would find one among the Athenians, for they had even fought Eurysthenes, who was then tyrant over Greece, on behalf of the children of Heracles.

There is also a story as follows, of how Callisthenes opposed Alexander over the matter of obeisance. Alexander had made an arrangement with the Sophists and the most distinguished of the Persians and Medes at court that this subject should be mentioned at a drinking-party. Anaxarchus began the discussion, saying that it would be far more just to consider Alexander a god than Dionysus and Heracles, not so much because of his many outstanding achievements but because Dionysus was a Theban and unconnected with the Macedonians and Heracles was an Argive, also unconnected except by Alexander's family descent, because Alexander was one of the Heraclidae; but that it was more just for the Macedonians to adorn their own king with divine honours. For there was no doubt that when Alexander passed away from among men they would honour him as a god; how much the more just to honour him while he was alive rather than when he was dead, when he would profit nothing by it.

11. When Anaxarchus had spoken to this effect, those who were parties to the plan praised what he said and indeed wished to begin the obeisance; but the majority of the Macedonians were hostile to the argument and kept quiet. Then Callisthenes intervened and said: 'Anaxarchus, I declare Alexander unworthy of no honour appropriate for a man; but a distinction has been made for men between those honours which are human, and those which are divine, in many ways. For instance, the building of temples and setting up of images, and the fact that precincts are set apart for the gods and sacrifices are offered to them and libations; and hymns are sung to the gods, but eulogies for men; but by no means least is the practice of obeisance. Men are kissed by those who greet them, but as the gods are set high

up and even to touch them is not lawful, therefore they are honoured by obeisance; and dances are performed in honour of the gods, and paeans sung to them. There is nothing remarkable in this, since among the gods themselves different honours are assigned to different gods; and moreover they are different among the heroes too, and also these honours are different from those given to the gods. So it is not right to jumble all this together, and to give mortals an exaggerated grandeur by excessive honours, while reducing the gods, as far as is possible, to an unseemly lowliness by honouring them equally with men. Alexander himself would not tolerate it, if some private person claimed royal honours by improper vote or ballot. With much more justification, then, would the gods be angry with any men who tried to take over their divine honours or submitted to receiving them from others. Alexander both is and is believed to be beyond measure the bravest of the brave, the most kingly of kings, the most worthy to command of all commanders.

'As for you, Anaxarchus, you above all ought to have been fore-most in putting this argument and opposing the contrary, since you attend Alexander as philosophical adviser and instructor. It was not at all fitting for you to begin this argument. You should have remem-bered that you are not attending and advising Cambyses or Xerxes, but the son of Philip, of the line of Heracles and Aeacus, whose fore-fathers came from Argos to Macedonia and continued in rule there not by force but constitutionally. Even to Heracles himself divine honours were not paid by the Greeks while he lived, nor even after his death until an oracle was issued from the god at Delphi that they should honour Heracles as a god. But if, since our discussion is taking place in a foreign country, we ought to think in foreign fashion, yet I ask you, Alexander, to remember Greece, for whose sake your entire expedition occurred, to add Asia to Greece. And consider—when you return will you compel the Greeks, the most independent of all men, to do obeisance to you, or will you excuse the Greeks and impose this disgrace on the Macedonians? Or will you draw a distinction, as regards honours, for all mankind, that by Greeks and Macedonians you shall be honoured as a man, and in Greek fashion, but by bar-barians alone in the barbarian fashion? If it is said concerning Cyrus, son of Cambyses, that he was the first of men to receive obeisance and that therefore this abasement became customary with the Medes and Persians, you must bear in mind that that same Cyrus was chastened by the Scythians, Xerxes by the Athenians and Lacedaemonians, Artaxerxes by Clearchus and Xenophon and the Ten Thousand with them, and Darius lately by Alexander—who had not been receiving obeisance.'

12. That was the gist of Callisthenes' speech, which greatly annoyed Alexander, but met with the approval of the Macedonians. Alexander realized this and sent bidding the Macedonians not to pay any more attention in future to obeisance.

VI. Hellenistic Justifications of Monarchy

All that is known of Diotogenes is that, according to Stobaeus, he was a Pythagorean. Ecphantus of Syracuse, also a Pythagorean, was active in the first half of the fourth century B.C. However, the passages on *Kingship* ascribed to him by Stobaeus are certainly not his. Estimates of their date vary, some putting them as late as the second century A.D., but they are at earliest Hellenistic.

Diotogenes' first paragraph is striking, especially in comparison with Anaxarchus' remarks on justice, as represented by Arrian. His Pythagoreanism is shown in the emphasis on harmony and the comparison with the order of the universe. There are echoes also of ideas we have found expressed in Plato and in Aristotle. The crucial difference, however, is that whereas they—the former especially—were talking of ideal kingliness, Diotogenes appears to be stating that certain qualities belong, in virtue of his office, to a king—or at least to a good king, but this is conceived of as a practical possibility, not an impossible ideal. This has profound political implications.

The second extract deals with the character of the king. The list of qualities discussed has some unexpected elements, most notable the rationalization of avarice and the emphasis on outward appearance and show. The justification of avarice may reflect the author's awareness of how Hellenistic monarchs actually behaved. The discussion of appearance is interwoven with a description of the king's function in creating harmony in the state. On one hand, Diotogenes is producing a philosophical justification for acceptance of kingship by subjects; on the other, he gives us some insight —particularly in his remarks on majesty—into the way kings presented themselves and were expected to present themselves to the public. In part, it might seem that popular tendencies are being exploited very similar to those on which Pericles played; at the same time, the repeated notion of resemblance to, or imitation of, a god is given both a philosophical and a popular application.

Ecphantus' exposition contains a blend of Platonic, Pythagorean and Stoic elements, with perhaps also a trace of the sun-symbolism of the Persian or Egyptian kingdoms. The king is to his subjects as God is to the universe; he mirrors and is in communion with God; he is to his people as law is to those who use it; they become better by imitation of him; he is the living Word . . . and so on.

What are the consequences of such views for the status of law? And to what extent does such argument on a philosophical level reflect a spiritual need in the Hellenistic world? The processions, royal epithets and panegyrics, such as those of the next chapter, perhaps reveal similar yearnings.

Erwin Goodenough ('The Political Philosophy of Hellenistic Kingship', Yale Classical Studies I, 1928, p. 98 ff.) has suggested that the epithets regularly used in the official titles of Hellenistic kings, particularly Soter ('Saviour'), Epiphanes ('Manifest') and Euergetes ('Benefactor') not only have both a religious and a political significance, but, as it were, epitomize the doctrines expounded in Diotogenes and Ecphantus of the king's relation to God and to his people, and his role both as intermediary and as model. To what extent this is true and whether the connection is likely to have been a deliberate one are questions that should perhaps be considered. Equally, the titles would have an obvious propaganda value taken at face value, with a populace lacking philosophical training. Which—if either— is likely to have been the starting point—the popular religion of gods and heroes, or the philosophical theories?

Certain ideas have now been given formal expression which present a question which is extremely important, although a definite answer may be hard to come by. To what extent, whether at the popular or the philosophical level, was there genuine belief in the divinity of the individual living king? The following chapter will yield additional material for study.

DIOTOGENES THE PYTHAGOREAN: FROM THE TREATISE *On Kingship*

61. The king would be the most just, and the most just is the most lawful; for no one would be king without justice, and there would be no justice without law. For what is just is contained in the law, and the law is the source of justice, and the king indeed is animate law, or one who rules by law; for these reasons he is the most just and most lawful.

The functions of the king are three, military command, the giving of judgment and the cult of the gods. Now, he will be able to exercise military command well if he has a good understanding of warfare, to give judgment and hear the causes of his subjects if he has thoroughly learned the nature of justice and law, and to conduct the worship of the gods reverently and piously if he has reasoned out the nature of the deity and virtue. Therefore the perfect king must be a good general and a judge and a priest; for these accompany and are appropriate to the supremacy and virtue of a king.

Now, it is the task of a helmsman to keep safe a ship, a charioteer his vehicle, a doctor the sick, and a king and general those who are in danger in war. For each supervises and constructs that system of which he is in command. Giving judgment and imparting justice, both in public law and in private cases, is the peculiar function of a king, as it is of God in the universe, of which he is leader and commander; that is, in general he is to harmonize the whole under one leadership and rule, and also to bring private matters of detail into accord with this harmony and leadership. Also as a king he does good to his subjects and bestows benefactions upon them, and for this he needs justice and law.

And the third function, namely the worship of the gods, needs a king to fulfil it; for the Best must be honoured by the best man, and the Ruling Principle by one who rules. Now, of those things in nature most deserving of honour, the best is God, and of those in the earthly and human sphere, the best is the king. As God is to the universe so the king is to the state, and as the state is to the universe so the king is to God. For the state, being composed out of many different elements, is an imitation of the composition and harmony of the universe, and the king, as he holds absolute rule and himself is animate law, has become like a god among men.

62. So, the king must not be overpowered by pleasure but must himself conquer it. He must not be like the multitude, but rather far different from them; he must consider that his proper aim is not pleasure but manly virtue. At the same time, it is fitting that one who claims rule over others should first be able to exercise command over his own passions.

Concerning avarice, there is this argument: he ought to possess wealth, in order to do good to his friends and help the needy and avenge himself on his enemies with penalties; for the enjoyment of good fortune, when accompanied by virtue, is most pleasant. Likewise in regard to pre-eminence; for a king should surpass others in virtue, and should be judged worthy to rule for that reason, and not on the grounds of wealth or power or military strength. The first is common also to many ordinary people, the second he shares with irrational creatures and the third with tyrants, but virtue alone is peculiar to good men. So a king who is temperate towards pleasures, generous in sharing wealth, and sensible and practised in virtue, that man is truly a king. The people have the same proportion of goods and evils as the parts of the individual soul; for avarice occurs in the leading part of the soul, since the desire is rational; and love of pre-eminence and ferocity belong to the spirited part, since this is the lively and energetic part of the soul; while love of pleasure belongs to the appetitive part, for this is the feminine and watery part of the soul; but injustice, which is the most complete wickedness and most compound in nature, involves the whole soul.

So, a king must tune a well-governed city like a lyre, establishing first in himself the most just measure and the standard of law, as he knows that harmony among the people, over whom God has given him leadership, ought to be attuned to himself.

And the good king, besides issuing decrees, must take pains to have the proper mental attitude and physical demeanour towards those who address him, moulding himself to the statesman and man of affairs, so as to appear to the people neither harsh nor contemptible, but agreeable and alert in all directions. He will achieve this, firstly if he is impressive both to look at and to listen to, and appears worthy of his position, and secondly if he commands esteem by his conversation and appearance, and in his bestowing of benefactions; and thirdly if he inspires fear by his hatred of wickedness and licence, and also by his conscientiousness and in general his skill and diligence in his kingly duties. For majesty is a kind of imitation of a god, and can rouse the wonder and awe of the multitude, while uprightness can win him affection and love, and impressiveness can make him appear formidable and invincible to his enemies and noble-spirited and a stimulating example to his friends. He must establish his majesty by taking pains to do nothing humble nor resembling the behaviour of the multitude, but rather like those who are the objects of admiration and are by nature fitted for leadership and the holding of the sceptre. He must match himself constantly not against inferiors or equals but against those greater than himself, and, according to the importance of his leadership, he must adopt the principle that the greatest pleasures are those derived from noble and great deeds, not from indulgence, and he must separate himself from the passions of ordinary men and draw nearer to the gods, taking upon himself, not out of arrogance but out of greatness of spirit and unsurpassable virtue, a seemly dignity, in appearance, thoughts, desires, dispositions of soul, actions and his very physical bearing and movements; and so he will exert an influence over those who look on him, marvelling at his dignity, his control and his fitness for distinction; for to gaze on something fine ought to affect the souls of those who behold him no less than the harmony of a flute.

So much for majesty; now I shall try to discourse upon uprightness. Every king will be upright who is in general just and fair and clement; for justice is a binding and unifying force in the community and such a disposition of the soul alone creates harmony between neighbours. Justice bears the same relationship to community life as rhythm does to movement and harmony to the voice, for it is a good common to ruler and to ruled, in that it is the harmonizing principle of the political community. Fairness and clemency sit by the side of justice, one softening the harshness of the injury, the other meting out forgiveness to those who in some way do wrong. The good king must be ready to help those in need, not in one way only, but in any way possible; and he must be grateful, not in proportion to the amount of the honour paid him, but to the manner and intent of the person honouring him. He must refrain from being burdensome to any men, and in particular to inferiors and those suffering from ill-fortune, for these, like men sick in body, are incapable of bearing burdens. Such are the characteristics of the gods, and especially of Zeus, the ruler of all things; for Zeus is august and revered because of his pre-eminence and the greatness of his virtue; he is noble in his bestowal of benefactions and blessings, so that the Ionian poet actually calls him 'father of gods and men'; and he is awful in that he pursues wrongdoers and rules and holds sway over all. He has in his hand the thunderbolt, symbol of his awfulness. In all these respects, it must be borne in mind, kingship is an imitation of divinity.

ECPHANTUS THE PYTHAGOREAN: FROM THE TREATISE *On Kingship*

64. From many indications it seems clear to me that the nature of every animal is in harmony with the universe and the things in the universe; for it breathes along with the universe and is closely bound to that sequence which is both inevitable and best, and so it accom-

panies the movement of the universe and is carried along in accord
with the general order of the universe and with the span of its own
duration. This is why the universe is called the Cosmos ('Order')
and is the most perfect of living things. Among its parts, which are
many and of differing nature, the leadership is held by a living being
most suited for this both in its origin and in having a greater share in
divinity. In the nature of the eternal god, those things that have the
foremost and greatest conformity (to divinity) cleave to [*lacuna*] and
the planets; and in the region of the moon, beneath where bodies
travel in a straight line, the nature of the daemon has its development;
and on earth among us the creature with the most excellent nature is
man, and the most divine is the king. He claims the larger share of the
better parts of our common nature; in his earthly tabernacle he is like
the rest of us, as he is made of the same material, but he is fashioned
by the best craftsman, who in making him used himself as model. So,
the king is a single and unique creation, as a copy of the higher King,
and he is always familiar to his maker, while to his subjects he appears
as it were in a light, the light of royalty. For it is by this light that he
is judged and proved, as is the mightiest of winged creatures, the
eagle, set face to face with the sun. This then is the explanation of
royalty in that it is divine and hard to look at on account of its brilliance, save for legitimate claimants. Bastard pretenders are refuted by
suffering dazzlement and dizziness, like those who climb to an unwonted height; but those who attain to it fittingly, because they are
akin to it, can live with it, and are able to make use of it.

Royalty, then, is something pure (as though tested by the sun) and
incorruptible, and very hard for a man to achieve, because of its
exceeding divinity. The man who takes up his stand in it msut be
very pure and radiant in nature, so that he may not dim its brilliance
by his own stains, just as some people defile the most sacred places
and some of those one meets pollute those whom they encounter.
One who lives in royalty ought to participate in its unsoiled nature
and to know how much he surpasses others in divinity, and how much
more divine than he are those others, by likening himself to whom he
would be doing the best for himself and his subjects. For other men,
if they do wrong, their most holy purification is to make themselves
like their rulers, whether it is the law or a king who governs matters
among them,* and the kings, if they fall short of the superiority proper

* Text corrupt.

to their nature, should notr emove far from god to find help.* For no one would seek for the cosmos who was in it and a part of it; likewise one who ruled over others would not be unconscious of his own ruler. Cosmic order has great power, as is shown by the fact that nothing is found which is not under rule, and that it is in a way a teacher of rulership. Its beauty blazes out at once, if the one who imitates in virtue is beloved both by Him whom he imitates and even more by those set under him.

No one who is dear to God could be hated by men, since neither the stars nor the whole cosmos are hostile to God—if the cosmos hated its leader, it would not obediently follow him; and it is because God rules well that the king's subjects also are ruled well. Now, I suppose that the earthly king can fall short in nothing of the virtues of the heavenly king, but just as the king is something alien and foreign which has come down from heaven to men, so one must suppose his virtues are the work of God, and are the king's through God. If one examines the fundamental truth, this is how it is: the foremost of all things and most essential for mankind is the communion shared in by the king among us and by the ruler of all things in the universe, for without love and communion things could not endure. One may observe this also in the case of bodies politic, leaving out of account what is usually called communion, which is inferior to the divine and royal nature. God and king have no such need of one another as to oblige them to work together to provide their wants and supply mutual assistance, for they are perfect in virtue; but the love in a city which shares in a common purpose is an imitation of the concord in the universe. Without the imposition of order by government, no city could be inhabited, and for this laws are necessary, and some sort of political organization, since this preserves the state. From these there arises a common good, a sort of good harmony and attunement of the many resulting from their concord in obedience.

The person who rules according to virtue is called and is a king, as he has the same love and communion with his subjects as God has with the universe and all in it. There must be secured complete goodwill, first from the king towards those he rules, second from the subjects towards the king, such as is felt by a father towards his son, a shepherd to his flock and a law to those who use it.

* Text corrupt.

65. He uses one and the same virtue in ruling over men and over his own life. He will not seek acquisitions through any lack, for his own personal service, but as pursuing a life of action according to nature. For although communion exists, each man lives sufficient to himself, and the self-sufficient man needs nothing else in carrying out his own life. If he must live a life of action, it is clear that he must acquire things in addition, but none the less he will keep his self-sufficiency. For he will have friends because of his virtue, and in making use of them, he acts in accord with no other virtue than he uses in his own life. Such conclusions must follow since no other special virtue is provided for this end. God, who has no ministers or servants, uses no one when commanding, nor does he crown or publicly proclaim those who obey, nor dishonour those who disobey. This is not how God himself rules over so vast a realm; but I think that in presenting himself as worthy of imitation he implants in everyone a desire for emulation of his nature. He is himself good, and this is his only function, and an easy one. Those who imitate him because of this do everything better than others. The resemblance for each man is self-sufficiency; for there is not one set of virtues which can do what is pleasing to God, and another which imitates him. Why should not our earthly king be just as self-sufficient as anyone else? In imitating the One he would liken himself to the most powerful, and everyone who tried to be like him * will be like that.* Any force or compulsion on subjects sometimes takes away from the individual his desire for emulation, for without goodwill imitation is impossible, and above all this is dissipated by fear. If only it were possible to remove from human nature the need for obedience; for this is a trace of our base earthly nature, that as mortal animals we are not exempt from it. An act of obedience is close to an act of necessity, for whatever escapes one is brought about by the other. Whatever things can by their own nature use the beautiful have no reverence for obedience, since they have no necessity for fear. The king alone can put this good into effect in human nature, so that through imitation of him, their better, men follow the way they should go. And those corrupted by evil nurture, as though by drink, his Word (*Logos*) strengthens; it heals the sick and drives out the forgetfulness which has taken up its abode in them owing to their wickedness, and establishes instead memory, from

* Text corrupt.

which is begotten so-called obedience. Taking its beginning from trifling seeds, this grows up as something good, though dwelling in an earthly environment, in which the Word, associating with men, supplies what is lacking owing to sin.

66. In so far as his thinking is holy and godlike, he is in reality a king; for by obeying such thinking he will be the cause of all good things and of nothing evil. Moreover, he will clearly be just, as he is in communion with all; for communion consists in equality, and while in the distribution of equality justice has the controlling part, communion also participates. For it is impossible to be unjust and give a share of equality, or to give a share of equality without having communion.

How could one doubt that the self-sufficient man is continent? For extravagance is the mother of incontinence, which in turn is the mother of insolence, from which the majority of human evils arise. But self-sufficiency will never breed extravagance or its offspring; self-sufficiency, being itself of primal entity, leads everything, but is led by nothing. Therefore it is a characteristic of God and of the king to rule by himself (whence he is called the 'self-ruling' [1]) and to be ruled by no one. It is clear that this could not happen without intelligence, and it is manifest that God is the intelligence of the Cosmos, for the universe is held together by orderliness and the necessary arrangement, and this could not happen without mind. Nor could the king have these virtues without intelligence; I mean the virtues of justice, continence, communion and those related to them.

---

[1] Ecphantus is representing the word *autarkes* as a derivative of *archein* (rule), instead of *arkein* (suffice).

VII. Hellenistic Practice

ATHENS: HONOURS TO A CONQUEROR

After the death of Alexander, his generals quarrelled among themselves for the possession of his empire, a struggle continued into the second generation. Antipater, the general whom Alexander had left in charge of Macedonia and Greece when he crossed over to Asia, left his own comrade Polyperchon to succeed to his command. He was ousted by Cassander, son of Antipater, under whom Demetrius of Phaleron had been installed as governor of Athens. Antigonus, former satrap of Greater Phrygia, after defeating Eumenes in the East attacked Cassander, with the aid of his son Demetrius Poliorcetes ('The Besieger'). The latter 'liberated' Athens in 307 B.C. and drove out Cassander's governor.

Plutarch gives an account of the reaction of the Athenians. It might be argued that the initiative of the Athenians influenced the definite establishment of kingships among the Diadochi ('Successors'), i.e. Alexander's former generals, who divided up his conquests to create personal kingdoms. It is in the period between Demetrius' two visits to Athens (306–305 B.C.) that Antigonus, Demetrius, Ptolemy and Seleucus begin to use the title 'king'. Plutarch assumes the insincerity of the movers of the Athenian decrees, and their intention simply as that of currying favour. Is this perhaps an over-simplification? Perhaps genuine gratitude and relief played a part. And might it also be that in such situations—and we shall find examples later—honours are voted to the ruler as an indirect attempt by the ruled at preserving their own self-respect?

Plutarch, *Demetrius Poliorcetes*

10. Returning to Munychia and making camp there he expelled the garrison, and razed the fortress, and only then in response to the invitation of the Athenians, who were ready to receive him, did he enter the city. He assembled the people and gave them back their ancestral constitution; in addition he promised that there would come

to them from his father one hundred and fifty thousand bushels of corn and enough ship timber to make a hundred triremes.

The Athenians recovered their democracy after an interval of fourteen years during which, after the Lamian War and the battle at Crannon, their government had been nominally a democracy but in fact an oligarchy, because of the influence of the Phalerean. Demetrius had shown himself magnificent and splendid in his benefactions, and they made him objectionable and burdensome by the immoderateness of the honours they heaped on him. They were the first of all men to address Demetrius and Antigonus as 'king', although both of them had until then carefully avoided the title, and this was the only remaining royal prerogative of the descendants of Philip and Alexander which it was thought that others could not take over or share. The Athenians were the only people who described them as 'Saviour Gods', and they stopped the tradition of giving the year the name of an archon, and elected every year a priest of the Saviours and put his name in the preface to decrees and contractual agreements. They also decreed that figures of Demetrius and Antigonus should be woven into the sacred robe of Athena, along with the gods; and the place where Demetrius first descended from his chariot they consecrated and set on it an altar, which they designated the altar of Demetrius Alighting. They created two additional tribes, Demetrias and Antigonis, and increased the membership of the council from five hundred to six hundred, since each tribe provided fifty councillors.

11. But the most outrageous idea of Stratocles (for it was he who was the deviser of these sophisticated and hyperbolical pieces of flattery) was his proposal that envoys sent officially by decree to Antigonus or Demetrius should be called sacred ambassadors instead of envoys, like those who escorted to Delphi and Olympia the traditional sacrifices on behalf of the cities at the Greek festivals. In others respects too Stratocles was audacious. He led a licentious life and was thought to imitate the coarseness and buffoonery of Cleon of old times in his familiarity with the populace (*examples follow*). . . .

12. But there is something even hotter than fire, as Aristophanes says. For someone else, surpassing Stratocles in servility, proposed that whenever Demetrius visited Athens he should be welcomed with the honours paid to Demeter and Dionysus, and that to the citizens who excelled in the splendour and expense of his reception a sum of money should be awarded from the treasury for a dedication. Finally they

changed the name of the month Munychia to Demetrion and the 'old and new', the last day of the month, to Demetrias; and they altered the name of the Dionysia to Demetria. Most of these doings met with manifestations of divine displeasure. For instance, the sacred robe, in which they had decreed that the figures of Demetrius and Antigonus should be woven along with Zeus and Athena, as it was being carried in procession through the Cerameicus was rent by a hurricane that swooped upon it; and around the altars of the Saviour Gods the ground was covered with great quantities of hemlock, a plant which did not grow at all in many other parts of the country; and on the day of the Dionysia, the procession was prevented because of an unseasonable spell of bitterly cold weather. There was a very heavy frost which not only blasted all the vines and fig trees with cold but also killed off most of the corn in the blade. So Philippides, an enemy of Stratocles, attacked him in a comedy, saying:

> Through him it was that frost blasted the vines,
> Through his impiety the robe was rent in twain,
> Because he gave the honours of the gods to men,
> This is what destroys a people, not comedy. . . .

13. But the most monstrous and unexampled of the honours was that proposed by Dromocleides of Sphettius. When the dedication of shields at Delphi was being discussed, he proposed that the Athenians should get an oracle from Demetrius. I shall transcribe the actual words of the decree, which runs: 'May it be well. It seems good to the people that the people elect one man from the Athenians who shall go to the Saviour and after sacrificing with good omens shall ask the Saviour how the people may most piously, nobly and speedily carry out the dedication of the shields; and whatever oracular answer he shall give, the people shall act accordingly.'

With such mockery they finally corrupted the man altogether, although even before his mind was not entirely sound. . . .

23. Now the Athenians called on Demetrius when Cassander was besieging the city. Demetrius sailed with three hundred and thirty ships and a great number of hoplites, and not only drove Cassander from Attica, but routed and pursued him in his flight as far as Thessaly, then took Heraclea, which came over to him voluntarily, and six thousand Macedonians who changed sides and joined him. Returning, he

gave the Greeks on this side of Thermopylae their freedom, made the Boeotians his allies and took Cenchreae. He also reduced Phyle and Panactum, fortresses in Attica which were garrisoned by Cassander, and gave them back to the Athenians. And they, although before this they had poured out upon him and used up all manner of honours, nevertheless discovered then also a way to show themselves the inventors and authors of flatteries. They assigned him the rear chamber of the Parthenon as his lodging; and he lived there, and it was said that Athena received and entertained him there—although he was not a very seemly guest and did not, while installed there, behave himself with the restraint due to the virgin.

EGYPT: A ROYAL PROCESSION

Ptolemy and his successors in the rule of Egypt were at pains to justify their rule both by alleging a connection with the Macedonian royal line and by adopting the claim to royal divinity associated with the Pharaohs of Egypt.

The first Ptolemy, Alexander's general, virtually kidnapped the corpse of Alexander and brought it to Memphis, and thence (although not until the following reign, according to Pausanias) it was transferred to a magnificent shrine, the Sema, at Alexandria, where it received heroic honours. According to the Hellenistic writer Eratosthenes of Cyrene (Arrian, *Anabasis* 5.3), it was not Alexander himself, but the Macedonians accompanying him on his Eastern campaigns who made the comparisons between him and the god Dionysus, altering details of the Dionysus legend to make it appear that Alexander's journey into India and back had repeated, and even surpassed, the achievement of Dionysus. The Ptolemies took over and exploited this.

One of the Ptolemies, possibly Ptolemy IV Philopator, had a genealogy constructed which represented the Ptolemies as descended, through the mother of Ptolemy I, from the early Macedonian kings and their mythical ancestor Heracles. Dionysus was worked in too; Satyrus in his history of Alexandria said, 'Dianeira was the child of Dionysus and Althaea, daughter of Thestius; and I believe her child by Heracles, son of Zeus, was Hyllus.' Ptolemy II Philadelphus seems already to have taken some pains to present himself as under the special protection of Dionysus, whose cult receives particular prominence in the procession described by Athenaeus. The connection with Alexander, however, is still mainly political; Ptolemy I accompanies him in a tableau clearly alluding to the campaigns launched

by Alexander as commander-in-chief of the forces of the League of
Corinth. The deceased Ptolemy I was deified by his son, with the cult-
title 'Soter', and the games of which this procession is a part were founded
in his honour *circa* 279 B.C. The lavishness and costliness of the show are
notable. Athenaeus' description deserves study as an account of a display
put on primarily as propaganda to a mainly illiterate audience.

Athenaeus 5

196. Masurius added an account of the procession held at Alexandria
by the most excellent king Ptolemy Philadelphus, which is recorded
in the fourth book of the work on Alexandria by Callixenes of Rhodes,
who says: (*the account is prefaced by a description of a pavilion erected
for the entertainment of royal guests.*)
197. 'The procession was held in the stadium of the city. First marched
the contingent of the Morning Star, because the procession began at
the time when the aforesaid star appears. Then came the section named
after the king's parents. After these came the divisions of all the gods,
each with attributes appropriate to the story of its god. Finally there
was the contingent of the Evening Star, as the season made that time
coincide with the end of the procession. If anyone wishes details, he
should acquire and examine the records of the quadriennial games.
    'In the Dionysiac procession there marched first Sileni, who kept
back the crowds. They wore purple cloaks, and some red cloaks. They
were followed by Satyrs, twenty to each section of the stadium, carrying gilded torches ornamented with ivy-leaves. After these came Victories with gold wings, carrying censers nine feet high ornamented
with gilded ivy sprays. They wore embroidered tunics and were decked
with a great deal of gold jewellery. After these there followed a double
altar nine feet tall, ornamented in high relief with gilded ivy-leaves,
and with a crown of golden vine leaves wound with white-striped
ribbons. One hundred and twenty boys followed, in purple tunics,
carrying frankincense and myrrh, and saffron as well, on golden
platters. After these came forty Satyrs with crowns of golden ivy-
leaves. Their bodies were smeared with purple, some with vermilion
and other colours, and these also wore a golden crown wrought of
vine and ivy. After them were two Sileni in purple cloaks and white
shoes. One of these had a broad-brimmed hat and a herald's staff, the
other a trumpet. Between them walked a man over six feet tall, in a
tragic costume and mask, bearing a golden horn of Plenty. He was

called "The Year". He was followed by a woman of corresponding
height, very beautiful and adorned with much gold and wearing a
becoming tunic, carrying in one hand a crown of *persea*, in the other
a palm branch. She was called "The Penteteris" (Four-year period).
There followed her the four seasons, suitably got up, and each carrying
the appropriate fruits. Next to them were two nine-foot censers, in ivy
pattern, of gold, and in the middle a square altar of gold. Then Satyrs
again in gold ivy-pattern crowns and red cloaks. Some of them carried
gold wine jugs, others goblets. After them marched the poet Philiscus,
who was a priest of Dionysus, and all the guild of the "artists of Dionysus".

198. 'Immediately after them were carried Delphic tripods, the prizes
for the athletes' managers, one for the manager of the boys' section
being thirteen and a half feet tall, the other for the men eighteen feet.
After these came a four-wheeled cart, twenty-one feet long, twelve
feet wide, pulled by a hundred and eighty men. On it there was an
image of Dionysus fifteen feet tall, pouring libation from a gold cup,
and dressed in a full length purple tunic with a transparent yellow
coat over it. On its shoulders was a purple cloak embroidered with
gold. In front of it was a Laconian mixing-bowl holding fifteen
measures, and a gold tripod, on which were a gold censer and two gold
saucers full of cassia and saffron.

'Above the statue was spread a canopy decorated with ivy and vine
and other fruits, and hanging on it also were wreaths, ribbons, Diony-
siac wands, tambourines, fillets and masks satyric, comic and tragic.
There followed the cart priests and priestesses and keepers of vest-
ments, and bands of initiates of every kind and women carrying win-
nowing-fans. After these were Macedonian bacchants, the so-called
"Mimallones" and "Bassarae" and "Lydians", with their hair flowing
and wearing wreaths, some of snakes, others of briony and vine and
ivy. Some held daggers in their hands, others snakes.

'After these, sixty men pulled a four-wheeled waggon twelve feet
wide, on which was a seated image of Nysa twelve feet high, wearing
a yellow tunic embroidered with gold and a Laconian shawl. This
image could stand up mechanically without anyone laying hand on it,
and, after pouring libation of milk from a gold saucer, sit down again.
In the left hand it held a Bacchic wand festooned with ribbons, and the
image itself had on a gold ivy-pattern crown with clusters of fruit
made of precious stones.

199. 'The cart had a canopy, and four gilded torches fastened at its edges. Then came another cart, thirty feet long, twenty-four feet wide, pulled by three hundred men. On it there was set up a wine press, thirty-six feet long and fifteen feet wide, full of grapes. Sixty Satyrs were treading the grapes, singing a vintage song to the sound of flutes, with Silenus supervising; and all along the route the juice ran. Then a cart was pulled thirty-seven and a half feet long, twenty-one wide, drawn by six hundred men. On it was a wine-skin holding three thousand measures, made of leopard skins stitched together. This also trickled all along the route, as the wine was slowly released. There followed it one hundred and twenty Satyrs and Sileni wearing crowns, some carrying wine jugs, others shallow cups, and others deep cups, all of gold.

(*After these there are long catalogues of silver- and gold-ware cups, mixing-bowls, amphorae, wine-presses—carried in procession—and a cart with fountains of milk and wine. A further section depicting ' The Return of Dionysus from India' has a cart with a figure of Dionysus on elephant-back, and further processions, including large numbers of animals—elephants, gazelles, ostriches, etc.—camel trains of spices and negroes carrying gold, ebony and ivory.*)

201. 'Then there were statues of Alexander and Ptolemy wearing ivy-pattern crowns of gold. The statue of Virtue which stood beside Ptolemy had a gold olive-crown. Priapus stood beside them with a gold ivy-crown. The city of Corinth, standing beside Ptolemy, was crowned with a diadem of gold. Beside all these was a cup-stand full of gold vessels and a mixing-bowl holding five measures. Following this cart were women in elaborate robes and ornaments. They had the names of cities; some were from Ionia and the rest were the Greek cities of Asia and the islands which had been ruled by the Persians; and they all wore gold crowns.'

THE PTOLEMIES AND THE EGYPTIAN PRIESTHOOD

Sister-marriage was first adopted in 277 B.C. by Ptolemy II, who married, ousting one wife to do so, his sister Arsinoe (whose blood-boltered previous career need not detain us here). This marriage was in accordance with the practice of the Pharaohs, whose divine blood had to be kept apart from that of mortals; to the Greek world, it was compared with the 'sacred marriage' of Zeus and Hera. However, deification was delayed. It appears that Ptolemy deified Arsinoe at her death in 270 B.C., with the cult-title 'Philadelphos' ('brother-loving'), and associated himself with her, as the 'Gods Adelphi'.

In the twenty-third year of his reign (seven years after Arsinoe's death) Ptolemy ordered that the duty on landed property, orchards and vineyards, formerly paid to the gods of Egypt, was henceforth to be paid to the goddess Arsinoe Philadelphos. The commemoration in two existing stelae of gifts to the gods made by the king may explain the apparent lack of resistance by the Egyptian priesthood. In any case, his action amounts to an expropriation of the revenues of the state religion for the benefit of the crown. However, it should also be remembered that the reign of this Ptolemy saw a great temple-building programme, of which Philae survives.

Thenceforth, the dynasty becomes a series of divine couples (and Soter's wife retrospectively achieves divinity in the reign of Ptolemy IV Philopator). The royal pair Ptolemy III Euergetes and Berenice are described as brother and sister in the dedicatory inscription of a Greek temple at Alexandria. Ptolemy's sister Berenice in fact married the King of Syria; his *wife* Berenice was a princess of Cyrene. They had a daughter, also Berenice, who died in childhood and was deified. A decree of the Egyptian priesthood assembled at Canopus adds further honours to the divine honours already assigned to the king and queen, and assigns divine honours to the dead child. The decree has certain similarities to the more famous Memphis Decree (the Rosetta Stone) from the reign of Ptolemy V, a translation of which is given below.

Ptolemy V Epiphanes succeeded to the Egyptian throne in 204 B.C., in his fifth year. There ensued a period of regency, during which the Ptolemaic dynasty lost once and for all its territories in Coele-Syria, Phoenicia and Palestine and there were nationalist rebellions in Egypt itself. The young king was declared of age in 197 B.C., and his coronation, the first among the Ptolemies to be so celebrated, was carried out with full Pharaonic ritual. The recognition by the government of the rights of the priesthood doubtless represents a bid by the foreign dynasty for support in nationalist quarters. The honours decreed by the priesthood to Epiphanes were not new, as can now be seen by comparison with the decree of Canopus passed in honour of Ptolemy III Euergetes; there is, however, a development in relations between the monarch and the priesthood somewhat to the advantage of the latter. The clergy are exempted from a number of their earlier obligations, while the king—as, to a certain extent, his father also had done —allows various Pharaonic titles to be applied to himself.

Decree of Memphis (Rosetta Stone), 27th March, 196 B.C.

Date

In the reign of the young king, successor to his father in the kingship; lord of kingdoms; great in glory; who has established order in
Egypt; pious towards the gods; victor over his adversaries; who has
improved the life of men; lord of the thirty-year-periods, like the
great Hephaestus; king like the sun, great king of the upper and lower
regions; offspring of the gods Philopators; approved by Hephaestus;
to whom the sun has given victory; living image of Zeus, son of the
sun, Ptolemy the everliving, beloved by Phthah—

In the ninth year, Aetes son of Aetes being priest of Alexander and
of the gods Soters and the gods Adelphi and the gods Euergetes and
the gods Philopator and the god Epiphanes Eucharistus '(Gracious');
the athlophore of Berenice Euergetis being Pyrrha, daughter of
Philenus; the canephore of Arsinoe Philadelphus being Areia, daughter of Diogenes; the priestess of Arsinoe Philopator being Irene
daughter of Ptolemaeus—

On the fourth of the month Xandicus, the eighteenth of the Egyptian
month Mechir.

Preamble

The chief priests and prophets and those who enter the sanctuary
for the investiture of the gods, and the pterophors and the hiero-
grammateis and all the other priests who have come from the temples
in the country to Memphis to the king, for the ceremony of the receiving of the kingship by Ptolemy the everliving, beloved by Phthah,
god Epiphanes Gracious, which kingship he has received from his
father himself, the priests, gathered in the temple at Memphis, on this
same day, said:

Whereas king Ptolemy everliving, beloved by Phthah, god Epiphanes Gracious, son of King Ptolemy and Queen Arsinoe the gods
Philopators, has conferred many benefits on the temples and those in
them and all those set under his rule; that being god, son of a god
and a goddess, like Horus the son of Isis and Osiris, who avenged his
father Osiris, beneficently disposed towards the gods, he has consecrated for the temples revenues in money and food; and has borne
great expenses to bring peace to Egypt and to establish order in sacred
matters; he has been generous to all his forces; and of the public

revenues in Egypt and the taxes collected some he has entirely abolished, others he has lightened, so that the (native) people and all
others might have abundance during his reign. The debts to the royal
treasury, owed by the inhabitants of Egypt and of the rest of his kingdom, which were considerable, he has remitted; those who were
imprisoned and those awaiting trial for a long time he has released
from indictment. He has moreover ordered that the revenues of the
temples and the donations made to them each year, in kind as well as
in money, like the portions assigned to the gods from vineyard plots
and gardens and the other lands belonging to the gods in the reign of
his father, are to remain on the old basis; and he commanded concerning the priests that they should pay no more into the 'ordination-tax'
fund than was fixed in the first year of his father's reign. He has
released those in the holy classes from the yearly voyage down to
Alexandria; and he has ordered that the levy for the navy is not to
be exacted. Of the sailcloth handed over in the temples to the royal
treasury he has remitted two-thirds. All that was previously neglected
he has brought back into proper order, taking care that all customary
observances towards the gods should be carried out as is proper.
Likewise he has imparted justice to all, like Hermes twice-great. He
has ordered moreover that those returning to the country, soldiers
and those others who were disaffected during the troubles, shall keep
their own possessions on their return. He provided that forces of
cavalry and infantry and ships should be sent against those who attacked
Egypt by sea and on land, undertaking great outlay of money and
food so that the temples and all the people in Egypt should be safe.
He went to Lycopolis in Busiris, which had been taken and fortified
against a siege by deposits of arms and all other sorts of equipment,
as the spirit of rebellion had become entrenched through the passage
of time among the impious people who gathered there, who had
done much harm to the temples and the inhabitants of Egypt. He
invested it with notable earthworks and ditches and solid siege-walls.
In the eighth year the Nile rose high and as usual flooded the plain, and
he dammed it in several places, fortifying the mouths of the streams
and spending large sums of money on these works. He stationed
cavalry and infantry to guard them, and soon seized the city by force
and destroyed all the impious men in it, just as Hermes and Horus,
son of Isis and Osiris, overcame those who revolted in those parts
before. As for those who led the rebels in his father's day, harassed

the country and violated the temples, he went to Memphis to avenge his father and his own monarchy. He chastised them all as they deserved, at the time when he came for the celebration of the customary ceremonies at his assumption of the kingship. He remitted moreover the temple debts owed to the royal treasury up to the eighth year, in food and in money, which were no small amount, and likewise the cost of the sailcloth which had not been delivered to the royal treasury, as well as the cost of verification for those that had been delivered, for the same period. He released the temples from the due of one artaba per aroura of sacred ground and one keramion per aroura of vine-land. He made many donations to Apis and Mnevis and to the other sacred animals in Egypt, taking much more concern than the kings who preceded him over matters to do with the animals, in all circumstances. The money for their tombs he gave generously and nobly, and the sums appointed for their particular worship, including sacrifices and processions and the other prescribed rituals. The privileges of the temples in Egypt he preserved on their existing basis, in accord with the laws, and he adorned Apis with elaborately-worked robes, supplying for this gold and silver and precious stones in no small quantity. He founded temples and shrines and altars; he restored, besides, those in need of repair, having towards what concerned the gods the zeal of a beneficent deity. On further information, he renewed the temples most venerated in his reign, as was fitting; in requital for which the gods gave him health, victory, might and all other blessings, the crown remaining to him and to his children for all time.

Decree

With fortune's favour.

The priests of all the temples in the country have resolved that all the honours paid to the everliving king Ptolemy, beloved by Phthah, the god Epiphanes Gracious, and likewise those of his parents, the gods Philopators, and of his forbears the gods Euergetes, and of the gods Adelphi and the gods Soters, should be greatly augmented. They also resolved to set up in honour of the everliving king Ptolemy, god Epiphanes Gracious, an image in each temple, in the most conspicuous place, which shall be given the name of Ptolemy, the avenger of Egypt. There shall be set there the chief god of the temple, giving him a weapon of victory, all depicted in the fashion of the country. The priests shall perform rites three times a day before the images and put on them sacred adornment and carry out the rest of the prescribed ceremonies, as for the other gods, in the processions in Egypt. They resolved to set up to the king Ptolemy, god Epiphanes Gracious, son of King Ptolemy and Queen Arsinoe, the gods Philopators, a statue of wood and a gilded shrine in each of the temples, and to set them in the sanctuaries with the other shrines, and in the great processions in which the shrines are paraded that of the god Epiphanes Gracious is is to be paraded also. . . .

(There follow specifications of the adornment of the shrine, and resolutions on priestly titles and annual ceremonies.)

A GREEK COURT POET

The Seventeenth Idyll of Theocritus is an encomium of Ptolemy II Philadelphus. It incorporates the genealogical claims of the Ptolemies already known to us; it also exemplifies the way in which Hellenic literary tradition could absorb and 'Hellenize' some of the salient features of the régime derived from Egyptian tradition—with certain significant exceptions. Theocritus stops short of actually calling the king a god. The poem should be compared, in content and in tone, with the Rosetta Stone Decree. Could it perhaps be argued that it is in Theocritus' poem, rather than the priestly decree with its overt apostrophes to the rulers as divine, that we find what can properly be called 'personality cult'? Or is the poem itself simply an impersonal exercise in conventional forms?

Theocritus, *Idyll 17: Encomium of Ptolemy Philadelphus*

Let us begin with Zeus and, Muses, end with Zeus, when we celebrate with our hymns the best of the immortals.

Of men, let Ptolemy be spoken of among the first, and last and in the middle, for he is pre-eminent among men.

Heroes, who in times past were born of demigods, did noble deeds and found skilled minstrels. I know how to speak well, and I would sing of Ptolemy; and hymns are the prerogative of the immortals themselves.

A woodcutter, going to wooded Ida, looks around, in the midst of plenty, to know where to begin his work. Of what shall I speak first? For a myriad are the ways in which the gods honoured the best of kings.

From his forefathers he had the ability to perform a mighty work, Ptolemy of the Lagids, when he should put in his heart counsel such as no other man could conceive.

His father made him honoured equally with the blessed immortals, and a golden throne has been constructed for him in the house of Zeus. Next to him sits Alexander, benevolent, a god in gleaming baldric, grievous to the Persians. Opposite is the seat of Heracles the centaur-slayer, wrought of solid adamant; there with the other descendants of Ouranos Heracles keeps good cheer, rejoicing exceedingly in his grandchildren's grandchildren, because the son of Cronos has taken old age from their limbs and they are called immortal, they that are born of his line. For the stalwart Heraclid is the ancestor of both (Ptolemy and Alexander), and both reckon back ultimately to Heracles.

And when Heracles goes from the feast, sated with sweet-smelling nectar, to the apartment of his dear wife, to one he gives his bow and the quiver under his arm, and to the other the staff of iron, marked with bosses, and they conduct into the ambrosial chamber of white-ankled Hebe the weapons and the bearded son of Zeus.

So among women of understanding the renowned Berenice is eminent, and has greatly benefited her begetters. On her fragrant bosom the ruler of Cyprus, lady, daughter of Dione, laid gentle hands. So they say that no man has ever yet so rejoiced in women as Ptolemy loved his spouse; and he was loved in return, even more. So a man might in confidence trust his entire house to his children whenever in love he goes to the couch of her who loves him. But a heartless woman has always her mind upon another, and conceives readily, but the children are not like their father.

Lady Aphrodite, excelling in beauty among the goddesses, she is your care, and thanks to you the beautiful Berenice has not crossed mournful Acheron, but snatching her up before she entered the dark ship and the ever-hateful ford of the dead, you placed her in a temple and gave her honours of her own. She kindly inspires tender feelings of love in all mortals, and makes the pangs gentle for the longing lover.

Dark-browed lady of Argos, you bore to Diomedes, slayer of men, Tydeus the man of Calydon. Deep-bosomed Thetis bore to Peleus, son of Aeacus, the spearman Achilles. And you, warrior Ptolemy, the famed Berenice bore to the warrior Ptolemy. The isle of Cos nurtured you when you were a new-born infant, receiving you from your mother when you first saw the light. There the daughter of Antigone, pressed by birth-pangs, called upon Eilithyia, looser of girdles; the goddess kindly assisted and shed painlessness over all her limbs; and the beloved child, resembling his father, was born. Cos cried aloud at sight of him, and touching the infant with loving hand, said:

'May you be happy, child, and honour me as Phoebus Apollo honoured Delos; pay the same honour to the promontory of Triops, rendering equal favours to the neighbouring Dorians—lord Apollo showed like love to Apenaia.'

So spoke the island; and from aloft a great eagle, bird of omen, cried out thrice aloud from the clouds. This was doubtless a sign from Zeus; reverend kings are the care of Zeus, son of Cronos, and this king especially, whom Zeus has loved since his birth. Great prosperity attends him; he rules over many lands and many seas.

Many thousands of lands and races of men nurture crops, aided by the rain of Zeus, but none bears so richly as the low-lying land of Egypt, when the overflowing Nile breaks up the dry clods, nor does any land have so many cities, the work of skilled men. Three hundred cities are built there, three thousand added to thirty thousand, twice three and again nine times three. Of all these the lordly Ptolemy is king. Moreover, he annexes part of Phoenicia, and Arabia, Syria, Libya and the country of the dark Ethiopians. He commands all the Pamphylians and the warriors of Cilicia, the Lycians, lovers of warfare, the Carians and the Cycladic islands, for he has excellent seafaring ships. The whole sea and earth and the roaring rivers are ruled by Ptolemy. Many horsemen are gathered about him and many infantry, equipped in gleaming bronze. In wealth, he could outweigh all kings, such abundance comes every day from all quarters into his rich house. His people work in peace at their occupations, for no foe has crossed over the Nile, full of monsters, and come by land to raise the war-cry in the villages of others, nor has anyone ever leapt in armour to the shore from a swift ship, with hostile intent against the cattle of Egypt. Such is the man who presides over the broad plains, Ptolemy of the golden hair, skilled in wielding the spear, whose chief care it is to guard all his inheritance, as a good king; and he himself adds to it.

But in his rich house the gold does not lie useless, piled up like the treasures of ever-labouring ants. The glorious houses of the gods have a great part, as he constantly makes first offering to them, with other honours. Much goes in gifts to mighty kings, much to cities, much to his worthy companions. Nor does any man who is skilled in singing a sweet song come to the sacred contests of Dionysus without the king granting him a gift worthy of his skill.

So the interpreters of the Muses hymn Ptolemy in return for his benefactions. What could be finer for a wealthy man than to obtain noble renown among men? The glory of the sons of Atreus abides; but those countless treasures they obtained when they captured the great palace of Priam are hidden somewhere in the darkness from which there is no return.

Alone, among men hitherto and those who still print the traces of their feet as they tread on the warm dust, Ptolemy has set up to his dear mother and his father incense-perfumed temples; in them, he has set up their images, beautiful with gold and ivory, bringing help to all on earth. He burns the thighs of many fat oxen on their reddened altars when the cycle of the months comes round, he and his noble wife, than whom no better woman encircles with her arms her bridegroom in their bedchamber. She loves from her heart her brother who is also her husband. Even so among the immortals was accomplished the sacred marriage of the children of Rhea, the rulers of Olympus. Iris, still a maiden, her hands washed in myrrh, prepared one bed for Zeus and Hera to sleep in.

Greetings, lord Ptolemy. I celebrate you equally with the other demigods, and I utter words which I believe men in the future will not reject. As for virtue, seek that from Zeus.

VIII. Rome: Seizure of Power and Honours to the Victor

We are fortunate in possessing such full accounts of the measures passed by the Romans in the period following Caesar's victory in the Civil War as are provided by Cassius Dio (early third century A.D.) and Suetonius (early second century A.D.). Dio, in particular, presents these in successive stages during the period from Pharsalus to 44 B.C., thus allowing us to try and trace, as it were, a kind of progression.

Several themes may be pursued here. There is the distinction between those honours which confer actual political power and those which enhance the status of the recipient. Of the latter, some are quasi-political, some quasi-religious, some neither. How and why do they have the effect of increasing Caesar's impressiveness in the public eye? There are differences also among the groups from whom proposals of honours emanated, and their motives. Caesar's own attitude is problematic—does he seem to have wished to take on the position and powers of a Hellenistic monarch? or even to have wished to be acknowledged as divine? Can Dio's distinction between the 'not undemocratic' honours and the others be upheld? And was the assassination plot a natural or inevitable outcome?

I have appended Dio's account of the actions of the triumvirs in the period immediately following Caesar's death, as providing some material for the study of what Weber called 'the traditionalization of charisma'—Ptolemaic Egypt and Imperial Rome provide parallels.

Suetonius, *Divus Julius*

76. However, other words and actions of his carry more weight, and support the view that he misused his power and was justly slain. For not only did he accept excessive honours, such as a succession of consulships, a perpetual dictatorship and prefecture of morals, and in addition the forename 'Imperator' and the additional title of 'Father of the fatherland' after his name, a statue placed among the kings and a throne in the orchestra at the theatre—he also allowed to be decreed to himself honours even surpassing human rank, such as a golden

seat in the Senate house and on the tribunal, a ceremonial carriage and litter in the Circus processions, temples, altars, images next to those of the gods, a ceremonial couch, a *flamen*, *luperci* and a month named after himself. There were no honours he did not receive or take as he liked.

His third and fourth consulships he exercised only in name, content with the dictatorial power he was granted at the same time, and in both years he appointed two consuls to replace himself for the last three months of the year. In the meantime, he held no elections save for the tribunes and aediles of the plebs, and he appointed prefects with praetorian rank to administer affairs in the city in his absence. On the last day of the year when a consul suddenly died, he gave the office for the last few hours to someone who asked for it. With similar contempt for regulations he disregarded ancestral custom and designated magistrates for several years, gave consular insignia to men of praetorian rank and took into the Senate men on whom he had conferred the citizenship, and some from the half-civilized Gauls. Moreover, he put his own slaves in charge of the mint and the public taxes. He demanded the charge and command of the three legions he left at Alexandria for Rufio, son of his freedman, his boy-friend.

77. Equally insolent were his public utterances, as Titus Ampius records: 'The republic is nothing, a mere title without substance or form. Sulla was a dunce to lay down the dictatorship. Men should talk with me more circumspectly and take what I say as law.' He went to such lengths in his arrogance that once when the seer reported unfavourable omens, that the victim lacked a heart, he said the omens would be favourable, as he wished it, and it was not to be taken as a portent if a creature lacked a heart.

78. But what he did that roused especially deadly hatred against him was the following. When the entire Senate went to him with a large number of decrees couched in the most honorific terms, he remained seated to receive them before the temple of Venus Genetrix. Some think that he was held back by Cornelius Balbus when he attempted to rise, others that he did not even attempt to, but that when Gaius Trebatius actually urged him to rise he looked at him in an unfriendly way. This behaviour of his seemed all the more intolerable because, on the occasion of his triumph, as he rode past the tribunician benches, he was so indignant at the failure of one of the college, Pontius Aquila, to rise that he exclaimed, 'So, then, tribune Aquila, ask me to restore

the republic', and for days on end he gave no undertakings to anyone save with the proviso, 'That is, if Pontius Aquila permits.'

79. To such notable insult, showing his contempt for the Senate, he added a still more arrogant action. For at the time of the Latin sacrifices when he was returning among the unrestrained and unprecedented acclamations of the people, someone in the crowd had put on his statue a laurel crown bound with a white ribbon and the tribunes Epidius Marullus and Caesetius Flavus ordered it to be taken down and the man carried off to prison. Then Caesar, annoyed either at the lack of success of the initial hint at the kingship or, as he put about, because he had been deprived of the glory of refusal, upbraided the tribunes and removed them from office. Subsequently he was unable to shake off the ill-repute of aiming even at the name of king, although when the populace greeted him as such, he said he was Caesar, not king, and at the Lupercalia, when the consul Antonius on the rostrum several times raised the diadem over his head, he pushed it away and sent it to the Capitol as a dedication to Jupiter Best and Greatest. There was even a widespread rumour that he was going to move to Alexandria or Troy, taking with him the resources of the empire, draining Italy with levies and entrusting charge of the city to his friends, and that at the next Senate Lucius Cotta, of the priestly commission in charge of the Sibylline Books, was going to propose that, since there was an oracle in the books of destiny that the Parthians could not be conquered save by a king, Caesar should be called king. This caused the conspirators to hurry on their intended action, to avoid having to agree.

Dio 42

18. When the news was reported of the battle of Pharsalus, the Romans for a long time did not believe it; for Caesar sent no despatch to the government, as he shrank from appearing to rejoice publicly in such a victory (and for the same reason he celebrated no triumph for it). Besides, it seemed very unlikely, in view of the resources of either side, and of people's expectations. When at last they became convinced, they pulled down the statues of Pompey and Sulla that stood on the Rostra, but did nothing more for the present. Many had not wanted to do even that much, and many were afraid that Pompey might renew the fight. They thought that even that was enough for Caesar,

and they expected that they would easily obtain pardon for it from Pompey. When Pompey had actually died, they believed that only belatedly and not until they saw his ring, which was sent to Rome (like Sulla's, it had three trophies carved on it).

19. So, when he had died, then they openly lauded the victor and re-viled the loser, and proposed everything they could think of to be given to Caesar. There was great competition in devising honours among virtually all the leading Romans, all striving to out-do each other with flattery, and also in the actual voting of honours. Everyone shouted and gestured so as to manifest the utmost zeal, as though Caesar himself were present and looking on, and, as though they were trying to please him and not acting from necessity, they expected to get some return—one a magistracy, another a priesthood, a third money.

I shall omit those honours—such as statues, wreaths, privileged seats, and the like—which had been voted to others before, and those which were new and were proposed now for the first time but were not confirmed by Caesar, in case I should become tedious if I enum-erated them all. I shall follow the same practice in the rest of my ac-count, the more so as the proposals grew constantly in number and absurdity. I shall relate only those which had some unique and speci-ally important feature and which were confirmed.

20. They granted to him permission to do whatever he wished with the supporters of Pompey—not that he had not already taken this right for himself, but so that his actions might be given some appear-ance of legality. They gave him authority to make war and peace with all mankind without having to refer either to the people or the Senate, the excuse for this being the rallying of the Pompeians in Africa. This also he already had in his power, inasmuch as he had so large an army. At any rate, the wars he fought had almost all been undertaken on his own initiative. However, as they wished to continue to appear autono-mous as Roman citizens, they none the less voted him these rights, and everything else that it was in his power to have even against their will. Thus, he was made consul for five consecutive years, and dictator not merely for six months but a whole year, and he acquired the tribunician power for life—virtually, for he got the right to sit upon the same bench with the tribunes and to be reckoned along with them for other purposes, an unprecedented privilege. All the elections, except those of the plebs, came under his control, and therefore they were post-poned until he should be present, and held towards the end of the year.

As for the provincial governorship, they themselves ostentatiously made the allotment for the consuls, but voted that Caesar should assign the others to the praetors without drawing lots (they had gone back to consuls and praetors contrary to their decree). They also granted another privilege, which was customary, but which in the current disturbed situation might rouse hatred and resentment; for they decreed that Caesar should hold a triumph as victor for the war against Juba and the Romans who fought with him, although Caesar did not even know as yet that this war was to occur.

Dio 43

14. Immediately after the African campaign, and before crossing into Italy, Caesar discharged the older men among the soldiers, in case they should mutiny again. He settled other matters in Africa as quickly as circumstances allowed and accompanied the whole fleet as far as Sardinia. From there he sent the troops on to Spain, with Gaius Didius, against young Pompey, while he himself returned to Rome, pluming himself chiefly on the brilliance of his achievements but also with some satisfaction in the decrees of the Senate. They had voted that sacrifices should be offered for his victory during forty days, and that in the triumph already voted him he should ride in a chariot drawn by white horses and be attended by all the lictors then with him and as many others as he had employed in his first dictatorship, as well as the number he had had in his second. They also elected him as overseer of every man's conduct (for he was given some such title— as though the title of Censor was not worthy of him) for three years, and dictator for ten years in succession. In addition they voted that he should sit in the Senate on a curule chair along with the current consuls and should always give his opinion first, that he should give the signal at all the games in the Circus, and that he should make the appointments of the magistrates and whatever other honour used previously to be bestowed by the people. They decreed that a chariot of his should be set on the Capitol facing the statue of Jupiter, that there should be a statue of him in bronze standing on the inhabited world, with an inscription saying that he was a demigod, and that his name should be inscribed on the Capitol instead of that of Catulus (because he had completed the temple after undertaking to bring Catulus to account for its construction).

These are the only decrees I have recorded, not because they were the only ones voted (for a great number were proposed and, of course, were also ratified) but because he refused all the rest, while these he accepted.

42. Although his conquest was not over foreign people but he had actually killed so large a number of citizens, he not only celebrated a triumph himself (for the Spanish campaign) but allowed Quintus Fabius and Quintus Pedius to hold a celebration, although they had been his subordinates and had achieved nothing on their own account. Of course, this caused ridicule, as also the fact that they used wooden instead of ivory representations of certain exploits, and other similar triumphal trappings. All the same, a brilliant triple triumph and triple procession of the Romans was held in celebration of those very events, and there was moreover a public thanksgiving of fifty days. The Parilia was honoured with games in the Circus in perpetuity, not because the city was founded on that day, but because the news of Caesar's victory had arrived on the day before, towards evening.

43. This, then, he gave to Rome. He himself, by decree, wore the triumphal garb at all the games and was adorned with the laurel wreath at all times and everywhere alike. He gave as excuse for it that his head was bald in front; but he occasioned talk by this very fact that, though no longer young, he took pains with his appearance. He openly displayed to everyone his liking for rather loose clothing, and the shoes he wore sometimes later were high and red in colour, like those of the kings who once ruled in Alba—for he claimed relationship to them through Iulus. In general, he showed great devotion to Venus, and wanted to persuade everyone that he had received from her a kind of bloom of youth. Therefore he used also to wear a carved ring depicting her in armour, and he made her name the watchword during most of his greatest dangers. Sulla had disapproved of the looseness of his belt, to the extent that he had even wanted to kill him, and had said to those who pleaded for him, 'I will grant him to you; but do you be very much on your guard against this ill-girt fellow.' Cicero could not understand it, and even after defeat he said: 'I should never have expected anyone so ill-girt to conquer Pompey.'

44. I have written this digression from my narrative so that no one might be ignorant of any of the things said about Caesar. In honour of his victory the Senate made all the decrees I have mentioned, and in addition called him 'Liberator' and had it entered in the public

records, and they voted for a public temple of Liberty. They also applied to him now first, and for the first time, as though it were his personal name, the title of *Imperator*. They were no longer merely following the ancient custom whereby others as well as Caesar himself had often been saluted for the outcome of wars, nor in the way in which those who received an independent command of some sort were so addressed, but were giving him once and for all the title which is now given to whoever holds supreme power. They went to such extremes of flattery as even to vote that his sons and grandsons should have the same title, although he had no child and was already old. From him this appellation has come to all subsequent emperors, as one peculiar to their position, like the title 'Caesar' also. However, the ancient custom was not abolished; both practices exist together. Therefore, when the emperors gain some notable victory, they are given the title a second time. For those who are *imperatores* in this special sense use the title once for all, like the others, and put it first; but those who have some success in war deserving the title acquire it additionally, according to the ancient custom; and so a man may be termed '*imperator*' twice or three times, or as often as this occurs.

These were the privileges they gave Caesar at this time, as well as a house, so that he might live at the state's expense, and a special thanks-giving whenever a victory should occur and sacrifices be offered for it, even if he had not been on the campaign or taken any part at all in the exploits.

45. All the same, these measures, even if in some people's eyes they were excessive and contrary to custom, were not actually undemo-cratic. However, they voted other things besides by which they dis-played him as a monarch outright. They offered him the magistracies —even those of the plebeians—and they elected him consul for ten years, as previously they had made him dictator. They decreed that he alone should have soldiers, and alone should administer the public treasury, so that no one else should have access to either except by his permission. And at this time they decreed that an ivory statue of him, and later that a whole chariot should be conducted along with the statues of the gods in the procession at the games in the Circus. Another statue they set up in the temple of Quirinus, inscribed, 'To the invincible god', and another on the Capitol beside the former kings of Rome. It strikes me that this is a remarkable coincidence. There were eight statues—seven to the kings and the eighth to that Brutus

who overthrew the Tarquins—and they set up Caesar's statue beside the one of Brutus; and it was as a result of this in particular that Marcus Brutus was stirred to conspire against him.

46. These were the measures in honour of his victory (I do not mention all, but only those I thought noteworthy). They were not all passed on one day, but just as it happened, at different times. Caesar began to make use of some, and intended to use others in the future, even though he very strongly rejected certain ones. Thus he took the office of consul at once, even before entering the city, but did not retain it to the end of the year. When he reached Rome, he renounced it, and handed it over to Quintus Fabius and Gaius Trebonius. When Fabius died on the last day of his consulship, Caesar at once chose another man, Gaius Caninius Rebilus, to replace him for the remaining hours.

Dio 44

1. This Caesar did in preparation for a campaign against the Parthians; but a baneful frenzy fell upon certain men, through their envy of his advancement, and this frenzy had him unlawfully killed, while adding a new name to recorded infamy. It shattered the decrees and, after a time of concord, involved the Romans again in dissension and civil wars. These men claimed that as slayers of Caesar they were at the same time liberators of the people; but in fact they plotted impiously against him and caused turmoil in Rome when it had achieved good government.

2. For democracy has a fair-sounding name, and appears to give equal rights to all through equal laws, but in practice it is found not to correspond to its name. Monarchy, on the other hand, sounds disagreeable, but is a most beneficial system by which to be governed. It is easier to find one sound man than many, and if it seems to some difficult to find even one, then to find many should be admitted to be impossible; for it is not in the capacity of most men to acquire virtue.

If any democracy has ever flourished, it has been at its peak for only a brief period, so long as the people were neither numerous enough nor strong enough to occasion insolence to arise as a result of their good fortune, or jealousy as a result of ambition. But for a city so great as Rome, and ruling over the finest and greatest part of the known world, controlling men of many diverse natures and having many men of great wealth, engaged both generally and individually in all kinds of activities and experiencing all sorts of fortune—for such a city it is impossible to exercise restraint under a democracy, and even more impossible, lacking restraint, for it to have concord. Therefore, if Marcus Brutus and Gaius Cassius had only taken these things into consideration, they would never have killed the leader and protector of the city, nor have been the cause of bringing countless ills upon themselves and their contemporaries.

3. This is how it happened: the cause of his death was as follows. The enmity he had roused was not altogether undeserved, except in so far as the senators themselves egged him on and puffed him up by their novel and immoderate honours, and then criticized him on account of these very honours, and spread reports of how he accepted them gladly and behaved more haughtily as a result of them. Caesar did sometimes make a mistake by accepting some of the honours voted him, and believing that he really deserved them, but most at fault were those who after beginning by honouring him as he deserved, then led him on and blamed him for what they voted to him. For he did not dare to reject all of them, in case he should be thought to be contemptuous, nor could he safely accept them, for excess of honour and praise makes even the most moderate men conceited, especially if they seem to be given sincerely.

4. The honours given him, besides those already mentioned, were as follows (I shall mention them all together, even if they were not all proposed or ratified at once). First they voted that he should always ride, even in the city itself, wearing the triumphal garb, and should sit in the curule chair everywhere—except at the games, for there he received the right to sit on the tribunes' bench along with the tribunes of the time. They gave him the right to offer *spolia opima* in the temple of Jupiter Feretrius, as though he had killed an enemy commander with his own hand, and to have his lictors always carrying laurel, and to ride into the city from the Alban Mount, after the Latin Festival, on horseback. In addition to these signal honours they named him 'Father of the fatherland', and stamped the title on the coins; they voted to have public sacrifices on his birthday, ordered that there should be a statue of him in the cities and in all the temples of Rome, and they set up two more on the Rostra, one of him as saviour of the citizens, the other as deliverer of the city from siege, with the customary wreaths for these exploits. They resolved to build a temple of New

Concord, as they enjoyed peace thanks to him, and to have an annual festival in honour of this goddess.

5. When he accepted these, they gave him the commission of filling the Pontine marshes, cutting a channel through the Peloponnesian Isthmus and building a new Senate-house, since that of Hostilius, though repaired, had been destroyed. The excuse for its destruction was that a temple of Felicitas was to be built there (and Lepidus, while Master of the Horse, did in fact carry this out), but the real reason was so that the name of Sulla should not be preserved on it, and so that another newly-built Senate-house might be called the Julian, just as they had called the month of his birth July and one of the tribes, chosen by lot, the Julia.

They voted that he should be censor without colleague and for life, and should enjoy the privileges of the tribunes, so that if anyone insulted him in word or deed that person should be outcast and accursed; and that his son, should he beget or even adopt one, should be appointed chief priest.

6. And as he was pleased with all this, a gilded chair was granted him, and a garb which was one worn by the kings, and a bodyguard of knights and Senators. Moreover they decided that prayers should be offered publicly for him each year, that oaths should be taken by his Fortune, and that all his future enactments should be regarded as valid. Then they gave him a four-yearly festival, as if to a hero, and a third priestly college, which they called the Julian, for the conduct of the Lupercalia, and one day on every occasion of gladiatorial contests in Rome and the rest of Italy.

And when he was pleased with these honours too, they then voted that his gilded chair and his garland, gilded and set with gems, should be carried into the theatre like those of the gods, and that at the circus games his chariot should be brought in. Finally they addressed him outright as Jupiter Julius, and ordered a temple to be consecrated to him and his Clemency, electing Antony as priest, like a *flamen Dialis*.

7. At the same time as these, they decreed another honour which most clearly showed their intention. This gave him the right to place his tomb inside the pomerium. The decrees on these matters they inscribed on silver tablets in gold letters and put them below the feet of Jupiter Capitolinus, thus pointing out to him very clearly that he was a mortal.

For they had begun to honour him in the expectation that he would show moderation; but as they went on and saw him pleased with what they voted (for he accepted all but a few), then different men kept proposing different honours, becoming more and more extravagant, some with exaggerated flattery of him and others to ridicule him—at any rate, some went so far as to propose that he should be allowed to have intercourse with as many women as he pleased because, even thought he was fifty, he still had many mistresses. Others, who were the majority, did this because they wanted to make him envied and hated as quickly as possible, so that he might the sooner be destroyed. This in fact happened, although Caesar was encouraged by these very decrees to believe that he would never be conspired against by the men who voted him such honours, and that no one else would do so, on account of them. As a result, he ceased to use a bodyguard—for he accepted nominally the guard of Senators and knights, and dismissed his previous bodyguard.

8. Once when in a single day they voted honours unusually numerous and unusually important (which were granted unanimously, except for Cassius and a few others, who gained notoriety in consequence, but came to no harm—whereby Caesar's clemency was most conspicuously demonstrated) they went to him as he was sitting in the entry of the temple of Venus, to announce to him in a body their decrees; for they dealt with such matters in his absence so as to appear to be acting not under duress but voluntarily. He received them seated— either through some divinely occasioned folly or even through excess of joy—and this provoked the anger of them all, not only Senators but the rest as well, to such an extent that it provided his murderers with one of their chief excuses for the plot. Some who later tried to defend him said that he could not control his bowels owing to an attack of diarrhoea, and remained seated to avoid evacuating. However, they could not convince the majority, because not long afterwards he got up and went home on foot. So men suspected him of being conceited and hated him for his haughtiness, when they themselves had made him so by the excessiveness of their honours. After this event, he increased suspicion still further by allowing himself, later on, to be appointed dictator for life.

9. When he had reached this point, those plotting against him no longer held back. In order to turn even his staunchest friends against him, they spread stories slandering him, and finally addressed him as king, a name they often used also among themselves. When he kept refusing this title, and rebuking those who addressed him in this way,

yet without actually doing anything from which it might be believed
that he was really annoyed by it, they secretly put a diadem on his
statue which stood on the Rostra. When the tribunes Gaius Epidius
Marullus and Lucius Caesetius Flavus took it down, he was violently
angry, even though they said nothing insulting, and actually praised
him before the populace as not wanting anything of that sort. For the
time being, although annoyed, he kept quiet;

10. but later, when he was riding back from the Alban Mount and
some men called him king, he said that he was not called king but
Caesar; and then when the tribunes brought a suit against the first
man who had called him king, he did not control his anger, but showed
extreme annoyance, as though the tribunes themselves were fomenting
sedition against him. He did them no harm for the moment, but later,
when they issued a proclamation that they were unable to speak out
freely and safely on behalf of the public good, he became very angry
and brought them into the Senate-house, where he denounced them
and ordered a vote. He did not kill them, although some demanded
that penalty for them, but first he deposed them from the tribunate
on the motion of their colleague Helvius Cinna and then erased their
names from the Senate.

   Some were pleased at this, or pretended to be, as they would not
need to run risks by speaking out frankly and as they themselves were
not involved and so could look on as though from a watch-tower.
Caesar, however, incurred additional odium from the fact that, while
he should have hated those who applied the name of king to him, he
let them go and arraigned the tribunes instead.

11. Something else that happened not long after these events showed
still more clearly that although he pretended to reject the title, in fact
he wished to assume it. At the festival of the Lupercalia, when he had
entered the Forum and was sitting on the Rostra on his gilded chair,
dressed in his royal garb and splendid in his gilded crown, Antony
with his fellow-priests addressed him as king and bound a diadem on
his head, saying, 'This the people offer you through me.' Caesar
replied, 'Jupiter alone is king of the Romans', and sent the diadem to
Jupiter on the Capitol. However, he was not angry, but had it entered
in the records that the kingship had been offered to him by the people,
through the consul, and he had refused it. So it was suspected that
this had been prearranged, and that he wanted the title, but wished to
be compelled to take it; so there was intense feeling against him.

Dio 47

18. While these three were behaving like this, they were at the same time exalting the late Caesar to the utmost degree. As they were eager for sole rule and were striving for it, they pursued furiously the rest of Caesar's murderers, their idea being that in this way they would be securing in advance immunity and safety for their own actions. They did zealously everything that tended to Caesar's honour, in the expectation that they themselves would one day be thought worthy of like honours. Therefore they exalted him not merely by the honours already voted him, but by others which they now added. One was that on the first day of the year they themselves took an oath, and administered it to the others, that they would consider binding all Caesar's acts. The same is still done today in honour of all those who successively hold supreme power, and also of those who once possessed it and have not been disgraced. They also laid the foundation of a shrine to him as hero, in the Forum at the place where he had been burned, and they had an image of him, together with one of Venus, carried in procession at the games in the Circus. If there was news of a victory anywhere, they assigned the honour of a public thanksgiving separately to the victor and to Caesar, though he was dead. They made it obligatory to celebrate his birthday by wearing laurel and revelling, and passed a law that those who neglected to do so should be accursed in the view of Jupiter and of Caesar himself, and that if they were Senators or the sons of Senators they should be fined one million sesterces. It happened that the games of Apollo fell on the same day, and so they voted that his birthday should be celebrated on the day before the games, as there was a Sibylline oracle forbidding a celebration at that time in honour of any other god save Apollo.

19. In addition they made the day of his murder, which had always been a regular meeting day for the Senate, an unlucky day. The room in which he was murdered they closed for the present, and later made it a privy. They also built the Curia Julia, named after him, beside the area known as the Comitium, as had been voted. Moreover, as though he were truly a god, they forbade any likeness of him to be carried in the funeral procession of his kindred, this being a very old custom which was still observed. They also decreed that no one who took refuge in his shrine for sanctuary could be driven or hauled

away. This was a concession granted not even to any of the gods, except those worshipped in Romulus' time. Yet that place too became an asylum in name only, not in fact, once men began to gather there, for it was so fenced round that it was impossible for anyone to go in at all.

IX. The Establishment of the Principate

The emperor Augustus, as Octavius (and presently Caesar Octavianus), began at the age of nineteen, with the illegal raising of a private army, the process that established him initially as the successor of Julius Caesar and then as Rome's first emperor. The next succession was not until fifty-six years later. Comparison between the two occasions is instructive. On both occasions, certain physical essentials of power are secured at once; on both occasions care is taken to appear to observe certain constitutional forms; on both occasions use is made of claims to a special connection with the illustrious predecessor. However, there are differences in the use thus made, and in the nature and gravity of the embarrassments which each in turn, Octavian and Tiberius, had to bring under control or conceal, especially because of the nominal maintenance of the forms of the Roman republican constitution.

The *Res Gestae Divi Augusti*, or 'Acts of the Deified Augustus', is an autobiographical document which Augustus left instructions to have inscribed and set up at his mausoleum. Our text is mainly from a copy set up at a temple in Ancyra. The opening chapters give the 'approved' version of his earlier career; Tacitus presents that alongside a hostile interpretation.

The document presents Augustus as he wished, presumably, to be remembered and so, one must suppose, includes those features he thought most effective in securing him public support and goodwill. Certain matters are skimmed over or omitted altogether. The Civil Wars receive very brief notice, none of his adversaries even being mentioned by name. In the record of military and diplomatic events (not given here) certain defeats and withdrawals are omitted. On his powers and prerogatives he is not frank. The 'transfer of power' mentioned in section 34 was far from complete; Augustus was given as his 'province' more than half the empire, with most of the legions, which he retained for the rest of his life. The constitutional crisis of 23 B.C., which resulted in his giving up the continuous tenure of consulship, is passed over, and so are the extra-constitutional consular power for life and censorial power for five years, which Dio says (54.10) were conferred on him in 19 B.C. (notice the careful wording of sections 7 and 34). His social legislation, particularly that on marriage, was unpopular; it does not figure in the *Res Gestae*.

The document may be studied in several different ways. One is as a description of the ways in which a monarch secures and stabilizes his position, and here the remarks of Aristotle on this subject may be recalled. Another is as an illustration of what is thought to have popular appeal— an exercise in the propaganda of government. Again, one may study the differences between the realities of power established and the façade that is maintained. Tacitus' account of Tiberius' succession in A.D. 14 provides a counterpoint here. Constitutionally, that might appear the most crucial moment—yet was there any real likelihood of a revival of the Republic?

The surviving part of the law of A.D. 70 is one of the most valuable documents we possess for the history of the Principate. In it, we have, set out in detail, a list of some of the strictly extra-constitutional measures taken under various emperors to ensure that the *princeps* should rule, despite the constitution. Dio (53.28) says that on Augustus' return from Spain in 24 B.C., 'the Senate freed him from all compulsion of the laws so that, as I have said, he might in reality be independent and absolute, both over himself and the laws, and might do everything he wished and nothing he did not wish.' Whether so sweeping a concession was ever made all at once is not certain; however, does it appear that the emperor by A.D. 70 at least was effectively freed from the laws' control?

Notice also how early the principle of hereditary succession as right and natural is assumed, and that in what was and had been for centuries a Republic. Yet is this altogether unexpected?

MONUMENTUM ANCYRANUM (RES GESTAE DIVI AUGUSTI)

1. At the age of nineteen I raised on my own initiative and at my own expense an army, by means of which I reasserted the freedom of the state when it was oppressed by the domination of a faction. On account of this the Senate bestowed honours on me by decrees in which it enrolled me in its order, in the consulship of Gaius Pansa and Aulus Hirtius (43 B.C.), according me the right to give my opinion among the consulars and giving me military command. It ordered me, as a pro-praetor, along with the consuls, to 'look to it that the state took no harm'. In the same year, when both consuls had fallen in battle, the people made me consul, and triumvir for the reorganization of the state.

2. The murderers of my father I drove into exile, and exacted ven-

geance for their crime in legally-established courts, and subsequently when they made war on the state I thrice defeated them in the field.

3. I fought many wars, civil and foreign, by land and sea throughout the entire world, and as victor I spared all citizens who sought pardon. Such foreign peoples as it was safe to pardon I preferred to preserve rather than exterminate. The Roman citizens who took the military oath of loyalty to me numbered about five hundred thousand. Of these I settled in colonies or sent back to their own towns on the expiry of their terms of service somewhat more than three hundred thousand, and to all those I allotted lands or gave money as rewards for their service. I captured six hundred vessels, not counting those smaller than triremes.

4. I had two ovations and three full triumphs, and was hailed twenty-one times as *imperator*. The Senate decreed further triumphs to me, all of which I refused. I laid in the Capitol the laurels which garlanded my *fasces*, after fulfilling the vows I had undertaken in each war. Fifty-five times the Senate decreed thanksgivings to the immortal gods for the successes gained on land and sea by me, or through my lieutenants acting under my auspices. The number of days on which thanksgivings were held in accordance with senatorial decree was eight hundred and ninety. In my triumphs nine kings or children of kings were led in front of my chariot. At the time of writing this I have been consul thirteen times and am in the thirty-seventh year of tribunician power.

5. The dictatorship was offered to me, both in my absence and when I was present, by both the Senate and the people, but I did not accept it. I did not refuse, at a time of severe shortage of corn, to undertake the supervision of the corn supply, which I so administered that within a few days I freed the whole state from fear and immediate danger at my own expense and by my own efforts. At the same time I was offered the consulship, to be held annually in perpetuity, but I refused it.

6. In the consulship of Marcus Vinicius and Quintus Lucretius (19 B.C.) and later in that of Publius Lentulus and Cnaeus Lentulus (18 B.C.), and for a third time in that of Paullus Fabius Maximus and Quintus Tubero (11 B.C.) the Senate and people of Rome agreed that I should be appointed superintendent of laws and morals, with absolute authority and holding office alone; but I would not accept any magistracy which conflicted with ancestral custom. The actions the Senate

at that time wished to be performed through me I carried out in virtue of my tribunician power, and on five occasions on my own initiative I asked the Senate for a colleague in this power, and received one.

7. I was triumvir for the reorganization of the republic for ten years running. To the day of writing I have been leader of the Senate for forty years. I am chief priest, augur, member of the fifteen sacrificial commissioners, member of the seven commissioners for sacred feasts, Arval brother, member of the guild of the Titii, fetial priest.

9. The Senate decreed that vows should be made for my health every fifth year by the consuls and priests. In fulfilment of these vows, games have frequently been celebrated in my lifetime, sometimes by the four principal priestly colleges, sometimes by the consuls. Also all the citizens, both individually and on behalf of their towns, have unanimously and continuously prayed at all the couches of the gods for my health.

10. My name was included in the hymn of the Salii by a decree of the Senate, and it was enjoined by law that I should be inviolable for ever and that I should have the tribunician power as long as I lived. I refused to be made chief priest in place of my colleague who was still living, when the people offered me this priesthood which my father had held. I accepted this priesthood some years later in the consulship of Publius Sulpicius and Gaius Valgius (12 B.C.), on the death of the man who had taken the opportunity of civil unrest to assume it, and such a multitude poured in from the whole of Italy to my election as is said never to have been at Rome before that time.

11. As thanksgiving for my return the Senate consecrated the altar of Fortuna Redux in front of the temple of Honour and Virtue at the Capena Gate, and ordered that the pontiffs and the Vestal Virgins should make a sacrifice there on the anniversary of my return to the city from Syria, in the consulship of Quintus Lucretius and Marcus Vinicius (October 12, 19 B.C.) and named the day Augustalia from my *cognomen*.

12. In accordance with the will of the Senate some of the praetors and the tribunes of the people, along with the consul Quintus Lucretius and leading citizens, were sent to meet me in Campania, an honour which to this day has been granted to no one save myself. When I returned from Spain and Gaul, after my successes in the provinces there, in the consulship of Tiberius Nero and Publius Quintilius (13 B.C.), the

Senate resolved to consecrate an altar of Augustan Peace near the Campus Martius, and ordered the magistrates, priests and Vestal Virgins to perform an annual sacrifice there.

13. Our ancestors wished that the gateway of Janus Quirinus should be closed when peace had been gained by victories on land and sea over the whole empire of the Roman people. Although, according to tradition, from the foundation of Rome to the time of my birth it was closed only twice in all, while I was leading citizen the Senate decreed its closure three times.

14. My sons, Gaius and Lucius Caesar, whom fortune snatched from me in their youth, were in my honour designated consuls by the Senate and people of Rome at the age of fourteen, to enter on the magistracy five years later, and the Senate decreed that from the day when they were escorted into the Forum they should be present in the councils of state. Moreover, the whole body of Roman knights hailed each of them as 'leader of the youth' and presented each with silver shields and spears.

15. To each member of the Roman *plebs* I paid under the will of my father three hundred sesterces, and in my own name I gave them four hundred sesterces each from the spoils of war in my fifth consulship (29 B.C.). Again, in my tenth consulship (24 B.C.) from my own estate I paid out a gift of four hundred sesterces per man, and in my eleventh consulship (23 B.C.) I bought up corn at my personal expense and distributed twelve rations. In the twelfth year of my tribunician power (11 B.C.) I gave each man four hundred sesterces for the third time. These largesses of mine reached a number of men which was never less than two hundred and fifty thousand. In the eighteenth year of my tribunician power (5 B.C.) and my twelfth consulship, I gave six hundred sesterces each to three hundred and twenty thousand of the urban *plebs*. In my fifth consulship (29 B.C.) I gave from the spoils of war one thousand sesterces each to the colonists from among my soldiers; this largesse at the time of my triumph was received by about one hundred and twenty thousand men in the colonies. In my thirteenth consulship (2 B.C.) I gave sixty denarii each to those of the *plebs* in recept of the public corn dole, who numbered a little more than two hundred thousand.

34. In my sixth and seventh consulships (28–27 B.C.), after I had extinguished civil wars, when with universal consent I had gained complete control of affairs, I transferred the state from my own power

to the authority of the Senate and people of Rome. In return for this service of mine I was by senatorial decree given the appellation 'Augustus', the door-posts of my house were publicly wreathed with laurel, a civic crown was fixed above my door and a golden shield set up in the Curia Julia. This shield, as attested by the inscription, was given to me by the Senate and people of Rome because of my courage, clemency, justice and piety. After that time I surpassed all in influence (*auctoritas*), but I had no more power than those who were my colleagues in each magistracy.

35. During my thirteenth consulship (2 B.C.), the Senate, the equestrian order and the whole Roman people gave me the title 'Father of the fatherland', and decreed that this should be inscribed in the porch of my house, in the Curia Julia and in the Forum of Augustus under the four-horse chariot set up there in my honour by decree of the Senate.

This is written in my seventy-sixth year.

Appendix

1. The amount of money he gave to the treasury or to the Roman *plebs* or to discharged soldiers was two thousand four hundred million sesterces.

2. His new buildings were: the temples of Mars, of Jupiter the Thunderer and Feretrius, of Apollo, of the deified Julius, of Quirinus, of Minerva, of Queen Juno, of Jupiter of Liberty, of the Lares, of the Di Penates, of Youth, of the Great Mother, the Lupercal, the sacred couch at the Circus, the Senate House with the Chalcidicum, the Forum of Augustus, the Basilica Julia, the theatre of Marcellus, the Octavian Portico, the Grove of the Caesars beyond the Tiber.

3. He restored the Capitol and sacred buildings to the number of eighty-two, the theatre of Pompey, the aqueducts and the Flaminian Road.

4. The expenditure he provided for stage spectacles, gladiatorial games, athletes, hunts and the sea battle, and the money given to colonies, municipalities and towns destroyed by earthquake and fire, or to individual friends and senators whose property qualification he made up, was incalculable.

TRANSMISSION OF POWER

Tacitus, *Annals* 1

1. At the beginning, the city of Rome had kings; liberty and the consulship were established by Lucius Brutus. They used to adopt dictators for brief periods; the power of the Ten Lawgivers did not last more than two years, nor did the consular authority of the military tribunes last long. Cinna's dominance was short-lived, as was Sulla's. The extra-legal power of Pompey and Crassus soon yielded to Caesar; the armed force of Lepidus and Antony yielded to Augustus, who under the title of *Princeps* received under his command the whole Roman state, exhausted by civil dissension. But the prosperity and adversity of the Roman people in earlier times have been related by distinguished writers, and there was no lack of able authors to tell of the times of Augustus, until the growth of adulation checked them. The reigns of Tiberius, Gaius, Claudius and Nero were dishonestly described in their lifetimes through fear, and after their deaths the accounts were influenced by grudges that were still fresh. So, I have decided to deal with just a little of the very end of Augustus' reign, then the principate of Tiberius and the sequel, without partiality or hostility, as I am far from having cause for either.

2. After Brutus and Cassius had been killed, when there were no longer any armies of the state, Pompeius had been overpowered off Sicily, Lepidus got rid of, Antony slain and even the Julian group had no leader left but Caesar, then he (Caesar) laid aside the title of triumvir. Presenting himself as consul, and satisfied with the tribunician authority to protect the common people, once he had won the favour of the soldiers with donatives, of the populace with corn, of everyone with the allurement of peace, then gradually he began to rise and to draw to himself the functions of the senate, the magistrates, the laws. No one opposed him, for the boldest had fallen in the battle or by proscription, and the rest of the nobles, in proportion to their servility, were exalted with wealth and honour and, in their prosperity under the new régime, preferred their present security to the dangers in the old dispensation. Nor were the provinces reluctant to accept this state of affairs, for the rule of the Senate and people was no longer trusted because of the struggles for power and the rapacity of the magistrates,

and the laws had been overthrown by force, bribery and, lastly, money, and rendered powerless.

3. But Augustus provided himself with supports for his dominance. His sister's son Claudius Marcellus, still quite a youth, he elevated by conferring on him a priesthood and the curule aedileship. Marcus Agrippa, a man of humble birth but a loyal associate during the fighting and after the victory, he made consul twice and presently, after the death of Marcellus, took him as his son-in-law. His stepsons Tiberius Nero and Claudius Drusus were distinguished with the title *imperator* while his own house was still intact—for he had taken into the family of the Caesars Agrippa's offspring Gaius and Lucius, and before they came of age he had them named 'Leaders of the Youth', and was keenly desirous that they should be designated to consulships, although he put on a show of refusing this. Then Agrippa passed away, and Lucius and Gaius were both carried off, the former on the way to the Spanish armies, the latter while returning, ill from a wound, from Armenia (whether the cause of their untimely deaths was destiny or the machinations of their stepmother Livia). Drusus was already dead. Then (Tiberius) Nero was the only stepson left, and everything converged upon him. He was made Augustus' son, his colleague in command, sharer in the tribunician power, and was paraded before all the armies, no longer by the secret contrivance of his mother, but with her open encouragement. She had gained such ascendancy over the aged Augustus that he sent off to the island of Planasia his only grandson, Agrippa Postumus, who certainly lacked refined accomplishments and was pig-headedly aggressive, relying upon his physical strength, though he had never been guilty of any outrage. All the same, Augustus put Drusus' son Germanicus at the head of eight legions on the Rhine, and ordered Tiberius to adopt him. Tiberius had a young son living, but Augustus wanted more props to shore up the succession. At that time there was no war outstanding save that against the Germans, which had to be carried on more in order to wipe out the disgrace of the loss of Quintilius Varus and his army than from any desire to extend the empire, or the prospect of any worthwhile gains. At home things were peaceful. The magistracies still existed in name. The younger men had been born after the victory at Actium, the old ones mostly during the civil wars. There were few left who had seen the republic.

4. So, now that the old order of the state was overthrown, there was

nothing left anywhere of the old honest ways. Equality was abandoned; everyone looked to the emperor's commands, with no apprehension for the present while Augustus was vigorous and maintained himself, his house and peace. When he was far advanced in age, broken by ill-health, and his end and the hope of a new order were in sight, a few began to talk ineffectually about the blessings of liberty; more were afraid of war, while some wanted it. The great majority gossiped widely about the masters who were about to come upon them. Agrippa, they said, was truculent and resented his disgrace, but was unfitted by his youth and lack of experience to bear such a burden. Tiberius Nero was mature in years and had proved his worth in war, but he had the old, ingrained hauteur of the Claudian family and many indications of a cruel temper, though checked, broke out. In addition, he had been brought up from infancy in the royal house, in his youth consulships and triumphs had been heaped upon him, and even in the years during which, under pretext of retirement, he had lived as an exile at Rhodes, he had occupied himself solely with anger, deceit and secret lusts. Moreover his mother was a woman who would not accept restraints. So they would be subjected to a woman, and two young men who would oppress the Roman state when they were not tearing it apart.

(*Later, Tacitus describes the aftermath of Augustus' death*)

7. At Rome, consuls, senators, knights rushed to demonstrate their servility. The more distinguished they were, the greater their insincere haste. They carefully controlled their expressions to avoid seeming pleased at the death of one emperor or sad at the start of another's rule; they mingled tears and joy, laments and adulation. The consuls Sextus Pompeius and Sextus Appuleius were the first to take the oath of loyalty to Tiberius Caesar, and they administered the oath to Seius Strabo, prefect of the praetorian guard, and Gaius Turranius, prefect of the corn supply, followed by the Senate, the army and the people. For Tiberius started everything through the medium of the consuls, as though it were the old republic and he were doubtful of his rule. Even the edict summoning the fathers into the senate house he issued only under the title of the tribunician power received from Augustus. The edict was brief and modest in sense. He was going to consult them on the honours due to Augustus; he was not leaving the body,

and this was the only official authority he was exercising. However, on Augustus' death he had given the watchword to the praetorian cohorts as emperor; he had guards, men at arms, all the appurtenances of a court. Soldiers accompanied him to the forum and into the senate house. He sent despatches to the armies as though he had taken over the principate. The only place he displayed hesitation was when he was speaking in the Senate. The prime reason was fear that Germanicus, who had at his disposal so many legions, and vast numbers of provincial soldiers, and who was a remarkable favourite with the people, might prefer to possess the rule rather than wait for it. Also he wanted to spread the impression that he had been summoned and chosen by the state rather than that he had crept into power through the influence of a wife and adoption by an old man. Later it was realized that his hesitation had been assumed in order also to allow him to descry the intentions of the foremost citizens—for he twisted words and looks into grounds for accusations, and stored them up.

8. He allowed no business to be transacted in the Senate on the first day except arrangements for the funeral of Augustus, whose will was produced by the Vestal Virgins and established Tiberius and Livia as heirs. Livia was adopted into the Julian family and given the name 'Augusta'. As the secondary heirs Augustus had written in the grandsons and great-grandsons, and in third rank the most prominent citizens. He disliked most of them, but his real aim was to impress posterity. The legacies did not go beyond bounds for an ordinary citizen, except that he left the populace and plebs 43,500 sesterces, and a thousand a man to the praetorian guardsmen, 500 to the urban cohorts, 300 to the legionaries and citizen cohorts.

Then the honours were discussed. The most notable of these, the proposal that the funeral should pass through the Triumphal Gate, was made by Asinius Gallus, and Lucius Arruntius proposed that the titles of laws enacted by him and the names of peoples conquered by him should be carried before the body. Valerius Messala added that the oath in the name of Tiberius should be renewed annually. When Tiberius asked whether he had instructed him to make this proposal, Messala replied that he had proposed it spontaneously, and that in matters pertaining to the state he would follow no man's opinion but his own, even at the risk of giving offence. This was the only form of adulation that was left. The fathers agreed by acclamation that the body should be carried to the pyre on the shoulders of senators. Caesar excused them from this with a haughty affectation of moderation, and issued an edict warning the people not to repeat the excessive popular enthusiasm which had disrupted the funeral of the deified Julius, by wishing to have Augustus cremated in the forum rather than at the intended site on the Campus Martius. On the day of the funeral, troops stood as though keeping guard. This occasioned great mockery on the part of those who had themselves seen or had heard from their parents of that day when servitude was still fresh and an unsuccessful attempt was made to rescue liberty, when the death of Caesar was regarded by some as the foulest, by others as the fairest of deeds. Now an aged prince, whose power had lasted long, and who had moreover provided plenty of heirs to his position in the state, had actually to be protected by military aid, so that his burial might be peaceful.

9. There ensued much talk about Augustus himself. The majority marvelled at trifles, e.g., that the first day of his taking over command had also been the last of his life, and that he had ended his days at Nola in the same house and room as his father Octavius. There was also talk of the number of his consulships, in which he matched Valerius Corvus and Gaius Marius put together, of his tribunician power held continuously for thirty-seven years, the title of *imperator* obtained twenty-one times, and other honours, either held more often than was usual, or entirely new. The more thoughtful variously lauded or criticized his life. Some said that it was dutiful feeling for his adoptive father and the needs of the republic, in which at that time the laws had no place, that drove him to take up arms in civil war, an act which can neither be planned nor executed by honourable means. He had made many concessions to Antonius, in order to ensure vengeance on his father's murderers, and many to Lepidus. After Lepidus collapsed into age and inactivity and Antony was ruined by his lusts, there was no cure for the disharmony in the state but that it should be ruled by one man. However, the republic was reconstituted not as a kingdom or a dictatorship but under the name of a *princeps* '(leading citizen'). The bounds of the empire were Oceanus or distant rivers; legions, provinces, the fleet were all interconnected; law reigned among the citizens, orderliness among the provincials; the city itself was magnificently adorned; violence had been used, but only in a very few instances, and so that the rest might have quiet.

10. Against this it was said that his filial feeling and the crisis of the state were merely used as a cloak. In desire for domination he had

roused up the veterans with bribes. An army had been prepared by a youth who held no office, and the consul's legions had been suborned, with a pretence of the approval of the Pompeians. Presently when, by a decree of the Senate, he had usurped the fasces and the rights of a praetor, when Hirtius and Pansa had been killed—either by the enemy, or Pansa by poison poured on his wound and Hirtius by own soldiers and a stratagem devised by Caesar—he took over the armies of both. He extorted a consulship from the unwilling Senate, and turned against the republic the forces he had received to fight Antony. The proscription of citizens and division of land were not approved of even by those who carried them out. Oh, yes, the deaths of Brutus and Cassius were a concession to enmities he had inherited—although it would have been right to let private hatreds give way to the public interest; but he *had* deceived Pompeius by a pretended peace, and he *had* deceived Lepidus, by a pretence of friendship. Then, after enticing Antonius with the treaties of Brundisium and Tarentum and marriage with his sister, he had made him pay the penalty for this treacherous alliance with his life. Certainly, after that there was peace, but a bloodstained one—there were the disasters of Lollius and Varus and the killing at Rome of men like Varro, Egnatius and Iullus.

His private life did not escape comment either. He had stolen Nero's wife and had a mockery of a consultation with the pontiffs as to whether a woman who had conceived but had not yet given birth could properly marry . . . there was the extravagant living of Vedius Pollio; and finally Livia, it was said, had been harmful to the republic as a mother and harmful to the house of the Caesars as a stepmother. No honours had been left to the gods, as he wished himself to be worshipped with temples and effigies like divinities, by flamens and priests. Nor had he adopted Tiberius as his successor out of affection or concern for the state, but because he was thoroughly aware of his arrogance and cruelty and wished to use him as a foil to enhance to the utmost his own glory. Indeed a few years previously when Augustus had requested the tribunician power from the Senate for Tiberius a second time, although he delivered an honorific speech, he let out various remarks about his manners, dress and habits by which he reviled him, under colour of excusing him.

But when the funeral was duly performed, a temple and divine worship were decreed to Augustus.

11. Then entreaties were directed towards Tiberius. He, for his part,

spoke of the greatness of the imperial command and of his own modesty. Only the mind of the deified Augustus, he said, was capable of undertaking such a burden. He had been summoned by him to share part of his cares, and had learned by experience how arduous and how much exposed to fortune was the load of one who ruled the whole. So, in a state that was supported by so many illustrious citizens, he asked them not to impose everything on one man; a number would, by uniting their efforts, more easily fulfil the tasks of government. There was more pomp than sincerity in such a speech. Tiberius, whether from nature or from practice, was always hesitant and obscure in expression, even on matters where he was not trying to conceal anything; and on this occasion, when he was indeed trying to hide his real intentions, he involved himself more than ever in indefiniteness and ambiguity. But the fathers, whose one fear was to be seen to understand, abandoned themselves to laments, tears, entreaties. They stretched out their hands to the gods, to the image of Augustus, to Tiberius' own knees. Then Tiberius ordered a document to be produced and read. This contained a statement of public resources, the numbers of citizens and allies under arms, how many fleets there were, subject kingdoms, provinces, tributes and taxes, calls on funds and bounties given. All this Augustus had written out in his own hand and had added the advice to keep the empire within its present bounds— advice prompted either by fear or by jealousy.

SPECIAL POWERS OF THE EMPEROR

Lex de imperio Vespasiani A.D. 70

(The surviving portion of the law passed on the accession of Vespasian to the principate, conferring various powers on him.)

And that he shall have the right to make treaties with whomsoever he wishes, as was the right of the deified Augustus, Tiberius Julius Caesar Augustus and Tiberius Claudius Caesar Augustus Germanicus;

And that he shall have the right to summon the Senate, put or refer proposals to the Senate, and carry senatorial decrees by presentation of a proposal and taking of a vote, as was the right of the deified Augustus, Tiberius Julius Caesar Augustus and Tiberius Claudius Caesar Augustus Germanicus;

And that when the Senate meets in consequence of his wish, authority, order or command, or in his presence, the legality of all transactions shall be considered and observed as if the meeting of the Senate had been summoned and held in accordance with the law;

And that any persons he has commended to the Senate and people of Rome as candidates for a magistracy, post of authority, command or curatorship, and to whom he has given or promised his vote, such persons shall at any election be given extraordinary consideration;

And that he shall have the right to extend and advance the sacred boundary of Rome, when he considers it to be in the interests of the state, as was the right of Tiberius Claudius Caesar Augustus Germanicus;

And that whatever he considers beneficial to the state and its majesty in matters sacred and secular, public and private, he shall have the right and the power to do and to perform, as had the deified Augustus, Tiberius Julius Caesar Augustus and Tiberius Claudius Caesar Augustus Germanicus;

And if in any laws or plebiscites it was written that deified Augustus or Tiberius Julius Caesar Augustus and Tiberius Claudius Caesar Augustus Germanicus should not be bound by its terms, the emperor Caesar Vespasian shall not be bound by such laws or plebiscites; and whatever by any law or bill the deified Augustus or Tiberius Julius Caesar Augustus or Tiberius Claudius Caesar Augustus Germanicus was called upon to do, all these things the emperor Caesar Vespasian Augustus shall have the right to do;

And all acts, decrees or commands issued by the emperor Caesar Vespasian Augustus, or by anyone else at his instance or command, before the enactment of this law, shall be held lawful and valid just as if they had been enacted by command of the people or the plebs.

Sanction: if anyone in consequence of this law acts or shall act contrary to the laws, bills, plebiscites or decrees of the Senate, or if in consequence of this law he shall not have done what was required of him by any law, bill, plebiscite or senatorial decree, he is not to be held liable for this, nor is he to pay any public fine nor may there be any legal action or judicial inquiry on this account, nor may anyone receive an action on this account before him in court.

X. The Princeps and Divine Honours

Tacitus, as we have seen (*Annals* 1.10), puts in the mouths of a section of Roman public opinion the statement that Augustus required the worship of himself with temples and statues, through priests and flamens. Other evidence makes it necessary to modify this statement to some extent. According to Dio (51.20) he granted in 29 B.C. permission for Ephesus and Nicaea, the leading cities of Asia and Bithynia, to establish sacred precincts dedicated to Rome and to Julius Caesar. 'He gave orders that Roman citizens there should honour these divinities, but the foreigners, whom he called Hellenes, he allowed to dedicate certain precincts to himself, the Asians to have one in Pergamum and the Bithynians in Nicomedia.' This, says Dio, set the pattern for future practice in the Roman empire; no subsequent emperor allowed such dedications to himself in Rome and Italy, although posthumous divine honours were accorded there to good emperors.

That is, in the Eastern provinces, Augustus allowed non-Romans to worship himself, but permitted to Romans only the posthumous worship of Caesar (a distinction which was hard to maintain with the conferment of citizenship on prominent provincials—the cult of Caesar seems to have disappeared early). Suetonius (*Divus Augustus* 52) adds that he allowed only dedications which coupled his name with that of Rome, and refused absolutely to allow them at Rome. As Suetonius notes, there were precedents in the Eastern provinces for dedications to Roman proconsuls. Cities in effect were offering the same kind of honours as they had become accustomed to pay to Hellenistic kings. Plutarch records dedications by the Chalcidians *circa* 191 B.C. to Titus Quinctius Flaminus, jointly with Heracles and Apollo, and a priesthood of Titus. The people of Cilicia built a temple in honour of Cicero's predecessor as governor, Appius Claudius, while Cicero declared that he himself had refused all statues, shrines, and ceremonial chariots. When he and his brother were offered a temple by the cities of Asia, when his brother was proconsul there, Cicero refused—in case, he says, those to whom such honours were not due should resent it.

In the West, the officially accepted practice in Augustus' lifetime was to make offerings not to Augustus himself, but to his Genius or his *numen*

—the attendant guardian spirit or beneficent divine power that, through him, secured blessings to the people of the empire. Traditionally, each Roman household had its Genius, thought of as attached particularly to the head of the family; we have here apparently an extension of this notion, perhaps also influenced by Greek public hero-worship. Already in 30 B.C., after Actium, the Senate had decreed that libations should be poured in his honour at banquets, and if we are to believe Horace and Ovid, this practice was widely adopted in private homes. In public, Augustus revived the community worship of the Lares of the Crossroads (Compitalia) in Italian cities and in the districts of Rome, and created a priesthood, with some local administrative functions, to serve it. The Genius Augusti was worshipped together with these Lares, now known as the Lares Augusti, and the priests were called Augustales.

In the Western provinces, the initiative seems to have come, to begin with, from the rulers rather than the ruled. Altars and priesthoods of the Genius or *numen* of Augustus were set up. Some—those at Lugdunum, Cologne and on the Elbe—were directly associated with the provincial league already made use of in administration. A noteworthy difference between the traditional family Genius worship and that of the Genius Augusti was that the former received only bloodless offerings, while the Genius of Augustus was worshipped with the offering of a bull, like the gods.

In theory, then, Augustus refused acknowledgment of his divinity during his lifetime, and indeed that would scarcely have been compatible with his avowed restoration of the Republic. However, the actual distinction drawn in practice was far from clear, and there were obvious political advantages to be gained from the organization of religious expression. The deification of his predecessor also played an important part, not least as having set a precedent. Tiberius also realized very clearly the political usefulness of a deified Augustus in securing his own position, while apparently genuinely reluctant to commit himself to the acceptance of divinity for himself in his own lifetime. His refusal (Tacitus, *Ann.* 4. 37–38) cannot have been persisted in very long or very effectively; there is inscriptional evidence for flamens of Tiberius in Italy, and in A.D. 29 a temple was set up to him—apparently without mention of Rome—in Cyprus (Ehrenberg & Jones, *Documents illustrating the reigns of Augustus and Tiberius*, no. 134). With Claudius, also, practice differs from personal avowal.

The political usefulness of the organized cult was undoubted and it does seem that later in the reign of Augustus, as well as in subsequent reigns, no very effective curb was kept on spontaneous dedications in various parts of the empire and even in Italy. The cult was not entirely organized—the real benefits conferred by Augustus on the Mediterranean world by bringing peace generated enthusiasm and loyalty, in part reflected by the accretion about him, before and after his death, of legends, many of which are reported by Suetonius.

Posthumous deification of the emperor became regular, though not invariable, and the cult of the Genius of the living emperor became a test of political loyalty.

Four documents are quoted below, all from the period of the Julio-Claudian principate. They deserve study for the light they throw on the social background of the state cult; on the character of particular emperors; and on both the differences and the resemblances between the emperor-worship of the Roman world and the king-cult in Ptolemaic Egypt.

HONOURS TO THE NUMEN OF AUGUSTUS AT NARBO. A.D. 11

Ehrenberg & Jones, *Documents*, no. 100

In the consulship of Titus Statilius Taurus and Lucius Cassius Longinus on 22nd September, the following vow was undertaken in perpetuity by the people of Narbo to the *numen* of Augustus.

Blessings and good fortune to Imperator Caesar Augustus, son of the deified (Caesar), father of his country, *pontifex maximus*, in the thirty-fourth year of his tribunician power, and to his wife, his children and his family, and the Senate and people of Rome, and to the settlers and inhabitants of the colony Julia Paterna, Narbo Martius, who have bound themselves in perpetuity to worship his *numen*. The people of Narbo have placed an altar in the forum at Narbo, at which annually on the 23rd September, on which day the felicity of our age brought him forth to be ruler of the world, three Roman knights from the people and three freedmen are each to sacrifice a victim, and are to supply to the settlers and inhabitants at their own expense on that day wine and incense, for making sacrifice with prayer to his *numen*; likewise on 24th September they are to supply incense and wine to the settlers and inhabitants; also on January 1st they are to supply wine and incense to the settlers and inhabitants; also on January 7th, on which day he first entered upon his *imperium* over the world; they are to make offerings of wine and incense with prayer and sacrifice a victim each and supply incense and wine on that day to the inhabitants and settlers. And on the last day of May, because on that day in the consulship of Titus Statilius Taurus and Manius Aemilius Lepidus he reconciled the people and the town-councillors, they are to sacrifice a victim each and to provide wine and incense to the settlers and inhabitants to make offerings with prayer. . . .

TIBERIUS' REFUSAL OF HONOURS

Tacitus, *Annals* 4

37. At about the same time, the province of Further Spain sent an embassy to the Senate and petitioned to be allowed to follow the example of Asia and erect a shrine in honour of Tiberius and his mother. Caesar was in general steadfast in rejecting honours; and he thought besides that he should take this opportunity of refuting the gossip that accused him of an inclination to self-aggrandizement. He began as follows: 'I know, Senators, that many think me inconsistent because recently, when the cities of Asia made the same request, I did not oppose it. Therefore I shall at one and the same time present the justification of my previous silence and also my decision regarding the future. Since the deified Augustus, all of whose deeds and pronouncements I regard as having the force of law, did not forbid the establishment of a temple to himself and the city of Rome at Pergamum, I followed the example he set, more readily because my own cult was conjoined with veneration of the Senate. However, although a single acceptance might be excusable, to allow oneself to be worshipped in all the provinces through statues with divine attributes would be vainglorious and arrogant. Moreover, the honour paid to Augustus would be diminished if it were merely a commonplace manifestation of adulation shared with others.

38. 'Gentlemen, I call you to witness that I am a mortal, and I behave as a man, and am content to take the leading place among men; and I wish future generations to recall this. They will do ample justice to my memory if they believe me to have been worthy of my ancestors, to have shown foresight in managing your interests, to have been steadfast in dangers and unafraid of causing offence for the sake of the public good. These are my temples, in your minds, these are the most beautiful and most lasting of images. Temples built of stone are as little regarded as tombs, if the judgment of posterity turns to hostility. So I call upon the allies, the citizens and the gods themselves; the gods

I beg to grant me, to the end of my life, a mind that is at peace and knows what is due to gods and men; men I ask that, when I pass on, they will honour my deeds and the renown of my name with praise and will recollect them with approval.'

Subsequently he persisted, even in private talk, in rejecting such worship of himself. Some explained this as modesty, many as diffidence, some thought it indicated an ignoble spirit—for, they said, the best of men have always deserved the highest honours. Thus, Hercules and Liber among the Greeks and Quirinus among ourselves have been added to the number of the gods. Augustus behaved better, in hoping for such elevation. Everything else is immediately available to an emperor, as soon as he becomes emperor; one thing he must never cease desiring to attain, a favourable memory of himself—for if reputation is despised, then the virtues fall into contempt also.

DECREE ON THE IMPERIAL CULT AND LETTER OF TIBERIUS. GYTHEION (LACONIA). A.D. 14.

Ehrenberg and Jones, *Documents*, no. 102

Let him set ... on the first pedestal the statue of the deified Augustus Caesar, father (i.e. of Tiberius), and on the second on the right that of Julia Augusta, and on the third that of the emperor Tiberius Caesar son of Augustus, the statues being provided to him by the city. A table is to be set by him in the middle of the theatre and an incense burner on it, and the councillors and all their fellow-magistrates are to offer sacrifice on it before the performers enter. The performances shall be in honour, on the first day of the deified Augustus, Saviour and Liberator, son of the deified Caesar, on the second of the emperor Tiberius Caesar Augustus, Father of his country, on the third of Julia Augusta, the Fortune of our people and our city, on the fourth of the victory of Germanicus Caesar, on the fifth of the Venus of Drusus Caesar, the sixth Titus Quinctius Flamininus. Care shall be taken that the participants are orderly. He is to present accounts of all the pay for the performers and the administration of the sacred money to the city at the first assembly after the games, and if he is detected in embezzlement or false entries in the accounts he is to be banned from all office in future and his property confiscated. The proceeds of all confiscations are to be sacred monies and from those funds extra adornments are to be provided by the annual magistrates. It shall be open to anyone of the people of Gytheion to bring prosecutions concerning the sacred funds without penalty.

Let the aedile present, after the days in honour of the gods and leaders, two more days of scenic performances, one in honour of Gaius Julius Eurycles, benefactor in many ways of the people and the city, and the second in honour of Gaius Julius Lacon, guardian of the protection and security of our people and our city. Let him present the performances on those days when he can, from the day of the Goddess. When he leaves office, let him hand over to his successor through a public record a statement of all the sacrificial offerings at the games, and let the city receive a written statement from his successor. When the aedile conducts the scenic games, let him have a procession from the temple of Asclepius and Hygeia, with the young adult men walking in procession, and the youths and other citizens garlanded with crowns of laurel and dressed in white. Let the sacred maidens also walk in procession and the women in ritual garments. When the procession reaches the temple of Caesar, let the superintendents (*ephors*) sacrifice a bull for the safety of the rulers and gods and the eternal continuation of their rule, and after sacrifices let them oblige the members of the messes and the other magistrates to sacrifice in the market place. If they do not conduct the procession, or do not sacrifice, or after sacrifice do not compel the messes and the other magistrates to sacrifice in the market-place, let them pay a fine of two thousand drachmae, to the sacred funds of the gods. It shall be open to any of the citizens of Gytheion to make accusation against them.

Let the superintendents whose leader is Terentius Bias, in the year when Chaeremon is general and priest of the deified Augustus Caesar, present three carved images, of the deified Augustus and Julia Augusta and Tiberius Caesar son of Augustus, and benches in the theatre for the chorus and four scenery doors and a dais for the instrumentalists. Let them also set up a stele inscribed with the sacred law, and deposit a copy of the law in the public record office, so that the law may be publicly and openly displayed to all and convey to all men the gratitude of the people of Gytheion to their rulers. And if they do not inscribe this law, or set up the stele in front of the temple or make a copy . . .

(*Nothing coherent remains of the rest of the decree.*)

Letter of Tiberius.

Tiberius Caesar Augustus, son of the deified Augustus, *pontifex maximus*, holder of tribunician power for the sixteenth year, to the superintendents and the city of Gytheion, greeting. Your envoy sent to myself and my mother, Decimus Turranius Nicanor, has conveyed to me your letter to which was attached the measures passed by you in veneration of my father and in our honour. I praise you for this and consider it fitting both for all men in general and for your city in particular to reserve special honours, befitting the gods, for the greatness of the benefits conferred by my father upon the whole world; but I myself am satisfied with more modest honours, fitting for men. My mother, however, will reply to you when she learns from you your decision about honours for her.

LETTER OF CLAUDIUS TO ALEXANDRIA. 10TH NOVEMBER, A.D. 41

Smallwood, *Documents Illustrating the Reigns of Gaius, Claudius and Nero*, no. 370

Lucius Aemilius Rectus states: since it was not possible, on account of the size of the city, for everyone to be present at the reading of the most sacred and beneficent letter to the city, I thought it necessary to publish the letter so that you may read it individually and marvel at the magnanimity of our god Caesar and be grateful for his kindness to the city.

The second year of Tiberius Claudius Caesar Augustus Germanicus Imperator, 14th of New Augustus (*10th November*).
Tiberius Claudius Caesar Augustus Germanicus Imperator, chief priest, holder of tribunician power, consul designate, greets the city of the Alexandrians. Your ambassadors, Tiberius Claudius Barbillus, Apollonius son of Artemidorus, Chaeremon son of Leonidas, Marcus Julius Asclepiades, Gaius Julius Dionysius, Tiberius Claudius Phanias, Pasion son of Potamon, Dionysius son of Sabbio, Tiberius Claudius Archebius, Apollonius son of Ariston, Gaius Julius Apollonius, Hermaiscus son of Apollonius, told me much about your city when they handed over your resolution. They reminded me of your good-

will towards me which, be well assured, I have for a long time trea-
sured. You are naturally loyal to the Caesars, as I have come to know
from many instances, and in particular you have given support to my
house, as it has to you—of which, to omit other examples and name
only the latest, my brother Germanicus Caesar, when he addressed
you, gave ample witness in most noble terms. Therefore I was pleased
to receive the honours you conferred upon me, although I am not
inclined to that sort of thing. First, I grant that you may celebrate my
birthday as an Augustal day in the way you have specified; and I
agree to the setting-up of statues of myself and my family in each
place, for I see that you are eager to establish everywhere memorials
of your loyalty to my house. Concerning the two golden statues, the
one of Claudian Augustan Peace, which my most esteemed Barbillus
proposed, with persistent importunity despite my refusal on the
grounds that it appeared too vulgarly ostentatious—that will be set
up at Rome. The other one shall be paraded among you in the manner
you ask on the days named after me, and let there be paraded with it a
chariot adorned as you wish. It would perhaps be foolish to allow
such honours and forbid the establishment of a Claudian tribe or
sacred groves according to the custom of Egypt; therefore I allow
you this also, and if you wish you may also set up the equestrian
statues of my procurator Vitrasius Pollio. I consent also to the
setting-up of the four-horse statues which you wish to install in my
honour at the approaches to your country, viz. at Taposiris in Libya,
one at the Pharos of Alexandria and the third at Pelusium in Egypt;
but I beg to be excused having a high priest of myself or temples
built, as I do not wish to appear to my contemporaries vulgarly conceited, and my view is that sacrifices and the like have at all times been
reserved to be given to the gods alone.

(*The rest of the letter concerns Alexandrian internal affairs.*)

XI. Justifications of the Principate

From Augustus onward, the Romans again had a king, but were unwilling to admit it. The result was an elaborate pretence whereby the bulk of the monarch's powers were made to appear in conformity with Republican usage, while those that resisted such classification were made the subject of grants from the (nominally) sovereign people. Ultimately, the princeps was declared exempt from the laws, as we have seen. However, Trajan revived the practice last followed by Claudius of making, on the occasion of his consulships, the two traditional magisterial avowals, on entry to office, that he would observe the laws, and on retirement, that he had observed them (Pliny *Paneg.* 65). One may doubt whether, in terms of real power, such a declaration cost him anything.

Dio 53.17 states succinctly the position already indicated in Augustus' *Res Gestae*, and in the opening chapters of Tacitus' *Annals*. From these passages, as also from the extracts from Pliny's *Panegyric* cited below, we can obtain some idea of the ways in which the conflict between republican theory and monarchic fact [1] was—not reconciled, but avoided, glossed over, or, especially, converted into praise of the monarch. It would be impracticable to give the entire text of the *Panegyric* here, but even in the small portion quoted ample material can be found to illustrate this process.

THE TITLES OF EMPERORS

Dio is partly concerned with a matter we have already considered, the acquisition of actual power, and more specifically with the titles relating to this power. His remarks, however, fall into two main categories, the second of which is concerned with titles conferring no power at all, but enhancing in various ways the image of the monarch. The latter, again, are not all of one kind. 'Caesar' and 'Augustus' in due course become

[1] 'Nerva reconciled things once incompatible—freedom and the principate'. Tacitus, *Agricola* 3.

125

simply part of the standard titulature of the emperor. The hereditary
succession of which Dio speaks ceases to be a fact, even in the loose sense
of restriction to the Julio-Claudian family, with Nero. The Flavians and
their successors are Caesars by title, and not by any tie of kinship. It is,
however, perhaps worth reflecting on the reasons that prompted Octavius'
original adoption of these (and, as interesting, Tiberius' following suit).
Politically, the memory of Caesar the dictator was an embarrassment;
what other associations was Octavius drawing upon, and for what ends?
Julius rapidly becomes Caesar the legend, and allegedly has joined the
ranks of the gods.

Suetonius, in a famous passage (*Aug.* 7), reveals that Octavian adopted
in 27 B.C. the name Augustus after a search for a title that would engender
in the popular mind notions of an especial sanctity and superiority attaching to him, and promote a quasi-religious reverence. Various etymologies
are suggested, connecting the name with the verb *augere* (to magnify,
exalt), and with the religious rituals of augury and the taking of auspices,
both connected with the welfare of the state. The adjective *augustus* in
ordinary usage seems to combine the notions 'venerable' and 'hallowed'.
The name—brilliantly successful idea though it turned out to be—was a
pis aller; 'Romulus' would in many ways have fitted the bill much better.
Unfortunately, Romulus had been a *king*.

Titles, however, can become routine, and consciousness of their real
sense fade. One might expect to find, in course of time, fresh appellations
devised. This duly happens (and also some emperors from time to time
resist, as we have seen also in the case of divine honours). Space does not
permit much detail, especially on the extravagances of Gaius Caligula
and Domitian (alluded to in Pliny *Paneg.* 2), but a few notes on the history
of one or two appellations are perhaps in place as a basis for consideration
of the attitudes of various emperors and of their subjects.

The title 'Father of his country' had Republican precedent; Cicero
will not allow us to forget that it was conferred upon him. Successive
first-century emperors, except Nerva, seem to have been reluctant to
accept it immediately on accession. Pliny, *Paneg.* 21, praises Trajan: 'You
refused even the title "Father of his country". What a long struggle we
had against your modesty and how belatedly we conquered! That title,
which others took straightaway on the first day of the principate, like the
titles of Imperator and Caesar, you postponed until you also—as the one
who set the least store by your own benefactions—should at last admit
you deserve it.' This is misleading. Trajan had accepted the title by October
98 (the year of his accession). Augustus refused it until 2 B.C.; Tiberius
never accepted it at all. The rest deferred acceptance for periods mostly
not specified in the sources, except for one year in the case of Nero, two
in that of Vespasian. Only Nerva took it immediately. Pliny can scarcely

be attacking him. Probably he intends an allusion to Domitian, but numismatic evidence indicates that he too deferred acceptance. In general, the Romans seem to have been more impatient to accord the title than their rulers were to accept it.

Dio does not mention *Dominus* ('Master') for the good reason that this was avoided as an official title by all save Domitian, who (Suet. *Dom.* 13) adopted 'Master and God' as a formal prefix in an edict issued through his procurators, and subsequently insisted on this form of address. Unofficially, however, its use seems to have been tolerated, as a generally respectful way of addressing the emperor; Pliny, for example, uses it in his letters to Trajan.

The Senate accorded to Trajan, early in his reign, the epithet 'Excellent' (*Optimus*). It can scarcely be doubted that an allusion was intended to the title of the Father of the gods, *Jupiter Optimus Maximus* (Jupiter Best and Greatest)—cf. Pliny *Paneg.* 80, below—and so a certain parallel may be drawn between this title and the new name *Augustus* taken by Octavian. The epithet does not, however, appear on coins during the early part of Trajan's reign; *optimo principi*, 'To the excellent princeps', as a form of dedication begins to appear on issues from 103, and after July A.D. 114 it eventually forms part of Trajan's official titulature. Throughout almost his entire reign, therefore, there is room for doubt whether the addressing of him as 'Excellent' was the official outcome of a legal decision or simply a demonstration of loyalty.

Dio 53

17. In this way, all the power of the people and of the Senate passed over to Augustus, and after his time there was, strictly speaking, a monarchy; for it would most correctly be considered a monarchy, even if two or three men did sometimes hold power together. Indeed, the name of monarchy was so hated by the Romans that they did not give their emperors the title of dictators or kings or anything of that sort; but as the final authority for government falls upon them, they must be kings. The offices established by the laws are still maintained, except for the censors, but the direction and control of everything is governed by the will of whoever is in power at the time. And in order that they may appear not to have this power in virtue of their own domination but from the laws, the emperors have laid claim to all the offices which, under the republic and with the consent of the people, were powerful, taking the titles as well, except for the dictatorship. So, they very often become consuls, and they are always called pro-

consuls when they are outside the pomerium. All of them hold in perpetuity the title of *imperator*, not only those who have won victories, but all the others as well, to denote their independent authority instead of the titles of 'king' or 'dictator'. These titles they do not use, since they first fell out of use in the government, but their function is secured under the title *imperator*.

In virtue of these titles they take the right to raise levies, collect money, declare war, conclude peace, rule foreigners and citizens alike everywhere, even with the power to inflict death on both knights and senators inside the pomerium, and all the other powers once held by consuls and other officials with independent authority. In virtue of holding the censorship they investigate men's lives and morals, and take the census, enrolling some in the equestrian and senatorial classes and deleting others, as they think fit. In virtue of being consecrated to all the priesthoods and also of bestowing most of them upon others, and since, even if two or three rule at the same time, one of them is high priest, they are in authority over all matters, profane and sacred. The tribunician power, as it is called, which the most influential men used to hold, gives them the power to stop the consequences of another's acts, if they do not approve of them, and protects them against outrage; and if they are thought to be wronged in the very slightest, not only in deed but even in word, they can destroy the guilty person without trial, as one accursed. For the emperors, as belonging entirely to the patricians, do not think it right to be tribunes; but they assume the full power of the tribunate, as it was at its greatest. They use it in numbering the years they have held power, as though they received it annually along with those who hold the tribunate each year. These are the functions they have taken from the republic, more or less in the form in which each existed then, and using the same names, in order to give the impression that they have no power save by its being granted them.

18. They have also acquired another privilege, which was not bestowed outright on any of the Ancient Romans, and this by itself would allow them to exercise the powers already mentioned and the others besides. For they have been released from the laws, as the actual words in Latin say (Ulpian, *Dig.* 1.3.31—*princeps legibus solutus est*); that is, they are free from all compulsion by law and bound by no written enactments. So, by using these democratic names they have donned all the power of the government, so that they have all the pre-

rogatives of kings, except the worthless title. For the title 'Caesar' or 'Augustus' gives them no particular power, but simply shows, firstly, that they are in the hereditary succession and, secondly, the resplendence of their status. The name 'Father' perhaps gives them a certain authority over us all, such as fathers once had over their children, although at first this did not confer authority but was a term of honour, and enjoined on them that they should love their subjects as their children, and on their subjects that they should revere them as their fathers.

That is the number and nature of the titles which those who hold power use in accord with the laws and with what is now the tradition. Nowadays they are all, as a rule, given at once, except that of censor, but they were voted to earlier emperors separately and at different times. As to the censorship, some took it in accordance with ancient usage, and Domitian took it for life. However, this is no longer done today, for as they have the function they are not elected to the office and do not use the title except for the census.

SOME THEMES OF EULOGY

Pliny's *Panegyric* was ostensibly an official address rendering thanks to the emperor on his (Pliny's) entering upon office as consul. It was by then common practice to have several successive pairs of consuls—the second and subsequent pairs known as 'suffect' consuls—in a year; Pliny was a suffect consul, for two months. Originally, thanks were rendered by consuls, in pursuance of a Senatorial decree of unknown date, to the gods and the emperor; from about the time of Claudius, the emperor alone was thanked.

The address was delivered in the Senate on September 1st, A.D. 100, but the text as we have it was considerably rewritten and expanded after delivery. Pliny himself tells us that the public readings he gave at the insistence of his friends extended to three sessions—i.e., more than four and a half hours of delivery.

Some of the themes of the passages cited below have already been mentioned. Attention may be drawn in particular to three others. These are adoption; the gods' aid and approval; and contrasts between Trajan and other emperors. All surely rest on the same basic assumption, made most explicit in chapter 53, and not overset elsewhere—whatever the stress on the 'citizenly' qualities of Trajan, and however bad some emperors may have been, there is no question but that the principate must continue to exist. It could be doubted whether the *Panegyric* is more a eulogy of the emperor or a declaration of the fitness and rightness of monarchic rule at Rome. The princeps (*any* princeps) has to be decked out in praises to fit the rôle, and the more that can truthfully be said the better.

Adoption is a particularly important theme. We have already seen how the principle of hereditary succession was followed from the start, and this seems to have been approved by the people of Italy and the empire and by the army. Eventually, however, succession failed; and the senatorial classes welcomed adoption as seeming to offer rule by the best man, irrespective of birth. That, at least, is part of the theory; but another, and equally important, part is that the adoption in a way revives the traditional claim of the senatorial class as a whole to be the ruling class. Tacitus (*Histories* 1.16) makes Galba say that his choice of Piso as his heir will be 'a substitute for freedom', and Pliny expresses a similar thought. Nevertheless, whenever an emperor appeared who did have sons (as, e.g. Marcus Aurelius, A.D. 161–180) it was accepted that there could be no question of adoption. The son must succeed even if, like Aurelius' son Commodus, he was unfit to be emperor.

Pliny, *Panegyricus*

1. Conscript fathers, our ancestors acted well and wisely in making it a practice that a speech, like an undertaking, should be prefaced with prayer; for they thought that men were not exercising due care and foresight unless they had the gods to help and advise them and unless they paid the gods due honour. Who more appropriate than a consul, or what time more suitable for the observation of this custom than when we are called upon by the command of the Senate and the will of the republic to render thanks to our excellent emperor? For what choicer or finer gift can the gods bestow than an emperor who is pure, virtuous and most like the gods? If any doubt remained whether earth received its rulers by mere chance or by some divine intent, it would be clear at least that our emperor was divinely appointed. For it was not by the hidden power of the fates but by Jupiter himself, openly and before our eyes, that he was revealed and chosen, among the very altars and in the very place where Jupiter presides as directly and immediately as among the stars in heaven. Therefore it is all the more fitting and due that I should pray to you, Jupiter most excellent, who once founded and now preserve our empire, that my speech may be worthy of a consul, of the Senate and of the emperor, that freedom,

loyalty and truth may abide in all my utterances and that my rendering of thanks may be as far from seeming adulatory as it is from the necessity of being so.

2. Indeed, I think that not only the consul, but all citizens, should strive to say nothing of our emperor that could equally have been said of any other citizen. So begone all those utterances that once were forced out by fear; let us say nothing in the style of former days, for we have nothing of the sufferings of former days. We shall not speak publicly of the emperor as we used to; for we no longer speak in private of him as we used to. Let our speeches show the difference in circumstances, and let it be understood, from the manner of our giving thanks, to whom they are given, and when. Let us at no point flatter him as a god, as a divinity, for we are speaking not of a tyrant but of a citizen, not of a master but of a father. His pre-eminence is all the greater for this, that he considers himself but one of us, and is as mindful of the fact that he is a man as that he is set above men. Let us therefore understand our good fortune, and show ourselves worthy of it in practice. Let us at the same time consider whether our deference is due more to princes who delight in the enslavement of their fellow-citizens than to those who delight in their freedom. The Roman people now has a prince of its choice. Not so long ago they sang in unison the praises of one emperor's beauty; now they praise another's bravery. The acclamations that once greeted the posturings and voice-projection of another, are now reserved for the present emperor's regard for duty, restraint and clemency.

But what of us, the Senate? Is it the divinity of the emperor that we are all accustomed to laud or, as love and joy direct, his humaneness, his moderation, his accessibility? What could be more fitting to a republic or to the Senate than that addition we made to his name, of the appellation, 'Excellent' (*Optimus*)? The arrogance of earlier rulers has made this his own property as of right. With what unity and concord do we call both ourselves and him blessed, and pray alternately that he do such-and-such, that he be called such-and-such —as though we would not say so, unless he were sure to do so! At these utterances he is overcome with modesty and weeps, for he is aware that these words are addressed to him personally, not to the emperor.

3. Therefore we ought each one of us to keep consciously in our minds that restraint we all observe even in the sudden heat of devotion, and know that the sincerest and most acceptable form of thanks are

those in which we emulate those acclamations that allow no time for pretence. In so far as in me lies, I shall try to accommodate my speech to the modesty and restraint of our emperor, and think as much of what his ears can endure as of what is due to his virtues. In giving thanks, I have more fear of his thinking me excessive in praise than deficient; this is a great credit to a prince, and an unusual one. This is my only cause for concern, and the only difficulty that faces me— for, conscript fathers, it is easy to thank one who deserves it.

There is no danger that, when I praise his affability, he may believe I am charging him with hauteur, or that when I praise him for frugality, clemency, generosity, kindliness, continence, industry and courage he may think himself attacked for extravagance, cruelty, greed, spite, lust, sloth and timidity. Nor indeed do I fear that I may find approval or disapproval as I say enough or too little. For I observe that the gods too are delighted not so much by the careful prayers of worshippers as by their innocence and piety, and that they welcome rather the man who brings a clean, pure mind into their temples than one who brings a prepared chant.

4. But I must obey the decree of the Senate, that 'it does appear in the public interest that, by the utterance of the consul in the form of a vote of thanks, good princes may recognize what they do, bad princes what they should do.' This is now the more solemn and necessary in that our parent prohibits private speeches of thanks and would prohibit public ones also, if he were allowed to veto the order of the Senate. Both, Caesar Augustus, show moderation in you, that you do not allow yourself to be thanked elsewhere and that you allow it here. For this honour is not paid by you to yourself, but to those who thank you.

Gentlemen, I have often asked myself what the nature and greatness of a man must be under whose sway and command are the seas, the lands, peace and war. And when I mentally fashioned a prince upon whom might sit becomingly power equal to the immortal gods, I have never succeeded in imagining one like him whom we see here. One was brilliant in war, but lax in peace; the toga became one, but not arms; one sought respect by intimidation, another wooed affection by humility. One squandered abroad the renown he won at home, another at home that he won abroad. In short, hitherto there has been none whose virtues were not damaged by the contact of some vices. In our prince, however, what a harmonious concord we find of all manner of praise and glory. His severity is not impaired by his cheerfulness, his dignity by simplicity, his majesty by affability. That firm, tall body, impressive head and dignified countenance, his age, in the prime of life, his hair which, by some divine intervention, has been given the premature signs of age to enhance his dignity—do not all these proclaim the prince?

5. Such should a man be, who has been given to us not by civil wars and a commonwealth oppressed by arms, but by peace, adoption and gods who at last have answered the prayers of the world. How could it be right that there should be no difference between an emperor made by men and one made by the gods? The gods' approval of you, Caesar Augustus, was made known when you were setting off to the army, at once and in unwonted manner. For all the other emperors were proclaimed to inspectors of omens by copious bleeding from victims or by flight of birds on the left; but when you ascended the Capitol, as is customary, the citizens, although there for another purpose, greeted you with cheers, as though already emperor. Indeed, the whole throng which beset the threshold, when the doors were opened for your entry, hailed as emperor the god—as was then thought—but, as events showed, you. And that is how all received the omen. You yourself refused to acknowledge it; for you refused to rule. You refused, as would one destined to be a good ruler. So, you had to be compelled, but this you could not be, save by the danger of the fatherland and the instability of the state. You were determined not to undertake the empire, were it not that it had to be saved. This, I believe, is why that riotous disturbance occurred among the troops—because great constraint and great alarm were required to overcome your modesty. And just as whirlwinds and storms make calm weather and calm seas more welcome, so that unrest, I believe, was harbinger to enhance the welcome nature of your peace. Such are the changes of human life, that prosperity comes out of adversity, and the reverse. God conceals the seeds of both, and in general the seeds of good and evil lie hidden under the appearance of the opposite.

7. A new and unheard-of route to the principate! What made you emperor was not your own desire, or your own fear, but the convenience of another, and his apprehension. You may seem to have attained the highest position in the world, but the one you left was happier. Under a good prince you ceased to be a private citizen. You were brought in to share toils and troubles, but what impelled you to under-

take that position was not its advantages and joys, but its difficulties and hardships. You undertook the empire, when another regretted having undertaken it. You had no ties of birth, or of close friendship, with the man who adopted you; the link was that you were both the best of men, one worthy to be chosen, the other to choose. You were adopted therefore not, like more than one predecessor, to please a wife; you were adopted not by a stepfather but by an emperor, and the deified Nerva became your father in the same spirit as he became father of all. This is the one way in which a son should be adopted, if he is adopted by an emperor. If you were about to hand over the Senate and people of Rome, the armies, the provinces, the allies, to one man—would you accept a successor from the lap of your wife, would you seek the heir to supreme power solely within your own house? Would you not cast your eyes around the whole citizen population, and consider the man nearest and most closely conjoined to you, whom you found to be the best and most god-like? The future ruler of all should be chosen from all, for you are not going merely to give your slaves a master —in which case you could be satisfied with the immediate heir—but you are going to give a prince to the citizens, and you are emperor. It would be an autocratic and tyrannical act if you did not adopt the man who is acknowledged to be the future ruler, even without your adopting him. Nerva did it realizing that there was no difference between begetting and adopting if children were adopted with as little discrimination as they are begotten— except that men put up more readily with someone a prince has been unlucky in begetting than one he had chosen badly.

8. Therefore he carefully avoided this eventuality. He called not only upon the judgment of men but upon the advice of the gods; and so it was not in the bedchamber but in the temple, not before the marriage bed but before the couch of Jupiter Best and Greatest, that the adoption was carried out. On that adoption was founded not our slavery, but our freedom, welfare and security. The credit for that the gods have claimed, because it is their work, done at their command; Nerva was merely the minister and he who adopted was as much obeying as you who were adopted. A laurel was brought from Pannonia. The gods saw to it that at the outset the unvanquished emperor should be decorated with the emblem of victory. This laurel the emperor Nerva had placed on the lap of Jove, when suddenly he was greater in stature and impressiveness than he was wont to be. Before the gathered

assemblage of men and gods he adopted you as his son, that is, the sole help for his travails. Then, as though he had resigned the imperial command, in what tranquillity and glory did he rejoice (for it makes very little difference whether you lay down or share the command, save that the latter is more difficult). Just as though you were present he leaned upon you, resting on your shoulders both himself and the fatherland, gaining strength from your youth and vigour. At once the whole disturbance settled down. The cause of this was not the adoption, but the person adopted. Nerva would have behaved recklessly had he adopted anyone else. Have we forgotten how, recently, after an adoption, mutiny did not cease, but broke out? The adoption would merely have stirred up angry passions and inflamed rebellion, had it not fallen on you. Can there be any doubt that the reason that an emperor who had lost respect was able to confer imperial command was the standing of the man on whom it was conferred? You were made at once son and Caesar, presently emperor, sharer of the tribunician power, everything all at once, which lately a natural father conferred on only one of his sons.

9. A strong proof of your moderation is that you have met approval not only as successor to the imperial power but as partner and joint ruler. For a man has to have a successor, whether he will or no, but a partner is a matter of choice. Future generations may not believe that a man whose father was a patrician, a consular and had triumphal honours, and who himself commanded a large army of brave men who were devoted to their general, was made emperor, *not* by the army; that the title 'Germanicus' was conferred on him by Rome while he governed in Germany; that he himself made no efforts to become emperor. All he did was to serve and to obey. You obeyed, Caesar, and that obedience brought you to the principate.

11. You honoured Nerva as a son should, first with tears and then with temples. You did not imitate others, who have done likewise but with different intentions. Tiberius deified Augustus—in order to introduce the charge of treason. Nero deified Claudius—to make him an object of ridicule. Titus deified Vespasian and Domitian deified Titus, because one wanted to be known as the son of a god, the other as a god's brother. You set your father among the stars, not to strike fear into the citizens, not to insult the gods, not to enhance your own position, but because you believe he is a god. This means less when it is done by those who believe themselves to be gods as well. You may

establish his cult with altars, couches and a priesthood, but you will not make him, and reveal him to be, a god any more than by the fact that he himself is such. For when a prince chooses his successor and then yields to his destiny, the one surest proof of his divinity is the goodness of his successor.

44. How advantageous it is to have attained prosperity through adversity! You shared our lives, our danger, our fear—such was the life of innocent men in those days. You know from experience how much rulers are hated even by those who made them bad. You remember what hopes and what complaints you joined us in expressing. For your conduct as emperor evinces the outlook of a private citizen; indeed, you show yourself a prince better than you prayed that another might be. You have so conditioned us that whereas the height of our hopes was once to have an emperor a little better than the worst, now we can tolerate none but the best. So there is no one who has such a false opinion either of himself or of you as to desire to succeed to your position. It would be easier for someone to be able to succeed you, than to wish to. Who would willingly undertake the burden of your responsibility? Who would not shun comparison with you? You yourself know from experience what a burden it is to succeed a good emperor, although you could support your claim with the fact of adoption. It is no slight thing, nor easy of imitation, to have a situation in which no one buys his safety at the price of his honour. All men's lives and dignities are safe, and the thoughtful and wise man is no longer he who spends his life in obscurity. Virtue finds the same rewards under the *princeps* as in the days of liberty, and the consciousness of good deeds is no longer their sole reward. You approve of steadfastness in citizens. Upright and energetic minds are not beaten down and repressed, as by other emperors; you foster and encourage them. Men's goodness is a benefit to them, though it would amply suffice if it did them no harm. These are the men on whom you bestow offices, priesthoods and provinces; they flourish in your friendship and approval. Men like them are stimulated by the prospect of such reward for honesty and diligence, those unlike are attracted to them—for men are made good or bad by the rewards for good or bad conduct. Few are of strong enough character not to be attracted or repelled by honest or brave conduct according to the rewards it gets or otherwise. The rest, when they see sloth, somnolence and extravagance reaping the rewards due to industry, alertness and thrift, seek these rewards

by the same methods by which they have seen others obtain them. They wish to be and to seem to be as those men are, and in wishing they become so.

45. Indeed previous emperors, save for your father and one or two others (I am indiscreet in saying this much) took more pleasure in the vices of the citizens than in their virtues—firstly because everyone is pleased to see his own nature in another, and secondly because they thought that men fit only to be slaves would bear enslavement more readily. They heaped everything into the laps of these men. Good men were thrust into the obscurity of idleness and unemployment; they were as good as buried, and were dragged into the light only when informed against and put on trial.

You choose your friends from the best men, and, really, it is right that those men who were most disliked by a bad emperor should be most dear to a good one. You know that as despotism and the principate are different in nature, so the very men who are happiest to have a *princeps* are those who chafe most under a despot. These are the men you advance, and you display as a pattern and model of the way of life and type of man that has your approval. And so, you have hitherto not accepted the censorship or the supervision of morals, because you preferred to test our characters by conferring benefits rather than imposing correction.

In general, I rather think that the emperor who allows men to be good does more to raise moral standards than one who compels them. We are easily drawn by him this way or that, as it were following his lead. For we desire his affection and approval, which men unlike him would hope for in vain; and by persistence in our conformity, we come to a point when virtually all of us live according to the morals of one man. To be sure, we are not so perversely constituted that, when we can imitate a bad emperor, we cannot imitate a good one. Only continue thus, Caesar, and your principles and your conduct will have the effectiveness of the censorship.

52. If anyone else had performed even one of these acts (*the immediate reference is to Trajan's—economical—building programme, including the enlargement of the Circus, and his donatives to the people*), he would long since have had a radiate crown about his head, a chair of gold or ivory set for him among the gods and prayers addressed to him at altars larger and more impressive than those of the gods. You enter the shrines only in order to worship. The greatest honour

for you is to be set (as a statue) on watch before the doorposts of the temples. So the gods preserve for you the supreme position among men, since you do not challenge a position of supremacy among themselves. Thus we see statues of you—one or two at most and those only of bronze—in the vestibule of the temple of Jupiter Best and Greatest; yet it is not long since all the approaches, every step and the whole precinct was ablaze on this side and that with gold and silver— or rather, was defaced, for the statues of the gods lost their splendour when mingled with the images of an incestuous emperor. So your statues, of bronze and few in number, remain and shall remain as long as the temple itself, while those countless golden ones have been sacrificed amid public rejoicing and have been overthrown and destroyed. It was a pleasure to dash to the ground those haughty countenances, to attack them with the sword and wreak one's fury on them with axes, as though blood and anguish followed every blow. There was none so lukewarm and tardy in his joy and delight as not to have a certain feeling of revenge at seeing the mangled arms, lopped-off limbs, and finally the ferocious, terrible faces thrown to the flames and melted down, so that by the action of fire they might cease to be a source of terror and threats to men, and instead serve to supply their needs and pleasures.

With the same reverence, Caesar, you do not allow thanks for your goodness to be made to your Genius, but to the will of Jupiter Best and Highest. It is to him that we owe whatever we owe to you, your good actions are the gifts of him who gave you to us. In times past, great herds of victims were, as it were, forestalled on the Capitoline Way and many of them were obliged to turn aside, for the abominable image of that savage despot required as much blood of victims for its worship as he himself had shed human blood.

53. Gentlemen, all that I say or have said about other emperors is intended to demonstrate how the nature of the principate, corrupted and depraved by long usage, is being reformed and corrected by our father. Indeed, eulogies are usually inadequate without comparisons. Besides, the chief obligation of a dutiful citizen towards the best of emperors is to attack those unlike him. No one can sufficiently love good emperors unless he sufficiently hates bad ones. In addition, the greatest and most far-reaching service done us by our emperor is to allow us to assail bad emperors with impunity. Did our troubles make us forget how Nero was lately avenged? As though *he* would allow

criticism of the life and repute of Nero, when he avenged his death. He would interpret as directed against himself whatever was said of one very like him. Therefore I am right, Caesar, to regard it as a boon comparable with all the rest you have bestowed and surpassing many, that we may daily avenge ourselves on bad emperors of the past, and warn those of the future, by our example, that there is no place or time in which the spirits of baneful rulers may find peace from the curses of posterity. Therefore, gentlemen, let us the more resolutely manifest both our sorrows and our joys. Let us rejoice in the benefits we enjoy and deplore the ills we suffered. Under a good emperor, both are to be done at once. Let this be the theme of our private talk, our conversations, our speeches of thanks, and let it be recalled that an emperor is best praised, while he lives, if his predecessors are criticized according to their deserts. For if later ages are silent about a bad emperor, it is clear that the current emperor's behaviour is the same.

54. No place could remain unacquainted with grovelling adulation, when laudation of the emperor was conducted by means of games and wild revels, dancing and a farrago of clowning, with effeminate utterance, rhythm and gesture. Particularly disgraceful was the simultaneous delivering of eulogies in the Senate and on the stage, by a play-actor and a consul. You have banished these mountebank skills from the honours paid to you. Respects are paid to you in serious poems and the eternal renown of chronicled history, not this short-lived and unseemly publicity. Indeed, the greater the silence on the stage about you, the more united are the theatre audiences in rising to pay you their respects. But why should I marvel at that, when even those honours offered to you by us you merely sample sparingly or refuse altogether? Formerly, no item of business, no matter how commonplace or trivial, was conducted in the Senate without being delayed by eulogies of the emperor on the part of those who happened to have to express their views. We would be consulted about increasing the number of gladiators or setting up an association of workmen, and as though the boundaries of the empire had been extended we would decree huge triumphal arches and inscriptions too long to fit the architraves of temples, or give months—several at a time—the names of the Caesars. The emperors put up with this, and were pleased by it, as though they had earned it. Nowadays, does anyone so far forget the subject under discussion as to use his time, when rendering his

opinion, in lauding the emperor? This steadfastness of ours is to your credit. We are complying with your wishes in meeting, not for a contest in adulation, but to see to the practice and exercise of justice, in order to render to your honesty and sincerity this tribute, that we believe you to wish what you do wish and not to want what you do not want. We start and end at the point where it was not possible to begin or end under another emperor. For there have been others, too, who refused very many of the honours decreed them, but no one before was so great as for it to be believed that he did not want them decreed. This I think is a more spectacular adornment than any amount of inscriptions, that your name is engraved not on wood or stone but in the memorials of eternal praise.

80. In every judicial enquiry, you are strict without being harsh, and clement without being lax. You did not secure the seat of office for the sake of enriching your private coffers; the only reward you seek for giving judgment is to have judged well. The litigants who appear before you are concerned, not to safeguard their own fortunes, but to earn your good opinion; they fear your judgment less on their cause than on their characters. Truly, it is the concern of a prince—indeed, of a god—to reconcile rival cities, and to quieten restless peoples by the use of reason as much as of command; to intervene against injustices by magistrates and to cancel whatever should not have been done, finally, like the swiftest of the stars, to survey all, hear all, and whencesoever a call comes for help to be there, like a divine power, ready to assist. Such, I believe, would be the way in which the Father of the universe ruled all with his nod, if ever he cast his eyes on the earth and deigned to count the fates of mortal among his divine concerns. Now he is free from all this part of his cares and at leisure to deal with heaven, since he has assigned it to you to fulfil his functions towards men. And you do fulfil it, and carry out the charge entrusted to you, since all your days are passed to our utmost advantage and your utmost glory.

88. Most emperors, though they were masters of their citizens, were the slaves of their freedmen; they were ruled by their counsels and their wishes; through them they gave audience, through them they spoke. Through them—rather, from them—even praetorship and priesthoods and consulships were sought. You treat your freedmen with the utmost respect, but as freedmen, and you think it enough for them if they have a reputation for honesty and sobriety. You know

that powerful freedmen are the surest sign that a prince lacks power. Firstly, you employ no one unless he is known and tried, either by you or your father or one of the best emperors; next, you yourself train them daily to measure themselves, not by your standing, but by their own. And so they are the more worthy of the great honour we pay them, because it is not forced from us. Did the Senate and people of Rome have good reasons for giving you the appellation 'Best'? A ready-made title and ready to hand, yet a new one. Be assured that no one hitherto has earned the title, which would not have had to be devised, had anyone earned it. Perhaps it would have been better to call you 'Fortunate'? That is a tribute to your fortune rather than your character. Or 'Great'? That would expose you to envy, rather than enhance you. The best of emperors by adoption gave you his own name, the Senate gave you the name 'Best'. This is as much your own personal name as the inherited one, and you are just as clearly and precisely designated by the name 'Best' as by 'Trajan'—just as in the past the Pisos were an example of frugality, the Laelii of wisdom, the Metelli of piety—all of which qualities are embraced in this one name. No man can appear best save he who excels all the best, each in his own several excellence. It is right therefore that this should be added as the last and greatest of your titles; for it is less to be emperor and Caesar and Augustus than to be better than all the emperors and all the Caesars and every Augustus. Therefore the father of gods and men is worshipped firstly under the title 'Best' and then 'Greatest'. All the more resplendent therefore is your glory, for you are known to be best and greatest. You have achieved a name which cannot pass to another, without seeming inappropriate for a merely good prince, false of a bad one, a name which, no matter if all hereafter use it, will always be acknowledged as yours. For as we use the name 'Augustus' to refer to him on whom it was first conferred, so this title 'Best' will never come to men's minds without the association with you, and as often as their descendants are obliged to call someone 'Best', they will remember who deserved to be so called.

THE NECESSITY OF MONARCHY

Dio sets in 29 B.C. a debate between Agrippa and Maecenas, arguing against and for Octavian's continuing in power. We do not have the complete text, as the end of Agrippa's speech is missing, and the beginning of Maecenas'; even so, the debate takes up almost the whole of Book 52. Chapters 19–42 are omitted here. There is an abrupt change of subject at the end of chapter 18; Maecenas ceases to argue in favour of Octavian's retaining monarchy and passes over to making a large number of detailed proposals for the actual running of the empire, proposals which do not relate to the situation in 29 B.C., but to the actual practice of the imperial government in Dio's own time, the first quarter of the third century A.D. It contains some proposals which were implemented only much later, or not at all. It is generally agreed that this latter portion of Maecenas' speech was in the nature of a pamphlet aimed at an emperor contemporary with Dio, although which emperor is uncertain—most likely Caracalla or Severus Alexander.

This portion has attracted the attention of ancient historians; but the first part, the balanced debate, is of interest in its own right.

The device of the debate we have already encountered in Herodotus. Of the actual arguments, many will recall to us the passages of Isocrates, Aristotle and even Euripides above, although some are indicated only sketchily and the speeches as a whole, Agrippa's in particular, are scarcely models of thoroughness or coherent development of thought. However, over and above the conventional themes, we find a number of topics particularly relevant to the situation of an emperor—especially with regard to the difficulty of collecting revenues, the invidiousness of patronage and the unpopularity attaching to the dispensing of justice. Agrippa's contribution also seems to contain a veiled description, as a warning, of the situation of Julius Caesar. Further, is the 'democracy' of Agrippa a thorough-going egalitarian one, or does it seem in fact kin to the government 'with your peers' on which Maecenas lays so much stress? Is Dio still harking back to the senatorial Republic, and what can we deduce of his attitude to it and to the principate?

Given the actual course of events after 29 B.C., it would be hard to make Agrippa's speech as cogent as Maecenas'. There is room, however, for question whether Maecenas' speech has really established the *necessity* of the establishment of a monarchy at Rome, or whether two-and-a-half centuries of hindsight and concurrence in its existence have conditioned him to take much for granted.

Dio 52

1. After this the Romans began again to have what was strictly a monarchic government, although Caesar planned to lay down his arms and to entrust affairs to the Senate and people. He made his decision in consultation with Agrippa and Maecenas, with whom he

was wont to share all his secret counsels, and Agrippa spoke first, as follows:

2. Do not be surprised, Caesar, if I try to steer you away from monarchy, even though I should derive many benefits from it, that is, if you were monarch. If it were to be advantageous to you also, I should urge it strongly; but monarchs by no means share the experience of their friends. The latter reap all the benefits they desire, without incurring envy or risk; it is the rulers who are exposed to jealousies and dangers. Therefore I thought it right that in this matter, as in all others, I should have regard for your interests and those of the state, rather than my own.

Let us consider at our leisure all the characteristics of monarchy, and then proceed in the direction in which our reasoning takes us. I assume that no one would assert that we should choose monarchy under all circumstances, even if it were not advantageous; otherwise, it would be thought that good fortune had been too much for us and success had robbed us of our wits—or else that we had aimed at monarchy all along, and that we had made a pretext of your father and our loyalty to him, and used the Senate and the people as a front, our intention being, not to free them from those conspiring against them, but to enslave them to ourselves. Both versions would incur blame for us. Who would not be indignant if he observed us saying one thing and found that we meant another? Surely he would hate us much more then, than if we had at the very outset exposed our wishes and aimed directly at monarchy. It has come to be believed that it is somehow a basic human characteristic to venture upon violence, even though it appear selfish; for everyone who excels in any respect thinks he deserves to have more than his inferior, and if he has any success he refers that to his superiority of mind, whereas if he fails he ascribes that to supernatural intervention. Suppose a man employs plots and chicanery; then he is thought to be tricky, crooked, malevolent and of an evil disposition—a reputation which I am sure you would not wish to have in men's speech or thoughts, even as the price of ruling the whole world. Further, if he succeeds, his power is thought unjust, and if he fails, his ill success is thought to be deserved.

3. Therefore, we would incur just as much reproach if we should now desire this position, even if we had no such ambition at the start. Surely it is much worse for men to be overcome by circumstances and not only fail to restrain themselves but abuse the gifts of Fortune, than

it is to wrong others as a result of failure. For men are often obliged by their misfortunes to do wrong, even against their wills, in defence of their own interests, while the others (i.e. those who succeed) allow themselves to abandon their self-restraint, even against their own interests. When men are not simple and straightforward in soul and are incapable of treating their good fortune with moderation, how could they be expected to rule well over others, or to deal properly with misfortunes?

Let us assume that we have neither failing, and that we do not wish to act irrationally, but intend to choose whatever course seems to us, upon deliberation, to be best, and let us consider accordingly. I shall speak frankly; for my part, I could not speak otherwise, and I know that you do not like to hear lies accompanied by flattery.

4. Well then: equality under law has a noble sound, and is most just in practice. Where men are endowed with the same nature, are of the same nation as each other, have been brought up among the same institutions and educated in similar laws, and join in putting their minds and bodies at the service of their country, then surely it is just that they should share in other things also, and surely it is best that they should receive special honour only as a result of excellence?

Equality of birth requires equality of privilege, and there is satisfaction if this is attained, displeasure if it is not. The whole of mankind, as being descended from the gods and destined to return to the gods, looks above, and is not willing to be ruled always by the same person, nor will it submit to sharing in the toils, hazards and expenses while being deprived of participation in the benefits. If men are obliged to submit to anything of this sort, they hate the force that has compelled them and if they find an opportunity they avenge themselves on the object of their hatred. For all men want to rule, and therefore they submit to being ruled in their turn; they are unwilling to be over-reached, and so they themselves are not obliged to over-reach others. They take pleasure in the honours conferred by their equals, and they approve of the penalties exacted by the laws. If they organize their society in this way, and consider all the good things and their opposite as being common to all, then they do not wish harm to come to any citizen, and they pray for all blessings for everyone. If any one of them has any particular excellence, he readily reveals it, is enthusiastic in practising it and displays it most willingly; and if he sees it in another, he is active in making it known, eagerly promotes it and bestows the most signal honour upon it. However, if anyone behaves badly, everyone hates him, and if anyone is unfortunate, everyone pities him—for they consider the damage and the disgrace arising from them as common to the whole state.

5. This is the situation of democracies. The condition of tyrannies is just the opposite, but there is no need to describe them at length. The main thing is that no one is willing to be thought to have any superior knowledge or possession, for this generally brings upon him the hatred of the ruling power. Everyone makes the ruler's disposition the yardstick of his own conduct, and seeks whatever advantages he may hope to gain through the tyrant by over-reaching others, without personal risk. So most people pursue only their own private advantage, and are hostile to everyone else, taking the good fortune of others as their own loss and the misfortune of others as gains to themselves.

As this is the situation, I do not see what reasonable ground you could have for wanting to be monarch. It would be difficult, in the first place, to apply that system to a republic; moreover, it would be much more difficult for you yourself to put it into practice—surely you see how the city and its affairs are still even now in confusion? Besides, it is difficult to overthrow our people, which has lived for so many years in freedom, and it is also difficult, when so many enemies beset us, to reduce once more to slavery the allies and subject peoples, some of whom have been democratically governed for a long time past and others of whom we ourselves set free.

6. To start with the least important matter—you will have to acquire a large amount of money from all quarters, for present revenues are insufficient to maintain the troops as well as pay all our other expenses. Democracies have the same problem too, for a government cannot be run without expenditure. However, in democracies many people make large contributions, in the best cases voluntarily, paying extra, vying among themselves and receiving due honours in return; if there should be any compulsory levies made upon all the citizens, they accept it because it is done with their own consent and they are contributing for their own benefit. Now, in autocratic governments, the people think that the ruling power is supremely wealthy and should bear all the expense alone; they eagerly inquire into the ruler's sources of income, but are less particular in calculating his expenses; they do not make personal contributions gladly or willingly nor are the public contributions made by their own choice. For no one would want to

make a voluntary contribution, any more than he would readily admit that he was rich—nor is it to the advantage of the ruler that anyone should, for such a person would at once get a reputation among the masses for patriotism, become puffed-up and start fomenting rebellion. On the other hand a general exaction oppresses the masses, specially as they undergo the loss, while others receive the gain. In democracies those who contribute the money usually also serve in the army, so that in a way they get it back again, but in monarchies, as a rule, one lot of men is occupied in farming, manufacturing, trading and politics, and from them revenues are mainly drawn, while another lot bears arms and is paid.

7. So that is one consideration which will give you trouble; and here is another one. In all situations, whoever commits a crime ought to pay a penalty, for most men are not chastened by argument or example, but need to be punished by loss of civic rights, exile, or death; and this happens regularly in an empire as large as ours and with so large a population, particularly when there is a change of government. If you appointed other men to judge these wrongdoers, they would compete with each other in acquitting them, particularly in acquitting those you might be thought to hate; for judges acquire a reputation for independence if they act contrary to the will of the ruler. And if any should be convicted, it would be thought that they had deliberately been condemned to oblige you. If you yourself act as judge, however, you will be obliged to punish many of your peers, which is an unfortunate situation, and you will certainly be thought to be bringing them to book out of resentment rather than regard for justice. No one believes that those who have the power to use force give judgment justly; everyone thinks that they are, out of shame, drawing an illusory semblance of constitutional government as a cloak over the truth, and that under the legal name of a law court they are satisfying their personal desires.

This is what happens in monarchies; whereas in democracies, if anyone is accused of private wrongdoing, he defends himself in a private suit before jurymen who are his equals, and if he is accused of a public offence, then he also has a jury of his equals, who are appointed by lot. Therefore it is easier for men to accept the verdicts given by such juries, since they do not think the penalty has been inflicted on them either because the judge had superior power or because he was obliged to grant a favour.

8. Again, apart from wrongdoers, there are men who pride themselves on their birth, or wealth, or something else, and who, though not otherwise bad men, are naturally opposed to the principle of monarchy. If a ruler allows them to become strong, he cannot live in safety, while if he attempts to curb them he cannot do so justly. So what *are* you to do with these? How will you handle them? If you exterminate their families, cut down their wealth and humble their pride, you will have no goodwill from your subjects. You could not expect to, if no one is to be allowed noble birth or honest wealth or any strength or courage or understanding. Yet if you allow these qualities to flourish you will find difficulty in dealing with them. If you were capable of managing single-handed the government and the conduct of war properly, and as circumstances require, and you needed no assistance for any of this, it would be a different story. As things are, it is absolutely essential for you to have many collaborators in administering this vast world and of course they ought all of them to be brave and strong-willed. Yet if you hand over the army and the official positions to such men, there is a danger that both you and your government may be destroyed —for no man of any account can be lacking in spirit, nor, conversely, could anyone derive such spirit from a habit of servile dependence; and if a man has spirit he cannot fail to desire independence and hate all mastery. However, if you entrusted nothing to these men but put everything in the hands of any commonplace fellows who were available, you would soon rouse the enmity of the others, thinking themselves distrusted, and your most important schemes would come to grief. What good could ever be accomplished by an ignorant and low-born man? Our enemies would all despise him, none of our allies would obey him, and even the soldiers would disdain to be commanded by such a man. Moreover, I need not specify for you the evils consequent on such a state of affairs; but this one thing I must say—if such a man failed in everything, he would do you far more harm than your enemies, and if he did anything properly, he would be a danger to you because his ignorance would make him lose his sense of perspective.
9. But this state of affairs does not occur in democracies. The more wealthy and brave men there are, the more they compete with each other and strengthen the state, and the state avails itself of them and rejoices in them—unless one of them aspires to a tyranny; such a man the citizens punish severely. This is shown by the experience of Greece, which demonstrates the superiority of democracies to monarchies.

While they had monarchy, they achieved nothing important, but when they began to live under democracy, they became most famous. The experience of other peoples also shows this. Those which even now still live under tyrannies are always slaves and always plotting against their rulers, while those which have officials for a year, or a longer specified period, remain free and independent. But why use examples from other peoples when we have some at home? We Romans ourselves originally had a different form of government, and then after many dreadful experiences we desired freedom, and when we attained it we advanced to our present prominence, deriving our strength solely from the benefits of democracy. It was on the basis of these that the Senate deliberated, the people ratified, the soldiers were zealous and their officers ambitious. None of this could happen under a tyranny. Anyway, the ancient Romans for these reasons had such a hatred of tyranny that they even put that type of government under a curse.

10. Besides, if one is to say something also about your own personal interests, how could you endure the administration of such weighty affairs day and night? How would you manage if your health gave out? What human blessings could you enjoy, and how could you be happy deprived of them? In what could you take real pleasure and when would you not feel great pain? A man holding such an office cannot but have many cares and fears, have very little enjoyment of what is most pleasant, and always and everywhere hear, see, do and undergo what is most disagreeable. That, I think, is why certain Greeks and barbarians refused to accept kingships even when they were offered to them.

You ought to foresee all these circumstances and think ahead before you become involved in them. It is discreditable—rather it is impossible—for a man to back out once he has got in. Do not let the greatness of the authority deceive you, or the abundance of wealth, or the size of the bodyguards or the array of courtiers. Men who have much power have many cares, those who possess much must expend much, the multitude of bodyguards is assembled because of the multitude of conspirators and the flatterers would sooner crush you than save you. 11. For these reasons, then, no sensible man would want to become supreme ruler. If anyone thinks that because monarchs are able to enrich others, save their lives, confer other benefits on them—*and* indeed to insult them, and ill-treat anyone they please—if anyone supposes that that makes tyranny worth striving for, he is utterly mistaken. I do not need to tell you that wantonness and ill-doing are shameful, are perilous and are hateful both to gods and men—for you are not, in any case, that sort of man nor would such considerations make you want to be sole ruler. I have chosen to speak now, not of all the evil that someone might do who set about the business badly, but of what even those who make the best use of their power are obliged to do and to undergo. As to the other point, that one has unlimited scope for bestowing benefits, this *is* something worth striving for; but, although in a private citizen it is noble, admirable, celebrated and free from danger, in monarchies it does not, in the first place, counterbalance the other, less pleasant features, so that a man might choose to accept them for the sake of getting this good, especially when he would be obliged to confer on others the enjoyment to be derived from it, and to have for himself the unpleasantness arising from the other things. Secondly, this advantage is not without complications, as people think; for a ruler cannot satisfy everyone who makes requests. Those who think they merit something from him are pretty well the whole of mankind, even if no benefit is due to them immediately—for everyone naturally is satisfied with himself and wants to enjoy some benefit from the man who is able to bestow it. The benefits that can be given (I mean honours and offices and sometimes money) would be found very easy to enumerate, in comparison with the vast number of persons. This being the case, the ruler will earn much more enmity from those who fail to get what they want than affection from those who succeed. The latter, as though they had received merely their due, do not think any particular gratitude is due to the giver, as they are getting no more than they expected; besides, they are actually reluctant to show gratitude, in case they reveal themselves as unworthy of their good fortune; and those who are disappointed in their hopes are aggrieved for two reasons, firstly because they feel deprived of what belongs to them (for everyone thinks he already possesses what he longs for), and secondly because they think they would be acknowledging some unworthiness on their part, if they accepted readily their failure to get whatever they expect.

All this happens because the ruler who bestows gifts in the right way looks first and foremost at the merit of the individual, and honours some and passes over others; and so, as a result of his judgment, some feel pride, others resentment, each being conscious of his own merit.

If a ruler tries to avoid this, and distributes honours arbitrarily, he will fail completely—for the bad, receiving honours contrary to their due, will become worse, supposing that they are being approved of as good or bought off as dangerous; and the good, finding themselves no better treated than the others, but regarded merely as equal to them, would feel more annoyance at being put on an equal footing with them than pleasure at being themselves thought to deserve some honour, and therefore they would abandon their course of good conduct and endeavour to emulate the worse. So this, which some would find the most attractive feature in monarchies, you find turns out to be the most difficult to handle.

13. Bearing in mind all of this, as well as what I said a little while ago, think carefully, while you may, and hand over to the people the army, the provinces, the offices and the monies. If you do it at once and voluntarily, you will be the most renowned of men and the most secure; but if you wait for some force to be applied against you, then you will probably suffer some harm as well as infamy.

History is evidence—Marius, Sulla, Metellus and Pompey initially when they gained control of affairs refused to take on sovereign power and came to no harm in consequence; whereas Cinna, Strabo, the younger Marius and Sertorius, as well as Pompey himself later on, desired sovereign power and perished wretchedly. It is difficult to induce this city, which for so many years has been democratically governed and rules over so many people, to consent to be enslaved to anyone. You hear how the people banished Camillus, because he used white horses for his triumph; you hear how they deposed Scipio, after condemning him for exceeding his powers; and you recall how they acted against your father, because they had some suspicion that he aimed at monarchy. Yet there have never been better men than these.

However, I am not advising you to give up the command and leave it at that; you should first do all that the public interest requires and, using decrees and laws, determine all matters of importance, as Sulla did. Even if some of his measures were later overturned, the greater number of them, and the more important, remain. And do not say that even then some people will engage in civil dissension, and so oblige me to repeat that the Romans would be much more likely to refuse to put up with a monarchy. Even if we should try to forestall every possible eventuality, it would be utterly unreasonable for us to be more afraid of the dissensions incidental to democracy than of the tyrannies that are innate in monarchy. I have not even attempted to say anything about the terrible nature of such tyrannies; for I wished, not just to tilt against so easy a target for condemnation, but to show you that monarchy is by nature such that even the best men. . . .

(Lacuna—the rest of Agrippa's speech and the beginning of Maecenas' are lost. According to Zonaras' epitome, Maecenas' line of argument was that Caesar had already been conducting a monarchy for a long time, and must either continue to do so, or perish.)

(Maecenas)
14. (. . . nor can they easily persuade by open speaking those who are not in a similar position), and they succeed in their undertakings because there is discord among their subjects. So, if you have any affection for your country, on whose behalf you have fought so many wars, and would gladly give even your life, bring it back into order and regulate it towards greater moderation. For while complete freedom to do and say what one pleases becomes, if you examine it in the case of sensible people, a source of happiness to all, in the case of the foolish it brings disaster. Therefore the man who gives such licence to the foolish is, as it were, giving a sword to a child or a madman, while he who gives it to the sensible is, besides everything else, saving these people even in spite of themselves. So I ask you not to pay heed to specious appellations and so be misled, but to examine the consequences, and so check the boldness of the populace and assign the management of the state to yourself and other best men, so that deliberation may rest with the most prudent, ruling with the best commanders, and that the strongest and most needy serve in the army for pay. In this way, each class will conscientiously perform the functions allotted to it, and they will readily give each other the assistance required. They will not be aware of inferiority, when they are at a disadvantage compared with others, and they will gain true democracy and true freedom—for that freedom of the mob is in fact the enslavement of the best people and brings destruction on both, while this freedom gives greater honour everywhere to prudence, and bestows equality on all according to their merits, so giving happiness to all alike who participate in this liberty.
15. For you must not think that I am advising you to enslave the

people and the Senate and be a tyrant. I would never dare say this nor would you bring yourself to do it. What would be honourable and expedient for you and for the city, is this—that you should, in concert with the best men, make all desirable laws, without any protest or opposition by anyone from the masses, and that you and your advisers should conduct wars according to your wishes, with all the other citizens immediately obeying your orders, and that the allocation of offices should be in your hands and those of your advisers, and likewise the determination of rewards and punishments. So, whatever you, with your peers, decided on would at once be laws, wars against our enemies would be carried on in secrecy and at the right time, and those appointed to any task would be chosen for merit and not by lot or as a result of competition for office. Good men would be honoured without arousing jealousy, wicked punished without causing conflict. So we would be most likely to conduct our affairs properly, without referring matters to the common assembly nor deliberating openly, nor entrusting them to acknowledged partisans nor submitting them to the dangers of competitive ambition. We would enjoy the blessings we have, and not engage in hazardous wars or impious civil strife. For all ills are found in democracy. The more powerful men, aiming at supremacy and hiring the weaker, turn everything upside down; and such ills have been most frequent among us, and there is no other way than this to put an end to them. The proof is that for a long time now we have been at war and engaged in civil dissension. The cause is the size of our population and the importance of our concerns. The population includes men of all sorts, in race and nature, and their dispositions and their desires are manifold; and the business of state has become so enormous that it can be administered only with great difficulty.

16. The past bears witness to the truth of what I say. While there were not many of us and we did not differ in any important respect from our neighbours, we were well governed and we subdued almost the whole of Italy; but ever since we were led outside Italy and crossed over to many lands and islands and filled all the sea and the earth with our name and our power, we have enjoyed no share of anything good. First we had quarrels among factions at home and within our own walls, and then we carried this disease into the armies as well. Therefore our city, like a great merchant ship, manned with a motley throng of all races and with no pilot, has for many generations now been

wallowing and tossing here and there in a heavy sea, as though without ballast. So do not let her go on suffering the storm; you see that she is waterlogged. Do not let her be smashed on a reef, for she is rotten and will not be able to hold out any longer. But since the gods have taken pity on her and set you over her as judge and overseer, do not betray your country, in order that, as now she has revived a little thanks to you, so she may continue in safety through all time to come.

17. I think you have long been convinced that I am right in advising you to put the people under a monarchy. In that case, take on the leadership readily and eagerly, or rather do not throw it away. For we are deliberating, not whether we ought to take something, but whether we shall take care not to lose it and run risks as well. Who will spare you, if you thrust control of affairs upon the people, or even if you entrust it to someone else? For there are very many men who have been injured by you, and pretty well all of these will claim the sovereignty and none of them will be willing that you should not pay for what you have done, or survive as a rival to him. Pompey is an example; when he gave up power, he was despised and plotted against, and as a result, when he was unable to recover his power, he perished. Your father Caesar also perished when doing exactly the same thing. Marius and Sulla would certainly have suffered a similar fate, if they had not died first. Yet some say that Sulla, fearing this very event, forestalled it by doing away with himself; at any rate much of his legislation began to be repealed in his lifetime. Therefore you also must expect to find many a man who will be to you a Lepidus, many a Sertorius, a Brutus, a Cassius.

18. So, looking at these facts and reflecting on everything else involved, do not abandon yourself and your country for the sake of avoiding the appearance of having deliberately sought the office. For, firstly, even if anyone else does suspect this, such a desire is not alien to human nature and the risk is a noble one. Again, who is unaware of the necessity that obliged you to take on your present position? Therefore, if there is any complaint to be made against this necessity, one might very justly blame your father's murderers; for if they had not so unjustly and pitiably slain him, you would not have taken up arms, would not have gathered your army, would not have resisted those men themselves. That you were right and just in doing all this, no one is unaware; so, even if there has been some error, still we cannot yet safely alter anything. Therefore, for our own sake and that of the

city, let us obey fortune, which offers you sole rule. And let us be very grateful to her, in that she has not only freed us from our civil troubles but has put in your hands the ordering of the state, so that, by bestowing proper care on it, you may show to all men that it was others who stirred up these troubles and wrought the mischief, whereas you are a good man.

XII. Christians and the Emperor

One might expect, on turning to Christian writers, to find oneself in an entirely different world of thought. In fact, this is not the case. Ideas, even whole arguments, that we have already encountered in pagan writers, in particular in Hellenistic philosophy, reappear. It is even possible for a Christian writer to talk of the relation of the emperor to God in much the same terms as a Hellenistic writer used in describing the relationship he conceived of as existing between the king and the divine.

Again, some may find a surprising degree of worldliness in the views expressed. There is a popular notion that the early Christians were interested exclusively in the next world and regarded the State and all its works as irrelevant, if not positively evil. This is far from being the case. Eusebius, in the fourth century, puts forward very eloquently the view that the establishment of the principate and of peace over the Roman world (the *Pax Augusti*) was providentially arranged to synchronize with Jesus' time on earth. The supreme ruler's government held in check enemies of the faith, and the prevailing peace facilitated the dissemination of the faith by the early disciples. The monarchy becomes associated, in his thinking, with monotheism, and the multiplicity of national states suppressed by the empire, with polytheism.

Frequent from Lactantius (early fourth century A.D.) onwards is the drawing of a parallel between the sole ruler of the world and God, sole ruler of the universe. Lactantius had used this as an argument for monotheism; in the mid fourth century, part of the bitterness and heat engendered in Church disputes over the nature of the trinity stemmed from the political implications of doctrines of the single or divided nature of God; moreover, by this time, the emperor was intervening very actively in ecclesiastical affairs.

Even Augustine, whose 'City of God' is explicitly distinguished from and contrasted with all earthly states, accepts the view, found as far back as Plato and Aristotle, that the state is based on natural law, and in his writings on the Donatist controversy more than once welcomes the help of the state in defending orthodoxy against schismatics.

CHRISTIANS' LOYALTY TO THE EMPEROR

The Christian community, especially in the first two centuries of its existence, was viewed with suspicion and hostility by the rest of the Roman world. There had always been uneasiness about private societies, even trade guilds being discouraged, because it was felt that they constituted potential centres for political disaffection and disturbance. Part of the hostility directed towards the Christians was the product of ignorance and superstition, which lent credulity to tales of immorality and sinister magic practices. It is clear, however, that Christians were believed to be politically unsafe. Nero, already in the middle of the first century A.D., was able to play on such notions; we are told that he blamed Christians for the great fire at Rome. In the famous case of the examination of Christians by Pliny in Bithynia (*Letters*, 10.96 and 97), the test he sets them—that they should make offerings to statues of the gods and the emperor, and revile the name of Christ—is one that would reveal their religion, but it is evident that to Pliny, unaware of the emotional hold such a religion can exercise, contumacy is evidence of disaffection to Roman government.

Tertullian in A.D. 197 produced his *Apologeticus* as a defence, in popular style, against popular charges of atheism and black magic made against Christians. Quoted below is the section concerned particularly with the emperor and with those ceremonies and titles in particular through which, as we have seen, the special status of the individual ruler was affirmed and justified. Tertullian is far from denying that special status; in chapter 30 he asserts it very definitely. Obviously, divinization of the emperor is not a means open to Christians of asserting it. He does, however, go so far as to cite God as the source of the emperor's power. In the *Liber ad Scapulam*, chapter 2, he states even more clearly the divine *warrant* for the emperor's power: 'A Christian is no-one's enemy, far less the emperor's. Knowing him to be appointed by his own God, he must love, reverence and honour him, and wish for his welfare, along with the whole Roman empire, while time endures.'

Tertullian's *reductio ad absurdum* of the pagan religious practices is lively and amusing. Section 35 sheds a lurid light on manners in the Roman world, at the same time revealing some of the unpleasant political facts. Avidius Cassius plotted against Lucius Verus (A.D. 161–169). Pescennius Niger and Clodius Albinus tried to seize the throne on the death of Commodus (A.D. 192), the former with the aid of the Syrian legions, the latter the British. Commodus was strangled by a wrestler with whom he used to train. The occasion of the bay-tree ambush is not known. Pertinax was killed by men who broke into the palace (A.D. 193). Sigerius and Parthenius were among the murderers of Domitian (A.D. 96).

Tertullian, *Apologeticus*

29. Therefore, let it be established first that those beings to whom sacrifice is made can provide for the welfare of the emperors or anyone else; and then you may accuse us of treason, if angels or demons, in their nature the worst of spirits, work any good, if the lost can save, if the damned set free, if—and here your withers are wrung—the dead protect the living. For if they could do this, then they would first protect their own statues and images and temples, which, in my view, are actually kept safe by Caesar's soldiers who mount guard on them. Besides, I reflect that the materials of which they are made come from Caesar's mines and the entire temples stand by Caesar's favour. Finally, many gods have suffered the wrath of Caesar; and it supports my argument if they have also found him propitious when he confers some benefaction or privilege on them. Therefore, since they are in Caesar's power and are entirely his, how can they have Caesar's welfare in their power, so as to appear capable of securing it, when they more readily secure their own from Caesar? So, are we offending against the majority of the emperors in not subjecting them to their own creatures, in not making a mockery of our duty towards their welfare, which we do not believe rests in hands of lead? It is you who are irreligious, who seek it where it is not, ask it from those who cannot give it, and passing by Him in whose power it is go on to inveigh against those who know how to seek it and in knowing can also obtain it.

30. For we pray for the emperor's welfare to the eternal God, the true God, the living God, whom the emperors themselves wish to be propitious to them above all others. They know who has given them power; they know, as men, who also has given them a soul. For they realize that He alone is God, in whose power alone they are, to whom they come second, after whom they are first, before and above all the gods. This is surely so; for they are above all men, and the latter are at least alive, and stand higher than the dead. They reflect how far the power of their empire prevails, and thus they recognize God, against whom they cannot prevail, and so they know that through Him their power avails. Finally, let the emperor challenge heaven, let him carry heaven captive in his triumph, let him set guard on heaven and lay taxes on heaven! He cannot. He is great because he is lesser than heaven; for he belongs to Him, whose is heaven and all creation. The source of his being emperor is the same as of his being a man, before

he was an emperor. His power comes from the same source as his life. . . .

33. Need I say more about the reverence and dutifulness of Christians towards the emperor? We must look up to him, as the chosen one of our Lord, so that I may justly say, 'Caesar is the more ours, as appointed by our God.'

Therefore as he is mine, I strive the more effectively for his welfare, in that not only do I ask it from Him who can bestow it, or as one who deserves to have his request granted, but also because in placing the majesty of Caesar below God I commend him the more to God, to whom alone do I make him inferior; and I make him inferior only to Him, with whom I do not put him on a level. For I shall not call the emperor God, whether because I cannot lie or because I do not dare to mock him, or because he himself will not want to be called a God. Given that he is a man, then it is for man's good to yield to God. Let him be satisfied with being called emperor; this too is a distinguished title, as it is bestowed by God. He who calls him a god, denies that he is emperor; if we suppose him not to be a man, then he is not emperor. Even when he is celebrating a triumph, he is reminded, in that lofty chariot, that he is a man—for someone at his back prompts him: 'Look behind you; remember you are a man.' And certainly he rejoices the more at being so resplendent in glory that a reminder of his condition is necessary. He would be lesser if he were then called a god, because he would not be truly so called. He is greater in that he is checked from thinking himself to be a god.

34. Augustus, who shaped the imperial power, did not wish to be addressed even as 'Lord'; for this too is an appellation of God. I shall straightforwardly call the emperor 'Lord', but in the common fashion, and not when I am put under compulsion, to say 'Lord' instead of 'god'. Yet in relation to him I am free; for my lord and master is one only, God omnipotent, eternal, the same who is also the emperor's master. How can he who is father of his country be master? Yet the title expressing a fatherly affection is more pleasing than that expressing power (and one speaks rather of the fathers of households than of their masters). So far is it from being our duty (indeed it is incredible) that we should call the emperor god, with a flattery not only base but dangerous. It is as if you had one emperor and used the title of another. Would you not cause strong and implacable resentment on the part of the emperor you already had, a resentment to be dreaded also by

him whom you thus addressed? Show more reverence for God, if you wish His goodwill for the emperor. Cease to believe that another is god, and therefore cease also to address as god him who has need of God. If flattery does not blush at its own mendacity in calling such a man god, let it at least fear the ill-luck; it is a bad omen to call Caesar god before his apotheosis.

35. So, the reason Christians are 'public enemies' is because they do not speak idly or lyingly or in unconsidered terms in honour of the emperor; and because men of true religion follow the observances their conscience dictates rather than folly. A noble display of dutifulness it is, I suppose, to set out hearths and couches in public, to have street feasts, to have the city reeking like an inn, to make mud with wine, to flock in crowds to all sorts of wrong-doing, shamelessness, incitement to lust. Is this how we express public joy, through public disgrace? Are those things seemly for the festivals of the emperors which are not seemly on other days? Those who observe discipline in respect for Caesar abandon it because of Caesar, and wanton immorality will be taken for dutifulness, and an opportunity for licence set down as a religious observance. Oh, *we* deserve damnation! Why do we perform our prayers and rejoicings for the Caesars in chastity, sobriety and uprightness? Why on a day of merriment do we not shade the doorposts with laurel and impinge on day with lanterns? It is a becoming thing, when a public festival demands it, to give your home the appearance of some new brothel!

Yet I could wish that in this observance also of a second majesty, concerning which we Christians are arraigned for a second sacrilege through not celebrating with you the festivals of the Caesars in a way which is allowed neither by modesty nor decency nor chastity, but commends itself as an opportunity for wantonness rather than by any worthy consideration—I could wish to make plain your fidelity and truth—it may be that in that respect too those who will not consider us as Romans, but enemies of the Caesars, may be found worse than the Christians.

I charge the Quirites themselves, the very native population of the seven hills—does that Roman tongue spare any Caesar of its own? The Tiber bears witness and the schools of beasts. If nature had put over our breasts a transparent covering, so that one could look inside, on whose heart would there not appear the scene of another, and yet another, new Caesar presiding over the distribution of largesse, at the very time when they are calling, 'May Jupiter take from our years and add to thine.' The Christian is as incapable of uttering this as of cherishing hopes of a new Caesar. 'These are the mob', you say. That may be, but still they are Roman, and no one is more vocal in denouncing Christians than the mob. Of course, all the other orders, as their status requires, are sincere in *their* observances. There is no breath of hostility from the Senate itself, from the knights, from the army, from the very palace. Then where did men like Cassius come from, and Niger and Albinus? Or those who ambushed Caesar between two bay trees? Or those who practised wrestling, to strangle him? Or those who burst into the palace in arms, bolder than all the Sigerii and Parthenii? If I am not mistaken, all these come from the Romans, that is, non-Christians. Yet all of these, right up to the very time of their impious outbreak, were sacrificing for the welfare of the emperor and swearing by his genius, both publicly and in private, and even gave the Christians the label of public enemies. Take also those who every day now are revealed as associates or supporters of the wicked faction, the gleanings of the vineyard left after the harvest of the parricides— with what fresh and thickly-branching laurels they adorned their doorposts, with what high and bright lanterns they made their porches smoky, with what ostentatiously magnificent couches they divided the Forum amongst them, not in order to join in the public rejoicing but to utter their own prayers during another's ceremonial and to inaugurate the form and image of their hopes by changing in their hearts the name of the emperor. The same is done by those who inquire about Caesar's life from astrologers and divines and augurs and magi—arts which were revealed by the fallen angels and banned by God, and which Christians do not employ even for their own sakes. Who need inquire after the welfare of Caesar, save him who meditates or desires some harm to it, or sustains hopes of benefiting from it? For inquiry is not made about masters in the same spirit as about loved ones; the one is prompted by the concern of kinship, the other of slavery.

A CHRISTIAN EULOGY OF THE EMPEROR

Constantine, the first Christian emperor, was converted to Christianity in or about A.D. 312. The Church in the Eastern Empire was disposed to concur in the way in which the emperor proceeded, for his own motives, to approximate and even identify the interests of church and state; the protection and support of the state would be of obvious value in furthering the dissemination of the true faith.

Eusebius, bishop of Caesarea from A.D. 314, as we have seen, represented the Roman empire as providentially instituted for the furtherance of Christianity. He is notable also in having been among the first to put forward a theoretical justification of rule by a sole emperor in which Hellenistic political philosophy was thoroughly assimilated to Christian premises.

His 'Tricennial Oration' was a speech delivered in A.D. 335 on the occasion of the celebration of the emperor's thirtieth year of rule. Chapters 2 and 3 in particular should be compared closely with the extract given earlier from Ecphantus' treatise on kingship. All the elements are there, including the mediating and guiding Logos (now, of course, identified with the Son). However, the God of Eusebius is not the vaguely-conceived, almost abstract divinity of Greek philosophy, but a divine person, taking an active and commanding interest in the ordering of earthly affairs. The political implications for monarchy in general are obvious, and are quite clearly stated in chapter 3.

There is, however, one very important difference. Eusebius does not extend to the emperor the Hellenistic definition of the monarch as 'animate law'—that is applied elsewhere. Can we draw conclusions from this about the Church's likely attitude in the event of a clash of interests with the Emperor?

For most practical purposes, however, the Church is putting behind the imperial rule the backing of a very powerful sanction indeed.

Chapter 5 is an elaborate restatement of a traditional theme—the description of a virtuous man, and the king eulogized in particular as an example. Again, many motifs familiar from pagan thought appear, with very slight alteration, to fit Christian doctrine. Notice that the Christian writer finds a rationalization for the worldly pomp and display of an imperial court. Here, as in the sun-symbolism of chapter 3, we find foreshadowed the formal visible elaboration of the Byzantine imperial court, just as the political ideas lay the foundations for Byzantine political structure.

Eusebius, *Tricennial Oration*

2. The only-begotten Word of God rules with the Father, from ages without beginning to time everlasting and without end; and our emperor is dear to Him, and derives the source of imperial authority from

above; and strong in the power of the sacred title, he has ruled for many circling years over things on earth. Moreover the Saviour of all orders the whole heaven and the universe and the kingdom above consistently with the Father's will; and our emperor, dear to Him, brings to the only-begotten and Saviour Word all those on the earth who are subject to him and renders them fit for the same (heavenly) kingdom. And that common Saviour of all by his invisible and divine power drives far off those rebel powers such as once flew about in the air above our earth and took a grip on men's souls—like a good shepherd driving wild beasts far from his flock; and the emperor, dear to Him, by divine aid is honoured with many trophies won from his enemies, and subjecting by right of war the manifest enemies of the truth he chastens them. The Word, subsisting before the world and Saviour of all, bestows on His devout the seeds of reason and salvation, renders them rational and possessing knowledge of the kingdom of the Father; while the emperor, dear to Him, like an interpreter of the Word of God, summons the whole human race to knowledge of the supreme Ruler, crying out in the hearing of all and proclaiming with loud voice the laws of true piety and of truth to all upon the earth. The Saviour of all opens the gates of the kingdom of the Father to those who go thither from here; and the emperor, following the example of the supreme Ruler, clears away all taint of godless error from the earthly kingdom, and summons all the choirs of holy and pious men into the royal mansions, taking forethought as it were for the preservation of that vessel with all its crew, piloted by him. Alone of all those who have ever governed the Roman empire, he has been honoured by God, the all-high King, with three full decades of reign, and he celebrates this festival not, as in old time, with earthly spirits or apparitions of demons to startle the populace, nor with the deceits and frauds of godless men, but gives honour to God Himself, who has honoured him, in consciousness of the blessings conferred upon him. He honours God not in the old ways, staining the royal halls with blood and filth, nor placating earthly demons with fire and smoke and holocausts of victims, but consecrating to the very King of all the most dear and acceptable sacrifice, that is, his own royal soul and mind most truly fitted for the service of God. For this offering alone is pleasing to God, and this our king has learned to make without fire and blood, in the pure reasonings of his mind. He strengthens his piety by the truthful doctrines in his mind; he adorns the praises of God with a

magnificent oration and emulates in his kingly actions the kindness of
God, devoting himself entirely to Him, and offering a mighty offering,
himself, as the first-fruits of the world entrusted to him. This then is
the noble sacrificial victim which the emperor offers on behalf of all,
sacrificing like a good shepherd, not 'slaying glorious hecatombs of
first-born lambs', but bringing to the knowledge and worship of God
those rational creatures who are his flock.

3. God, delighting in such a sacrifice, gladly welcoming the offering
and well-pleased with the priest who made it in so august and seemly
a fashion, adds long cycles of years to his rule, returning with an
increase of benefactions the emperor's acts of piety towards Him. He
allows each festival to be celebrated with the empire in a state of peace,
and as each decennial celebration comes round He advances one of the
emperor's children to a share in the rule. First, him who bears his
father's name He proclaimed a partner in the royal lot at the first
decennial term of the rule, the second, who was next in time, at the
second, and the third likewise at the third festival which we now celebrate.

Now the fourth term has begun to pass, and as the time of his
reign is prolonged Constantine wishes to extend the imperial authority
through the participation of more of the family and the proclamation
of Caesars, and fulfils the predictions of the divine prophets, by whom
long since it was uttered: 'The saints of the most High shall take the
kingdom' (Dan. 7.18). So, as God, the ruler of all, bestows time and
children upon the dearly-loved king, he makes his rule over the peoples
of the earth strong and flourishing, as though it had only just begun to
bloom. And He Himself achieves for him this celebration, making him
victorious over all foes and enemies, and displaying him to all upon the
earth as an example of true piety. The emperor sheds light upon the
dwellers in the most remote places, like the light of the sun, through
the presence of the Caesars like rays sent forth from himself. And so
on us, whose lot it is to live in the East, he bestows a son worthy of
himself, and his other son he sends to another portion of mankind, and
another elsewhere, like bright reflectors of the light shed forth from
himself. Then joining the four stalwart Caesars like four steeds to one
imperial carriage, steering them with the reins of divine harmony and
unanimity, riding over all the earth that the sun surveys, he is present
everywhere and inspects all things.

Then, adorned with an image of the divine authority, fixing his eyes above, he steers and directs men below according to that divine pattern [*idea*], strengthened by imitation of the supreme monarchy. For this the King of all things has bestowed upon men alone of all creatures that inhabit the earth; for He is the law of kingly power, and decrees that all shall be subject to the rule of one; and monarchy surpasses all systems and constitutions. The rule of the many, sharing power equally, which is opposite to this, should more properly be called anarchy and civil discord. Therefore there is but one God, not two or three or more, for polytheism is the negation of God; and there is one king, one royal Word and law, not enunciated in words and syllables nor written and engraved, to be corrupted by time, but the living and substantive word of God, which enjoins the kingdom of the Father upon all who are beneath him and come after him. Heavenly hosts attend him, and tens of thousands of the ministering angels of God, the multitudes of the hosts above and of the unseen spirits of heaven, who look after the order of the world. All these are led by the kingly Word, as it were by the regent of a mighty king. This the oracles of the sacred writers call the general-in-chief, the high priest, prophet of the Father and angel of His mighty counsel, radiance of the light of the Father, only-begotten Son and countless other such titles. And in establishing this living Word, law and wisdom and fulness of all blessing, the Begetter has given to all under his rule the greatest good gift; and the Word, passing through all things and journeying everywhere, unfolding the bounties of the Father unstintingly to all, even unto the rational creatures upon the earth, affords a representation of the sovereign potency, providing with divine powers the soul of man made after His image. Whence the soul of man participates also in other virtues, flowing from the same heavenly source; for God alone is wise, who also alone is God; and likewise He alone is by nature good, and alone is mighty in strength; and he begets justice and is the father of reason and wisdom, the fount of light and life, dispenser of truth and virtue and author of kingly rule and of all command and power . . .

5. Of which hope [sc. of Heaven] our emperor, dear to God, already partakes here on earth. God has adorned him with native virtues and from God he has received the out-pourings of divine favour in his soul. He is rational, from that universal reason, wise through participation in divine wisdom, temperate from the pattern of temperance and valiant from participation in the heavenly might. So he might truly

be called king, in that he has his soul fashioned by kingly virtues in the likeness of that kingdom yonder.

But the man who is alien to all this, and who denies the King of the universe and does not acknowledge the heavenly Father of souls; who does not clothe himself in the adornment becoming a king but covers his soul in unsightliness and disgrace, putting in the place of royal clemency the rage of a wild beast, the incurable poison of wickedness in place of a generous disposition, stupidity in place of sense and instead of reason and wisdom the unseemliest of all the vices, unreason, from which, as though from a bitter draught, there ensue harmful growths, a life intemperate and past redemption, greed, slaughter, rebellion against God, impiety—the man given up to these vices, though he may be thought for the time being to dominate by tyrannical might, will never truly be called a king. How could he present a likeness of the true monarchy when his soul is stamped with countless false images of demons? How could he rule and be lord of all, when he has drawn upon himself countless grievous masters, and is the slave of foul pleasure, the slave of unrestrained lusting after women, the slave of unjustly-got wealth, the slave of wrath and anger, the slave of fear and alarms, the slave of murderous demons, the slave of spirits that destroy the soul?

Therefore let him alone be proclaimed to us as emperor, with the witness of truth, who is dear to God, the Lord of all, who alone is free, or rather who is truly master, being above desire for money, superior to lust for women, victorious even over natural pleasures, in command of wrath and anger, not subject to them. He truly is emperor, bearing a title corresponding to his acts; truly victor as he has conquered the feelings that cause human nature to fall. He is fashioned in the likeness of the divine pattern of the supreme sovereign, and in his mind, as in a mirror, reflects the beams of the virtues that come from it, by which he is rendered temperate, good, just, brave, pious and devout. Our emperor alone is truly a philosopher—he knows himself, and he knows that all the fortune that attends him comes from outside himself, or rather from heaven. He manifests the august title of monarchic power by the special mantle he wears, and he alone is deservedly clad in the royal purple that befits him.

He is king, who night and day calls upon the heavenly Father, who implores His aid in his prayers, who reaches out towards the heavenly kingdom. He knows that the things of this world cannot compare with God, the universal king, and that mortals perish and are like rivers that flow and pass away, and he longs for the imperishable and incorporeal kingdom of God and prays to attain it, through the loftiness of his mind raising his thoughts above the vault of heaven and stricken with an ineffable longing for the lights that are there, in comparison with which he thinks that those things that are esteemed in this life are but darkness. For rule over men, in this mortal and transitory life, he sees is but a slight and brief dominion, not much superior to the charge of goatherds or shepherds or herdsmen, but rather more toilsome and with a less tractable flock. The acclamations of the populace and the utterances of flatterers he regards as an annoyance rather than a source of pleasure, through the steadfastness of his character and the true discipline of his soul. When he looks at the hordes of his subjects, the countless soldiers, the heavy and light infantry and cavalry who are his slaves and hearken to him, he is not impressed; he is not puffed up by ruling over these, but turns his thought inward upon himself and sees in himself that nature that is common to all. The garment interwoven with gold and patterned with many-coloured flowers, the imperial purple and the diadem itself, he laughs at, when he sees the multitude awe-struck by them and gazing at this show like children staring at a hobgoblin. He himself has no such emotion, because of his knowledge of the divine; for the cloak he wraps himself in is the soul, and it is patterned with temperance and justice, piety and all the other virtues, which is the adornment truly becoming to a king. Moreover, the wealth so strongly desired by the multitude, that is gold and silver and such stones as are admired, he knows to be really just useless stones and rubbish, seeing them in their true nature, and knowing that they can do nothing to avert evils. What use are they for relieving sickness or averting death? None the less, although he knows this well, the use of them for the showy adornment of his subjects leaves him unmoved, and he smiles at the witlessness of those who, in their simplicity, admire such things. As to drunkenness and insobriety, and excessively elaborate dishes, such as are usual with gluttons, he refrains from them all, thinking that such things suit others, but not him; for he is convinced that they do great harm, and they darken the intellect.

For all these reasons, the emperor, educated in divine wisdom and lofty in spirit, strives towards things greater than this present life, calling upon the heavenly Father and longing for His kingdom, acting with devoutness in all things and setting forth to all those ruled by him, as a good teacher to his pupils, the divine knowledge of the supreme King.

THE DEIFICATION OF EMPERORS: A FOURTH-CENTURY CHRISTIAN VIEW

Athanasius, a deacon at the time of the Council of Nicaea in A.D. 325, made bishop of Alexandria in A.D. 328 and subsequently deposed and exiled five times in the course of his bitter struggle against the defenders of the Arian heresy, wrote A.D. c. 318–320, when he was in his early twenties, a work, *Against the Heathen*, in which he mounted a vigorousa ttack against pagan religion. This was bound to include some reference to the deification of emperors and the imperial cult.

The polemic is not addressed to the emperor. It is hard to determine how far Constantine went in suppressing pagan worship. Some temples were despoiled of their more valuable treasures, but there does not seem (despite the assertions of Eusebius) to have been any attempt to enforce a general prohibition on pagan worship. Indeed, it is doubtful whether it could have been enforced, since in the Roman world Christians were very much in the minority, and in particular in the upper classes on whom the emperor depended for his official staff. As far as the imperial cult was concerned, the emperor seems to have made some effort to prevent specifically religious acts, such as sacrifice, but tolerated priesthoods for the organization of theatrical and similar spectacles in honour of the imperial house. To have swept away an institution of such social and political value would certainly have brought considerable unpopularity.

Athanasius' argument is in general on a more lofty philosophical plane than that of Tertullian, but comparison between the two is interesting. It could perhaps be said that the basic difference between the two is in the posture taken. Tertullian is on the defensive, while Athanasius confidently takes the offensive.

Athanasius, *Against the Heathen*

7. It is now necessary to say how men descended to the madness of idol-worship, so that you may know that the invention of idols did not arise from good but from evil; for something whose origin is evil should not be judged good in any respect, as it is utterly bad.

8. The soul of man was not satisfied with having devised wickedness,

but gradually began to impel itself towards the worse. It had learned the diversity of pleasures, and began to live in forgetfulness of everything to do with the gods. It took pleasure in the sensations of the body, and in things present only, attending to the manifest aspects of these, and considered that nothing existed save what could be perceived and that only what was temporal and corporeal was good. So it is perverted and forgets that it was made in the image of the good God and no longer sees, by the faculty in itself, God, the Word, in whose likeness it was created. Going outside itself, it devises and fashions what does not exist; for it hides away in the entanglements of physical desires that mirror, as one may call it, within itself through which alone it was able to see the image of the Father; and it no longer sees those things which the soul should apprehend. It is carried hither and thither and sees only those things which fall within the range of sensation. Hence it is burdened with all the fleshly desires and harassed by the opinions relating to them, and in consequence the God which it forgot in its thoughts it fashions in the corporeal and visible world, giving the appellation of 'god' to visible things and esteems only those things which it wants, and sees as pleasant.

So, then, the foremost cause of idolatry is wickedness; for as men learned to devise for themselves wickedness which did not exist, so likewise they fashioned for themselves gods which did not exist. It is as if a man were to be immersed in a deep pool, so that he no longer saw the light or those things which are visible in the light, because his eyes were turned downwards and because of the water that overwhelmed him; seeing only what was in the depths, they would think nothing else existed save these and that these visible objects were the chief objects in the universe. So men of old in their folly were immersed in the desires and illusions of the flesh, and forgetting the thought and belief in God, using a blurred reasoning, or rather irrationality, they made out visible objects to be gods, and esteemed the creation rather than the Creator, and honoured as divine the works of God rather than their author and artifex, the Lord God. Now with the people in the example given, who are immersed in the depths, the deeper they progress the more they rush into darkness and deeper abysses; this is what has happened to mankind. For they have not embraced simple idolatry and stopped at those idols with which they began. The longer the time they have spent in their first error, the more they have devised fresh superstitions for themselves. They have not been sated with the first wickedness, but filled themselves again with others, proceeding in abominations and extending ever further their blasphemy. To this the holy Scripture testifies, saying: 'When the wicked cometh, then cometh also contempt and with ignominy reproach.' (Prov. 18. 3.)

9. For as soon as man's mind turned away from God, men went downwards in their thoughts and reasoning, and first gave the honour due to God to the sky, the sun, the moon and the stars, thinking not only that they were gods, but that they were the creators of everything else. Then, descending still further in their darkened reasonings, they gave the appellation of gods to the aether and the air and the things in the air.

Advancing in evil, they hymned as gods the elements, the prime bases composing physical bodies, namely the hot and the cold, the wet and the dry. And as those who fall utterly down creep around on the earth, in the mud, like land-snails, so the most impious of men, when they had fallen right down away from the very notion of God, finally made gods of men and the shapes of men, both men living and men after death. They even pondered and devised worse things— they applied the divine and transcendent name of god to stones and timbers and to reptiles, both aquatic and terrestrial, and to wild brute beasts, bestowing on them all the honour due to God and shunning the true and real God, Father of Christ. Would that the boldness of these foolish men had stopped there, and that they had not gone further and embroiled themselves still deeper in impiety. For some of them were so utterly fallen in mind and darkened in intellect that they even imagined for themselves, and made gods of, things that did not exist at all, and were nowhere to be seen in creation. For they mingle rational beings with brutes, twining together things dissimilar in nature, and devotedly worship them as gods; examples are the Egyptian gods with the heads of dogs and snakes and donkeys, and the Libyan ram-headed Ammon. Others have separated off parts of the body, the head, shoulder, hand, foot and placed each among the gods and given them divine honours, as though they were not satisfied with worshipping the whole body.

Others, extending impiety further, as the excuse for their inventions and their wickedness, deified and adored pleasure and desire, like their Eros and Aphrodite in Paros. Some of them, as though vying in seeking the worse, dared to set among the gods their own rulers or their children, either because they honoured their rulers, or because they feared a tyrant. Such are the notorious Zeus in Crete and Hermes in Arcadia, Dionysus among the Indians, and among the Egyptians Isis, Osiris and Horus, and in our times Antinous, the boy favourite of Hadrian, the Roman ruler, whom men worshipped although they knew he was a man, and not an honourable man but one full of licentiousness, because of their fear of their ruler. For when Hadrian was staying in Egypt and the servant of his pleasure, Antinous, died, Hadrian ordered him to be worshipped. Thus he showed that he loved the boy even after his death, and so provided cause of reproach against himself and at the same time gave glaring evidence against all idolatry, that it was devised by men no otherwise than to satisfy the desire of those who manufactured gods. This the wisdom of God testifies in these words: 'The beginning of fornication is the invention of idols.' (Wis. 14.12.)

Do not marvel, nor think what is said to be beyond belief, since not long ago (and perhaps it is still so), the Senate of Rome decreed that their emperors whom they had ruling them from the beginning, either all of them or those whom they pleased and thought fit, were among the gods, and ordered that they should be worshipped as gods. For those whom they hate they admit are enemies by nature, and call them men; those with whom they are pleased, they order to be worshipped because of their virtue, as though they had it in their power to make gods, in spite of being men themselves and not denying that they are mortal. But since they make gods they themselves ought to be gods. For the maker ought to be better than what is made and the judge must necessarily rule over what is judged; and he who gives something must necessarily give what he himself has, just as, of course, every king bestows what he has, and is greater and better than those who receive. So if they decree to be gods those whom they wish, then they themselves ought first to be gods. But this is the remarkable thing, that since they themselves die as men they prove that their own vote on the men whom they made gods was false.

10. This is not a new custom, nor one that began with the Roman Senate. It originated and was practised long before for the invention of idols. Those who were of old celebrated as gods among the Greeks, Zeus, Poseidon, Apollo, Hephaestus, Hermes, and among women Hera, Demeter, Athene, Artemis, it was decided were to be named gods by the decrees of Theseus which are related in the history of the

Greeks. So, those who decreed, having died as men, are mourned; and those for whom they decreed divinity are worshipped as gods. Incredible perversity and madness! They know the man who decreed that these were gods, yet they honour those to whom he decreed divinity rather than himself. If only their idolatry had stopped at men and had not applied the title of divinity to women also. For even women, whom it is not safe to admit to deliberations on public matters, even them they worship and revere with divine honours, as for instance those deified by the decrees of Theseus already mentioned, and among the Egyptians Isis and the Maiden and the Goddess of Youth and among others Aphrodite—for the names of the rest I do not think it seemly even to mention as they are mere nonsense. Many men, not only in ancient times but in our own times also, after losing their dearest ones, their brother, relatives and wives, and many women too, who have lost their husbands (all of whom nature revealed were mortal men), because of their extreme grief for them had their pictures painted and devised sacrificial rites and consecrated them. So people later because of their painted images and the fame of the craftsman, revered them as gods, acting quite contrary to nature.

CHURCH AND STATE

During the reign of Constantine a close relationship developed between Church and Emperor, based essentially on mutual advantage and so obscuring the fundamentally different outlook of the two. Constantine's conversion seems to have been at least in part prudential; in a letter of the year of his conversion he says that 'annulment of the worship in which the highest reverence of the most holy heavenly power is maintained' (presumably a reference to the great persecution of the Christian church at the end of Diocletian's reign) had brought the greatest dangers to the empire, while its revival had restored peace and prosperity; the Christian God was evidently a very powerful one. He also doubtless appreciated the strength of the loyalty within the Christian church, and wished to secure this loyalty for his empire. The Church for its part welcomed the protection now afforded them. They began and continued repeatedly to refer their disputes to him. The reign was prolific in controversy within the church—especially the Donatist, Melitian and Arian disputes. Constantine established a precedent by convening the first general council of the whole church, at Nicaea in A.D. 325, at which he himself presided. It came to be accepted that it was the emperor's right to convene and direct church councils and that only the decisions of those councils actually convened by him could be regarded as valid. Even when he began to depose and exile individual bishops and to impose penalties on dissenting sects on his authority, the church acquiesced; and indeed, in terms of the kind of theory of monarchy we have seen in Eusebius' address, was it not bound to do so? Constantine himself may have seen nothing untoward in these proceedings; in the pagan empire, it had been part of the function of the emperor, as earlier it had of the chief Republican magistrates, to manage the state's relations with its gods. In the Christian church hitherto, however, there was no such tradition; the church itself determined on the basis of the scriptures what best pleased God.

So long as the intervention of the emperor was on the side of orthodoxy, his *de facto* function as supreme judge in Church matters was not merely accepted but gained the authority of usage. In A.D. 351, however, the emperor Constantius declared in favour of the Arians, and proceeded to attempt to impose their view of the Trinity throughout the church. Logically Arianism accorded better than the orthodox view of the divided Trinity with the highly-developed Hellenistic-based theory of a single monarchy on earth as a parallel to, and mirror of, the single divine monarchy of God. Whether Constantius came to put a political interpretation on the orthodox divided Trinity or not, the church preferred to abandon the precise parallel between earth and heaven sooner than accept the heretical Arian view.

The result was a direct challenge to the doctrine, operative for so long subsequently in the Byzantine Empire and in the West later after the Reformation, and known to later ages as 'Caesaropapism'—the view of the king as not only head of state but head of the church.

Athanasius, who in earlier writings (e.g. parts of *Against the Heathen*) had spoken in much the same terms as Eusebius, in the *History of the Arians* (a pamphlet published anonymously in A.D. 358 and sent to the monks in Egypt with strict instructions not to allow copies to be made) bitterly attacks the emperor for his support of the Arians. The sacerdotal character of the emperor is challenged (chapter 44):

Remember you are a mortal man. Fear the day of judgment and keep yourself pure against that day. Do not involve yourself in church matters, nor give us orders on these matters, but rather be informed on them by us. God has put in your hands the *imperium* (*basileia*); to us He entrusted the church. . . . As it is not permitted to us to rule the world, neither is it yours to wield the censer.

The passage quoted below comes from Athanasius' account of events at the Milan Synod of A.D. 355. The tone is highly emotional. One may ask, however, whether either Constantius acted in an utterly authoritarian way, or Athanasius himself is utterly rejecting all royal intervention. The passage contains more than one indication that the emperor stopped short of attempting to force his opinions on the bishops.

As for Athanasius' attitude, do his words convey a direct denial of the emperor's right to intervene at all in ecclesiastical matters, or does he envisage rather a co-operation between church and state with the emperor providing protection and advice and acting in some sort of accepted executive capacity? One should perhaps remember the anxiety of Athanasius to ensure that the *History of the Arians* should remain strictly private and limited in circulation.

Athanasius, *History of the Arians*

32. These were the actions of the emissaries of the Palace. Those remarkable men, relying on their support from the emperor, set to work earnestly. They summoned some of the bishops to the emperor, and deceived others by means of letters and invented charges against them, with the intention that the former would shrink in the presence of Constantine, and the others, in fear of the emissaries and the threats of false information against them, would put aside their correct and devout opinion. In this way the emperor forced such a multitude of bishops—some by threats, others by promises—to say: 'We have no further communion with Athanasius.' For those who went to him were not admitted into his presence or given any kind treatment or even allowed to leave their abodes until they either signed, or refused and were driven into exile. This he did because he observed that the heresy was hated by all; and so for this reason especially he obliged so many to count themselves along with the few. The latter made efforts to build up a great mass of names, both in order to create ill-will against the bishop and to put a fair face on the impiety of Arius, which had the support of Constantine, who thought that he could pervert the truth, as he did men. He did not know and had not read that the Sadducees and the men of Herod, with the aid of the Pharisees, had not availed to conceal the truth but rather because of that it shines more brilliantly every day; and they, even though they cried, 'We have no king but Caesar' (John 19.19), and obtained the judgment of Pilate, none the less were deserted and expected to be left in utter ignominy, all but stripped, like the partridge (cf. Jerem. 12.11), when they saw their patron dead.

33. But if it was unseemly for some of the bishops to change their opinions for fear of such things, still more unseemly was it, and a sign of men who had not confidence in their own beliefs, to use violence and compel the unwilling. So the devil when he has no truth, takes to axe and hammer and breaks down the doors (cf. Ps. 74.6) of those who receive him. But so kind is the Saviour that He teaches: 'If any man will come after me' (Matt. 16.24), and 'He who wishes to be my disciple', and when He goes to anyone He does no violence, but rather knocks and says: 'Open to me, my sister, my love' (Song 5.2). And when they open He enters, but if they shrink and will not, He goes away. For truth is proclaimed not with swords and javelins or by means of soldiers but by persuasion and advising. Now, how can there be persuasion, when there is fear of the emperor? Or advice, when the man who opposes suffers in the end exile and death? Indeed David, though he was a king, and had his enemy in his hands, when his soldiers wished to kill his enemy, prevented it, not by use of his power but, as the Scripture says (I Sam. 24.7), David persuaded his men in words and did not allow them to take up Saul and kill him. But this one, who lacks the Word, uses his power and does violence to all, so that he may be revealed to all, that he has wisdom not of God but of man, and that those who follow the view of Arius truly do not have any king save Caesar—for it is through him that the opponents of Christ accomplish whatever they wish. Whereas they think that thanks to him they conspire against many, they do not realize that they have made many confess the faith, among whom are the men who now have made the clear profession, those devout men and good bishops, Paulinus bishop of Trèves, the metropolis of the Gauls, Lucifer, bishop of the metropolis of Sardinia, Eusebius of Vercelli in Italy, and Dionysius of Milan, which is the metropolis of Italy. For the emperor summoned them and ordered them to subscribe against Athanasius, and communicate with the heretics. When they were amazed at this strange behaviour and said that this was not the ecclesiastical canon, he at once said: 'What I will, you are to consider as canon; for the bishops of Syria accepted it when I spoke thus. So obey, or you too will be exiled.'

34. Hearing this, the bishops, greatly amazed and stretching out their hands to God, spoke frankly to the man, and informed him that his kingdom was not his own, but God's, who gave it, and they bade him fear God, lest it should suddenly be taken away. They threatened him

with the day of judgment and advised him not to destroy the authority of the Church, nor to mingle the Roman empire with the statutes of the Church, nor to bring the Arian heresy into the church of God. But he did not listen, nor would he allow them to say any more, but rather threatened them and drew a sword against them and ordered some of them to be led away. Then, like Pharaoh, he changed his mind. So these saintly men, shaking the dust from them and looking up to God, were not frightened by the threat of the king, nor did the drawn sword induce them to betrayal, but they accepted exile as part of the service of their ministry.

THE CHURCH OVER ALL

Augustine's *City of God* (*c.* A.D. 413–416) is, as it were, the founding document of a tradition of political thought which developed in the Western Empire with very different results, for relations between church and state, from the Eastern Empire. It would be impossible to reproduce the entire work here—its length would fill several volumes, and much of the exposition is not relevant to our theme. An attempt has been made to select a few of the more salient passages relating (*a*) to the position of the emperor, and (*b*) to the church's attitude to the state.

Augustine, as said earlier, agreed with the view that the state (that is, the earthly state) was based on natural law and therefore was not necessarily and in its nature bad (see, e.g. 19.17) and that Christians had a duty to obey their earthly rulers, and could also welcome their help against enemies. This seems to be his general opinion, and the definition of the state which he regards as the more correct, although in 19.21 he seems to adopt a different view: 'without justice, there can be no state . . . where there is no justice there can be no gathering of men united in fellowship by agreement on what is right, and therefore no people, according to the definition of Scipio or Cicero (*de Re Publica*); and if no people, then no people's state (*res publica*) but merely a mob, not worthy of the name of people.'

The duty of obedience to earthly rulers, however, must be both limited in scope and contingent upon the fulfilment of certain conditions. This is perhaps most overtly stated at the end of 19.17, although it is implicit in Augustine's account of the origins and nature of his two kinds of state, the earthly and the heavenly. Would his argument, if pursued further, lead to the conclusion that the Church should have authority over the temporal government?

His comments on the emperors are very different in tone from those of the Eastern divines already quoted. In subsequent generations, successive barbarian invasions made Rome and Italy, and the Western Empire, increasingly isolated from the East. It was Augustine's thought that most strongly influenced the development of political thought in the West, while the East remained under the influence of a tradition ultimately stemming from the ancient Hellenistic monarchies. The 'special relationship' between God and the emperor is little in evidence in Augustine (although even he perhaps has still a trace of the traditional deference in his account of the career of Theodosius, divine miracle included). Kings, says Augustine, may be good or bad, for 'God bestows earthly kingship on both good and bad, not at random and as it were by chance (for he is God, not Fortune), but according to the secret ordination of circumstances and times hidden from us but known to Him' (4.33).

In the Eastern world, the 'cult of the personality' of the monarch flourished, aided and abetted by the church; in the West, the Church was its constant rival and alleged superior, at least until the Reformation.

Augustine, *The City of God*

(a) *The Emperors*
5.24. *The happiness of Christian emperors and how true it is*

We call certain Christian emperors happy, not because they have had a long reign, or died peacefully and left sons to rule, or conquered the enemies of the state, or been able to prepare against and subdue disaffected citizens rising against them. Such boons, or consolations in this troubled life, have been achieved also by some of the worshippers of demons, who, unlike these, do not belong to the kingdom of God; and this came to pass through the mercy of God, so that those who believe in Him will not look to him for these things, as though they were the supreme good. We call them happy if their rule is just, if, amid the utterances of those who pay them extravagant honours and the fawning of those who greet them with excessive humility, they are not puffed up but remember they are men; if they make their power a handmaid to the majesty of God, to extend His worship as widely as possible; if they fear God, love Him and worship Him; if they love more that kingdom in which they do not fear to have partners; if they are slow to avenge and readily forgive, if that vengeance is exercised through the necessity of controlling and preserving the state and not to satisfy hatreds arising from private enmities, if that leniency is shown not in order to leave wickedness unpunished but in hope of reformation; if the harsh judgments they are so often obliged to make are balanced by mercifulness and generosity in doing good; if they are all the more severe in checking extravagance because they could indulge in it freely; if they prefer to exercise rule over their evil desires rather than over any number of nations; and if they do all this not from a passionate desire for empty glory but out of love for eternal felicity; if, for their own sins, they do not neglect to make to their own true God the offering of humility and mercy and prayer.

Such Christian emperors we say are happy—for the moment, in hope, later in reality, when that which we await arrives.

5.25. *The prosperity God bestowed on Constantine, a Christian emperor*

God did not wish that men, who believe He should be worshipped for the sake of eternal life, should think that no one can attain the loftiest heights of earthly rule save by praying to demons, as though these spirits availed greatly in such matters. Therefore upon Constantine, who did not pray to demons but worshipped the true God, He bestowed such worldly blessings as none would dare to pray for. He allowed him to found a city allied to the Roman empire, as it were the daughter of Rome herself, but without a single temple or statue of the demons. He reigned a long time, he held and defended the entire Roman world as sole Augustus; in the conduct and waging of wars he was most victorious, in oppressing tyrants uniformly successful. He died at a great age, of illness and old age, and left sons to rule.

But so that no emperors should be Christian simply in order to earn the fortune of Constantine (since the reason for which each man should be a Christian is eternal life), God carried off Jovian much quicker than Julian; he allowed Gratian to be killed by a tyrant's sword, though his fate was far milder than that of the great Pompey, worshipper of the Roman so-called gods. For Pompey was not able to be avenged by Cato, whom he had left as, in a fashion, his heir to the civil war; Gratian, however—though a devout soul needs no such comforts—was avenged by Theodosius, whom he had taken to share in his rule, doing so although he had a younger brother of his own, because he was more eager for reliable associates than for excessive power.

5.26. The faith and devoutness of Theodosius Augustus

Wherefore, not only did Theodosius maintain the loyalty he owed to Gratian during the latter's life, but after his death when his young brother Valentinian was driven by his murderer Maximus into Theodosius' own part of the empire, as a Christian he received the boy as his ward and looked after him with a father's care, although he could easily have made away with him, destitute as he was of all help, if he had burned with a lust to extend his rule rather than with love of doing good. So he received the boy, maintaining his imperial status, and consoled him with kindness and favour. Then, when that success made Maximus formidable, Theodosius was not driven by the pressure of his anxieties to sacrilegious and unlawful inquiries. He sent to John, who was established as a hermit in Egypt, whom he had learned from growing repute to be the servant of God endowed with the spirit of prophecy, and he received from him news of most sure victory. Then, when he had done away with the tyrant Maximus, he restored the boy Valentinian to his own part of the empire, from which he had been put to flight, with all compassion and respect.

Valentinian presently perished, either by treachery or through some other chance or circumstance. He obtained another prophetic response, and in the assurance of faith he suppressed another tyrant Eugenius, who had been unlawfully appointed in the place of Valentinian; and against the stalwart army of Eugenius he fought rather with prayers than with blows. Soldiers who were there told me that the weapons they were throwing were wrenched out of their hands—for a strong wind came from Theodosius' side against his opponents and not only carried off speedily whatever they were throwing against Theodosius' men but even turned their own weapons back against themselves. So the poet Claudian, although he is aloof from the name of Christ, said in his praise:

'Oh, too dearly beloved of God, for whom Aeolus sends forth armed tempests from the caverns, for whom the air fights and the winds swear allegiance and come to join the ranks.'

Being victorious, then, as he had believed and foretold, he took down the statues of Jupiter which, to oppose him, had been 'consecrated' by some pagan rites or other and set up in the Alps. Their thunderbolts were made of gold, and some scouts said in joke (such jesting being permitted) that they would not mind being blasted by such bolts. He was amused and kindly gave them the bolts. The sons of his enemies, who had been swept away, not by his command but by the fury of battle, took refuge in a church, although they were not yet Christians. He took this opportunity to have them become Christians and loved them with Christian charity, not depriving them of their property and elevating their status. He allowed no indulgence of private enmities after the victory. He was not like Cinna and Marius and Sulla and others of the like kind, who would not make an end of civil war even when the war was over. He did not wish to harm anyone once the war was ended—he regretted rather that it had ever begun.

Amidst all this, from the very beginning of his rule without rest he brought aid against the unbeliever to the struggling Church, which had been grievously afflicted by Valens, who supported the Arians. He rejoiced more in being a member of this Church than in reigning over the world. He gave orders for pagan statues everywhere to be thrown down, knowing that the gifts of this world are in the power not of demons but of the true God.

Nothing could be more remarkable than his devout humility in the matter of the heinous crime at Thessalonica. In response to the pleas of the bishops he had promised pardon, but was obliged by the outcry of some of his associates to exact punishment. He submitted to the discipline of the Church and so did penance that the people praying on his behalf rather wept at seeing the exalted might of the emperor prostrated than feared his wrath for their sin.

This, and other like good acts, which it would take too long to relate, Theodosius took with him out of this temporal life, which is but a vapour, no matter what peak of human eminence one occupies. The reward for these deeds is eternal bliss, which is bestowed by God, and only upon those who are truly devout. The other adornments or aids to this life—the world itself, light, air, earth, waters, fruits, the soul and body of man himself, senses, mind, life, He gives to the good and bad alike; and these include any sort of great power, which He dispenses according to His plan governing the ages.

(b) *The State*
14.28. *Of the nature of the two cities, the earthly and the heavenly*

So the two cities are the product of two loves, the earthly one of love of self leading to contempt of God, the heavenly one of love of God even unto contempt of self. The former takes pride only in itself, the latter in God. The former seeks glory from men; for the latter, the witness of God to its intention is the greatest glory. The former holds up its head in its own glory; the latter says to its God, 'My glory, and the lifter of my head' (Ps. 3.3). The former is ruled by a lust for domination among its leaders and the peoples it subjugates. In the latter, they serve one another in love, those set in command by taking thought for the city, those set under them by obeying. The former loves its own strength, in its powerful persons; the latter says to its God, 'I will love thee, O Lord, my strength' (Ps. 18.1). So in the former its wise men, living a life according to man, pursue the goods of body or mind or both, or those capable of recognizing God, 'They glorified Him not as God, neither were thankful, but became vain in their imaginations and their foolish heart was darkened', that is, in the mastery of pride, 'Professing themselves to be wise, they became fools, and changed the glory of the incorruptible God into an image made like to corruptible man, and to birds, and fourfooted beasts, and creeping things' (Rom. 1.21–23) (for they led or followed the people in worshipping images of this kind), 'and worshipped and served the creature more than the Creator, who is blessed for ever' (Rom. 1.25). In the heavenly city however there is no human wisdom save devoutness, by which the true God is rightly worshipped, in expectation of that reward in the company of the holy, not men alone but angels also, 'That God may be all in all' (I Cor. 15.28).

15.1. *On the two classes of human creation, tending from the beginning to different ends.*

Many have thought and said and committed to writing much about the bliss of paradise or paradise itself and the life of the first men there and their sin and punishment. I too have spoken of these matters in the preceding books according to the Holy Scriptures, either what I read in them or what I could understand from them, in agreement with their entirety. However, if these matters are subjected to closer inquiry, they need manifold arguments and multifarious, which would require to be worked out in more books than time and the present work permit; for I have not enough time at my command to justify lingering on all the points that the idle and niggling inquirers, more ready to question than capable of understanding, might raise. However, I think I have dealt adequately with the great and very difficult questions relating to the beginning of the world or the soul or the human race itself. The human race I have divided into two categories, one living according to man, the other according to God; these we allegorically call two cities, that is two societies of men, one of which is predestined to reign for ever with God, the other to endure everlasting torment with the devil. But that is their end, of which I must speak later. Now, concerning their beginning, since enough has been said about angels, whose number we do not know, or about the first men, now it seems to me I must undertake to describe their careers from the time when those two began to procreate until men shall cease to procreate. For the whole of this temporal age, in which men die and pass away, or are born and succeed, is the course of these two cities which we discuss.

So—Cain was the elder child of those two parents of the human race, and he belonged to the city of men; Abel was the second and he belonged to the city of God. For just as in one man we experience what the apostle said, 'Howbeit, that was not first which is spiritual, but that which is natural; and afterward that which is spiritual' (I Cor. 15.46) (whence every offspring of Adam is bound to be evil and fleshly, as springing from a damned stock; but if he progresses by being reborn into Christ, thenceforward he will be good and spiritual) —so in the whole human race, when these two cities began their advance, by birth and dying, the first born was the citizen of this temporal world, the second was a visitor to this world, belonging to the city of God, predestined by grace and elect of grace, by grace a visitor below, by grace a citizen above. For he himself arises from the same matter, which was originally damned in entirety; but God like a potter (a simile the apostle introduces not impudently but sensibly) from the same clay made one vessel for honour, the other for disgrace. The latter was made first, the former second, because in one and the same man, as I have already said, there is first the bad part, from which we must begin but where we need not stay, and later the good, to which we progress and arrive at, and where we stay. Not every bad man will become good; but no one will be good who was not bad; but the more quickly someone changes to the better, the sooner he gains the name belonging to the status which he has attained and covers over the earlier title with the later one. So it is written of Cain that he founded a city, and of Abel that he was a traveller, and did not.

For the city of the holy is above, though it produces here its citizens, in whom it sojourns abroad until the time of its reign comes, when it will gather all together to rise in their own bodies, when the promised kingdom shall be given them, when with their prince, the king of ages, they shall reign time without end.

15.3. *Strife and peace in the earthly city*

The earthly city, which shall not be everlasting (for when it is condemned to the last punishment, it will no longer be a city), has its good here, and has such joy in its present existence as there can be in such things. Since it is not the kind of good that causes its lovers no hardship, then this city is often divided against itself in litigation, war and fighting, seeking victories that are deadly, or at least mortal. For whatever part of it rises in war against another part seeks to be conqueror over the nations, though it is the captive of its own vices; and if it is too puffed up when it conquers, its victory is deadly too, while if it thinks of the common lot and is more distressed by what can happen in adversity than puffed up by the results of success, the victory is only mortal. For it will not be able always to remain dominant over those whom it managed to subdue by conquest. It is not right to say that the desires of this city are not good, when it is itself better in its own human kind; for it wants a kind of earthly peace, to obtain the lowest kind of good, and it seeks to arrive at that by fighting. If it conquers and there is none to resist, there will be peace, which the contending parties did not possess while they strove in ill-starred desire of those things they could not both have. This peace is sought through toilsome wars and won by what is thought to be a glorious victory. When the conquerors are those who fight with the juster cause, who would hesitate to say the victory calls for congratulation and a desirable peace has been obtained? This is good and is doubtless the gift of God. But if one neglects those better things belonging to the city above, where there will be eternal victory and peace free from care, and desires these goods, thinking them better or loving them more than those that are believed better, the consequence must be misery, and the increase of existing misery.

15.5. *Of the first author of the earthly city, the fratricide, whose crime the founder of Rome copied in killing his brother*

So the founder of the earthly city was the first fratricide; for he was overcome by envy and slew his brother, a citizen of the eternal city, who was a traveller here on earth. So it is no wonder that so long after, in founding that city which was to be the head of that earthly City of which we speak, and was to reign over so many nations, there corresponded to that first example, or *archetype*, as the Greeks call it, a sort of image of its own nature—for there too, as one of their poets describes the crime, 'the first walls were soaked in brother's blood' (Lucan 1.95). This is how Rome was founded, for Roman history testifies that Remus was killed by his brother Romulus. However, they were both citizens of the earthly city. Both sought renown from the establishing of the Roman state, but each sought so much glory as he could enjoy only alone—for someone who wanted the glory of domination would be less dominant if his power were diminished by having a partner alive. So, in order that one might have entire domination, his ally was removed, and he grew greater and worse through crime when innocence would have made him lesser and better. Now, the brothers Cain and Abel did not share the same desire for earthly things. One, who killed the other, did not bear the other a grudge because his dominance would be less, if both ruled: Abel did not seek power in the state his brother founded. The cause was that devil-sent envy that makes the evil bear a grudge against the good, for no other reason save that the one is good, the other evil. For possession of good is in no way diminished by the occasional or permanent existence of a sharer; rather, the more widespread it is, the more it binds individuals together in affection. Therefore he who refuses to possess goodness in common will not have it at all; and he will find it the more abundantly the more he is able to love him who shares it. The former is shown by the strife that arose between Romulus and Remus, in the way it divided the earthly city against itself; but the strife between Cain and Abel showed the difference between the two cities, that of God and that of man. Bad fights against bad; so does bad against good; but good, if it is perfect, cannot fight against good. So those who are progressing towards goodness but not yet perfect may engage in strife against another, from the same cause as they fight against themselves, and in one single man, 'the flesh lusteth against the Spirit, and the Spirit against the flesh' (Gal. 5.17).

So one's spiritual desire may fight against the fleshly desire of another, and vice versa, just as good and evil fight each other; and the fleshly desires of two who are not yet perfectly good may contend against each other, as bad fights bad, until the soundness of those who are cured leads to ultimate victory.

19.17. *The origin of peace and discord between the heavenly and the earthly city*

But the house of a man who does not live according to faith seeks earthly peace from the circumstances and advantages of this temporal life, whereas the house of a man who lives by faith awaits that which is promised for eternity in the future, and treats earthly and temporal things as a mere traveller among them, not seduced by them and led aside from progress towards God, but using them for support in bearing more easily and increasing as little as possible the burdens of the corruptible body, which weigh down the soul. Both men and both houses alike use those things which are necessary to this mortal life; but each has his own aim in using them which is quite distinct and separate from the other.

So the earthly city likewise, which does not live by faith, seeks earthly peace and fixes there the harmony of command and obedience among the citizens, so that there may be an agreement of human wishes on those matters relating to human life. But the heavenly city, or rather part of it, which is a stranger in this mortal life and lives by faith, must of necessity make use also of that peace, until it passes through the mortal state to which that peace is necessary. And during this time, while it passes its life of, as it were, imprisonment abroad in the earthly city, having received as a pledge the promise of redemption and the gift of the spirit, it does not hesitate to obey the laws of the earthly city, which administer all that is necessary for the maintenance of mortal life, so that, since mortality is common, harmony may be preserved between both cities in matters pertaining to mortality.

However, the earthly city has certain philosophers of its own, who do not agree with the divine doctrine in that, either because they surmise or because they are deceived by demons, they believe that many gods must be made favourable to human concerns and that different spheres of command are assigned to the charge of different gods, one looking after the body, another the mind, and within the body one concerned with the head, another with the neck, and so severally for each part; and likewise in the mind one cares for intellect, one learning, another anger, another lust; and in the matters connected with living, one is assigned to the herds, another to wheat, another to wine, another to oil, another to woods, another to money, another to sailing, another to war and victories, another to weddings, another to childbirth and fertility, and so severally. But the heavenly city knows there is only one God to be worshipped and with true piety believes that He alone must be served in that servitude which the Greeks call *latreia*, which is due to God alone.

As a result, the heavenly city could not have laws of religion in common with the earthly city, and it thought it necessary to differ from the earthly city on behalf of these laws, and to be a burden to those of different views and bear their wrath and enmity and the assaults of persecution, save when the spirits of their opponents were at some time cowed by fear of their numbers and the ever-present aid of God. So while this heavenly city sojourns abroad on the earth, it summons its citizens from all nations, and forms a society of travellers among speakers of all tongues, having no regard to differences in customs, laws or institutions, not cancelling or destroying any of the means whereby earthly peace is sought or maintained, but rather preserving and following them, for though they may differ from one nation to another, still they share the common aim of peace on earth—all this providing that it does not stand in the way of the religion by which is taught the obligation to worship the one true God.

Therefore the heavenly city also makes use of the earthly peace in its sojourn abroad, and so far as religious duty permits it preserves and strives for the agreement of human wills in regard to what pertains to man's mortal nature; and it makes that earthly peace serve towards the heavenly peace, which is truly peace, in that it is the only kind which may truly be thought and considered to be peace for a rational creature, being a most orderly and harmonious union in the enjoyment of God and of one another in God. When one attains to that, life will not be mortal, but clearly and certainly alive, nor the body something animal whose corruption irks the soul, but spiritual with no needs, subjected to the will in all respects. This peace it has while it sojourns abroad in the faith, and in accordance with this faith it lives justly, relating to the achievement of that peace all good actions towards God and towards one's neighbour, since the life of the city is certainly a life in society.

Chronological Summary

415	Athenian expedition to Sicily
	Alcibiades recalled, goes into exile
413	Death of Nicias in Sicily
407	Alcibiades recalled to Athens
406	Alcibiades goes into exile
404	Athens surrenders to Lysander
405–367	Dionysius I tyrant of Syracuse
359	Accession of Philip II of Macedon
354	Demosthenes' first extant political speech
388	Battle of Chaeronea: Philip in control of Greece
	League of Corinth formed
336	Assassination of Philip
	Accession of Alexander
334	Alexander starts expedition against Persia
323	Death of Alexander
	Wars of the Diadochi
	Seleucid, Ptolemaic and Antigonid kingdoms established
3rd–1st cents	Ptolemaic rule in Egypt

ROME

B.C.

753	Foundation of Rome (traditionally)
753–716	Romulus
716	Accession of Numa
509	Expulsion of last king, Tarquinius Superbus
	Republic established
451–50	Laws of the Twelve Tables
449–367	Struggle of the Orders
218–201	War with Hannibal (Second Punic War)
210	P. Scipio appointed to proconsular command in Spain
133	Tiberius Gracchus tribune
123–2	Gaius Gracchus tribune
108	Marius' first consulship; appointed to command in African War
81–79	Sulla dictator
77	Pompey given proconsular command in Spain
70	Pompey consul
67–62	Pompey in eastern Mediterranean with proconsular command
60	First triumvirate formed—Caesar, Pompey, Crassus
59	Caesar consul

58–50	Caesar in Gaul with proconsular command
49	Civil War starts
48	Death of Pompey
	Caesar made dictator
44	Assassination of Caesar
31	Octavian defeats Antony
30	Conquest of Egypt
27	Octavian takes name Augustus

31 B.C.–A.D. 138	The Principate	
	Augustus	31 B.C.–A.D. 14
	Tiberius	14–37
	Claudius	41–54
	Vespasian	69–79
	Trajan	98–117
A.D. 138–284	The Monarchy	
	Marcus Aurelius	161–180
	Commodus	176–192

THE DOMINATE

Diocletian	284–305
Constantine	Emperor of the West 308–337
	Emperor of the East 324–337
	Vision at the Milvian Bridge 312: Constantine's conversion to Christianity
Constantius	Emperor of the East 337–361
	Emperor of the West 351–361
Theodosius	Emperor of the East 379–395

Index

Index